Computer-Mediated
Communication

STUDIES IN RHETORIC AND COMMUNICATION
General Editors:
E. Culpepper Clark
Raymie E. McKerrow
David Zarefsky

James W. Chesebro and
Donald G. Bonsall

Computer-Mediated Communication

Human Relationships in a Computerized World

The University of Alabama Press   Tuscaloosa and London

Copyright © 1989 by
The University of Alabama Press
Tuscaloosa, Alabama 35487
All rights reserved
Manufactured in the United States of America

∞
The paper on which this book is printed meets the
minimum requirements of
American National Standard for Information Science-
Permanence of Paper
for Printed Library Materials, ANSI A39.48–1984.

Library of Contress Cataloging-in-Publication Data

Chesebro, James W.
    Computer-mediated communication : human relationships in a
computerized world / James W. Chesebro and Donald G. Bonsall.
        p.   cm. — (Studies in rhetoric and communication)
    Bibliography: p.
    Includes index.
    ISBN 0-8173-0460-6 (alk. paper)
    1. Interpersonal relations.   2. Interpersonal communication.
3. Information technology—Social aspects.   I. Bonsall, Donald G.,
1956–   . II. Title. III. Series.
HM132.C4257   1989
302—dc20   89-32991
                                                                           CIP

British Library Cataloguing-in-Publication Data available

To our parents,
Jeanette M. Campbell Chesebro, and Floyd J. Chesebro
and Nancy J. Bahl Bonsall, and Donald L. Bonsall

Contents

Preface

We reserved the Preface, written after all of the chapters of the book were completed, to discuss our motives for writing the book. We have clearly reacted to science, its technologies, and its related vocabularies. In our view, scientific inspiration and curiosity have consistently permeated the American vision and experience, yet during the 20th century science has undergone a tremendous transformation. No longer merely an inspiration, science has become an overwhelmingly powerful sociopolitical and economic institution. Its vocabulary has become a dominant feature of American thought. Its technologies have increasingly invaded the American home.

The home personal computer is a controlling metaphor for these scientific influences. It has created a direct link between science and the individual, affecting the language and life-style of the average American. In this sense, the issues created by computers and their related vocabularies are both public and personal. For us, the critical issue turns not on the content of computer systems but on how computerization functions as a medium of communication. We see the home personal computer as a medium that is redefining and realigning the relationships among science and the individual, the public and private domains, and the national rhetoric of science and the private thoughts of individuals. From our perspective, we are witnessing nothing less than the computerization of America.

We have approached these new relationships as critics, humanistic critics, concerned about the self-actualization of every individual within a computerized world. We particularly view our efforts in this book as rhetorical criticism, a rhetorical and critical view of the home personal computer. As rhetoricians, we are concerned about the messages created and conveyed by the personal home computer and about the new social relationships now in the making as a result of these messages. As critics, we seek to describe, interpret, and evaluate the patterns of communication that exist between computers and people.

Our approach to these issues can stem from no other viewpoint but our own, a viewpoint that represents the merging of two distinctly different perspectives. Donald G. Bonsall is a computer specialist. He has worked as a computer programmer in data-entry fields and was formally trained as a computer scientist. In contrast, James W. Chesebro was originally trained in classical and contemporary rhetoric and later specialized in theories of contemporary rhetoric. These very different perspectives influenced the conception and development of this book.

It seems to us that our methodological approach must be viewed as eclectic, for we have found much of use in a host of different methodological approaches. The pragmatism of the neo-Aristotelian method has decisively affected our analysis: We have frequently found it appropriate to consider how specific target audiences have used and been used by home personal computers. An experiential or phenomenological method often governs our analysis, for we have found it impossible to ignore our own experiences with computers. We have also found valuable Kenneth Burke's dramatistic approach, for the computer-human communication process is profoundly dramatic, and our analysis has often sought to reveal the symbolic nature of this relationship. Our approach is also decidedly generic in its formulation: Indeed, the five major types of computer-human relationships described in this book are explicitly labeled as generic. Finally, a poststructural or postmodern influence is evident, particularly in our concluding assessment in chapter 9 of computerization as a national rhetoric. In all, diversity characterizes the methods used to complete the analysis guiding this book.

We invite the reader to consider how these motives materialized in the chapters that follow.

JWC
DGB
Forest Hills, New York

Acknowledgments

Two members of our discipline read earlier drafts of this manuscript. Both offered critical responses that we found invaluable in subsequent revisions.

Carroll C. Arnold approached the manuscript as an editor. He painstakingly read and reacted to every sentence and concept in this manuscript. He challenged; he offered revisions; he encouraged. He deserves his reputation as one of the finest editors in our discipline.

Michael Calvin McGee approached the manuscript as a colleague. He reacted to our approach, methods, ideas, and role as rhetorical critics. He was decisive, helpful, and supportive. He deserves his reputation as one of the finest critics in our discipline.

We sincerely appreciate the time, energy, and thought that Professors Arnold and McGee devoted to this manuscript.

JWC
DGB

Computer-Mediated
Communication

Introduction

Computers now pervade the typical American home. Dedicated computers are now embedded in dishwashers, clothes washers and dryers, refrigerators, televisions, radios, freezers, ranges, telephones, heating and cooling systems, stereos, microwaves, security systems, and automobiles. As Broad (1984, March) has so aptly noted, the "biggest change" in the American home has been the "introduction of digital electronics, which made its debut in the late 1970's" (p. C8). Yet these computers are predominantly "concealed," for the computers built into home appliances can be used by a consumer without his or her conscious recognition that an entire set of computers may be repeatedly employed during an average day.

The introduction of the small desktop computer into the American home and workplace has forced people to respond to the computer as a new technology affecting their everyday lives. Small desktop computers made their most decisive impact in the American home during the first half of the 1980s. Both Dataquest (cited in Sanger, 1985, July) and Software Access International (cited in Marcom, 1985, July) reported that less than 1 million home computers existed in 1980. By 1983, the home-computer "explosion" was clearly imminent. Gallup (1983) reported that 2 to 4 million American households had personal computers by 1983, that an additional 13 million families were "very interested" in buying a home computer, and that yet another 15 million families were "fairly" interested in purchasing their own home computers. By 1984, the commercial value of desktop computers sold

1

in the United States exceeded for the first time the sales value of mainframe or supercomputers (Sandberg-Diment, 1984, February). By 1985, the most precise numeric data, provided by Christensen (1985) and Dataquest (cited in Sanger, 1985, July), indicated that some 15 million, or almost 20 percent, of all American households had desktop home computers. Thus by the mid-1980s the computer age had become a matter of record in a significant portion of American homes.

Yet, as the 1980s came to a close, it was also clear that the personal computer had not equaled the television's and telephone's prevalence in the American home. During 1988, the Electronic Industries Association reported that home-computer "household penetration" had reached only 20 percent by January 1988 (1988b, p. 54) and 21 percent by June 1988 (1988a, p. 22). As was stated in the *New York Times* ("A Computer in Every Home?" 1987), the home computer was originally viewed as "the greatest thing to happen since refrigeration, [but] a great many Americans have been able to cope nicely without the home computer" (p. 48). At the same time, however, Future Computing (cited in Sherwin, 1987) reported that sales of home personal computers increased 10 percent in 1986 and 17 percent in 1987; that 16.8 million, or almost 20 percent, of American households had personal computers by the end of 1987; and that "healthy growth will continue for the next five years" (p. XQ1; also see "Personal Computers Grow," 1987; Schlender, 1988). Others predicted that sales of home personal computers would continue to increase throughout the 1990s (Sanger, 1987, December). Indeed, Abraham Peled (1987) has argued that computing has entered "a new passage"; in this new phase,

by means of developments in hardware and software, computing will grow more powerful, sophisticated and flexible by an order of magnitude in the next decade. At the same time the technology will become an intellectual utility, widely available, ultimately as ubiquitous as the telephone. Visual and other natural interfaces will make the machines easier to use, and a flexible high-capacity network will be capable of linking any combination of individuals who need computing, whether they are physicians trying to reach a difficult diagnosis, investment bankers structuring a deal, aeronautical engineers creating a new airframe, astrophysicists modeling the evolution of the universe or students studying for an examination. (p. 57)

The most fascinating social questions do not turn on the number of computers Americans have purchased; rather, they deal with why people have purchased these machines, how they use them, and, probably even more important from a communication perspective, how they respond to such high technology within their homes. Indeed, Philip D. Estridge (cited in Sanger, 1985, August), who pioneered the extraordinarily successful entry of International Business Machines (IBM) into the personal-computer field, aptly captured the controlling issue: "The most important thing we learned was that how people reacted to a personal computer emotionally was almost more important than what they did with it" (p. D8).

Responding to the Computer

We explore the ways in which people respond to personal computers. As one might anticipate, responses to computers vary tremendously. Some of the more obvious responses to personal computers are reflected in the popular jargon of the day, in such terms as *computer obsession* and *computerphobia*. Excessive involvement with or excessive fear of computers is perhaps infrequent but is a possible and significant response (see, e.g., Sandberg-Diment, 1982, August 17; Schmidt, 1985), but other responses are equally important.

For some, operating a personal computer is nothing more than a "trade skill," as David Weinberger (1986, p. 431) has put it. For these seasoned users, operating a computer is equivalent to driving a car: The skills required to operate a computer become habitual and of second nature. They conceive of a computer as a kind of sophisticated and elaborate typewriter and nothing more. For example, Erik Sandberg-Diment (1986, August 17) has maintained that "the computer itself, as a machine, is of no particular interest, any more than the typewriter and the calculator once utilized in the performance of similar tasks were" (p. F13). The computer is thus cast as a tool employed solely as the user determines. While this genre of responses appears perfectly logical, it ignores the actual and psychological impact of the extended capabilities and increased power provided by personal computers. Although an important response to recognize, this reaction is too simplistic to accept as a definitive and complete response.

For others, a computer can become an extension of the self or a potential friend and can create a self-contained world. In her interviews with some 400 computer users, Sherry Turkle (1984) discovered two groups for whom the computer functioned as more than a tool. Not unexpectedly, Turkle found that one group, young children exposed to computers at the age of 6 or so, frequently found it extremely difficult to determine whether a computer did or did not possess awareness, consciousness, feelings, or the ability to cheat during games. In Turkle's view, when responding to computers these children employed a "psychological" metaphor that generated questions regarding the "aliveness," intelligence, morality, and feelings that a computer might possess. By the age of 9, 10, or 11, when the typical child can distinguish between human and machine behaviors, the children used computers in ways that were powerful reflections of primary role formulations usually adopted by children of these ages. During this socialization period, these children began to display either "hard" or "soft" social development mastery patterns, which roughly paralleled the different mind-sets of the engineer and the artist. Later, when these children reached adolescence and played video games, Turkle found that the video games constituted a new, independent, self-contained, and apparently real world—at least for the children—which they believed promised them infinity and perfection. Thus, Turkle implied that computers were capable of exerting profound influence upon the socialization of children, regardless of their stage of development.

A similar kind of observation is embedded in Turkle's conception of a second group, "computer hackers." Although far more serious games are played by hackers, Turkle ultimately concluded that these computer specialists regarded the computer as an extension of the self and a friend and employed it to create a self-contained reality and to substitute for direct face-to-face contact with other human beings. In Turkle's view, the hacker functions within the realm of the sciences, which she has distinguished from sensuality. Among scientists, Turkle argued, hackers are "the ostracized of the ostracized" (p. 199), and indeed many computer-science students perceive themselves as "nerds, loners, and losers" (p. 200). Thus hackers develop an "overintensity" with "machines," a "fascination" with "the machine itself," and ultimately "a way of life" with the computer (pp. 200–201). Hackers eschew social contacts. As Turkle put it, "The hacker culture appears to be made up of people who need to avoid complicated social situations, who for one reason or another got frightened off or hurt too badly by the risks and complexities of relationships" (p. 216). In this conception, hackers are intensely linked to computer machinery itself and to the mastery of the computer, which apparently compensates for social inadequacies but ultimately functions as a substitute for face-to-face social contact.

In sharp contrast, for other users the computer creates new social contacts that could not have existed without computer technologies. Utilizing the communication capabilities of computer systems, these users link computers by telephone lines to form computer networks. The computer-phone connections allow individuals to dial a network, read and leave messages, and, on some of the multi-telephone-line systems, "chat" by typing in messages on their computer keyboards and receiving messages on their computer screens. While many of these computer networks are owned by corporations, research institutions, government agencies, and educational systems, others are created locally, responding predominantly to users within immediate telephone area codes and offering concentrated attention to certain subjects, which may vary from explorations of specialized computer technologies to dating services. Located throughout the United States, some 600 local computer bulletin board systems (CBBSS) are listed in the *On-Line Computer Telephone Directory*. In his examination of a 10-percent random sample of these local computer bulletin board systems, Chesebro (1985) analyzed the content of the messages left on the public forums of these systems and found that although many of the messages dealt with computer issues, roughly 30 percent of the messages possessed a decidedly interpersonal dimension. Messages offering or requesting self-descriptions, sexually oriented notices, and requests for social contacts or for a specific user to contact another user all appeared far more socially oriented than task related. These computer bulletin board systems thus appear capable of affecting the personal life-styles of the users. Even though one cannot see the person one is chatting with, interpersonal relationships and friendship can apparently be readily formed through these systems. As one user of these systems reported to Kerr (1982, September), "I have talked to some people for years without knowing where they live or their real names. Yet they are as much a presence in my life as if they were in the room. They are my friends" (p. C7). Carpenter (1983) likewise argued that these computer bulletin board systems constitute nothing less than "an entire society on-line . . . a town, a club, a clique, a fantasy world, a dating system . . . or anything one wants it to be" (p. 9). She concluded that "when you build a computer system, you're building a social system" (p. 11). Similar results are reported with other kinds of groups. In her survey of 120 educators, Aitken (1985) found that computer-telephone links were frequently used "to make new friends." In her judgment, "most of the interviews and questionnaires indicated that the computer had a neutral to positive association with interpersonal communication." Likewise, in Hellerstein's (1986) survey of 236 network participants, users—particularly "heavy users"— were found to employ computers "for social purposes." "This social utility function," observed Hellerstein, "includes the use of the computer to facilitate communication as well as providing a common source of conversational material and a common group activity" (p. 7). In the same context, Williams and Rice (1983) have argued that electronic media and the interpersonal realm are increasingly blurring the distinctions among interpersonal, private, group, and public communication: "The traditional categorized distinctions among different types of communication are being reduced by technological change," which is "blurring lines between interpersonal and mass-mediated contexts. We must increasingly account for the coalescence of personal, organizational, and public contexts of human communication" (p. 220).

For yet another group—an adult and frequently distinguished group of users—the computer is anthropomorphized and personalized. The computer is intentionally treated as if it were a person, a human being with a discernible personality. The rationale for anthropomorphizing and personalizing a computer has been explicitly defended (see, e.g., Frude, 1983; Jernick, 1984). John McCarthy (1983), often identified as the founder of artificial intelligence, has argued that it is frequently useful to anthropomorphize a computer. He has noted that "as our daily lives involve more sophisticated computers, we find that ascribing little thoughts to machines will be increasingly useful in understanding how to get the most good out of them." Although he observed that "anthropomorphism is often an error," he distinguished "good" anthropomorphism from "bad" and maintained that "it is going to be more difficult to understand machines without using mental terms": "The reason for ascribing mental qualities and mental processes to machines is the same as for ascribing them to other people. It helps to understand what they will do, how our actions will affect them, how to compare them with ourselves and how to design them" (p. 46).

By no means exhaustive, this listing of responses nevertheless serves to illustrate the diversity of responses that have been generated by the introduction of the computer. These dramatically different, sometimes contradictory responses to the computer are the point of departure for this book, yet they are symptomatic of a far larger set of social and communication issues. The divergent responses identified here are, for example, undoubtedly due to the attitudes people have developed about computers before coming into actual contact with them, the functions people execute with computers, what computers do, the environment in which people use computers, and the reasons why people use computers. In a systematic analysis, all of these variables must be considered when describing computer-human communication. Such a description necessarily requires the development of a theoretical framework to account for these diverse variables. In addition, in terms of even more fundamental communication issues, it is appropriate to ask how and why human-computer communication functions as it does and to attempt to detail the basic principles governing the computer-human communication process. Moreover, these responses generate tremendously important issues for those studying human communication. For example, if the reports of computer bulletin board users are taken seriously and confirmed, it may be essential to redefine the meanings of such words as *friendship* and *interpersonal communication* as well as to reconsider the usefulness of the distinction between interpersonal and mass communication. Finally, this survey of computer responses also suggests that the sociopolitical and cultural implications of extensive computer use must be explored. At virtually any stage in life, from early childhood through adulthood, a person may be exposed to or directly involved with a computer, computer technologies and terminologies, and the social mores and consequences created by computer use. As these computer uses and consequences emerge as increasingly dominant social patterns, the resulting new societal and cultural norms require definition and explanation. The implications of these changes also need to be anticipated and described. It seems appropriate to initiate such an exploration by identifying its governing perspective.

The Governing Perspective of This Book

The framework controlling this book stems from five interrelated viewpoints. First, computerized communication now dominates information exchanges within the United States and is rapidly controlling global communication systems. Second, computers do and will increasingly alter how people execute their daily activities. Third, computers now and will increasingly alter users' life-styles and values. Fourth, as computerization continues to infiltrate the American household, computerization will become a highly personal concern for Americans. Fifth, computerized communication is altering human communication itself. In the pages that follow, the reported evidence seems to leave little reason to doubt that computerized communication is altering how, if, and when people talk to each other in all social systems and even in the privacy of the American home. As we argue in the last chapter of this book, this same reported evidence also provides a foundation for concluding that computerization is establishing an archetypal metaphor for human talk that is emerging as a controlling philosophy, if not ideology, in the United States. Technology and communication are now intimately interrelated. The terminologies, attitudes, and values utilized to describe a technology are increasingly becoming the foundation for characterizing and understanding human communication and therefore each person who finds that communication reflects and defines himself or herself. In other words, the computer revolution is now a personal issue, an issue that requires exploration, definition, and analysis.

The Objectives of This Book

This book is designed to achieve five specific ends. First, it functions as an introduction to basic concepts in computing, to computer-human communication as a process, and to the role of personal computers in everyday life. The survey of basic concepts is designed to provide not a comprehensive introduction to computer science but rather a commonly shared set of terminologies as a base for exploring the social issues created by computerization. In addition, because of the diverse ways in which computer-human communication can be discussed, the basic assumptions and communication principles governing computer-human communication are explicitly identified. Moreover, while focusing upon the role of computers in the personal environment, we do not wish to detract from the role of computers in other kinds of societal environments. The distinction between the private life and the public sector is slowly losing its explanatory power, and computers are one of the factors transcending, blurring, and dissolving that distinction. An exploration of how computers are experienced in the personal realm (the focus of the first part of this book) therefore provides a basis for revealing public issues related to the computerization of America (the focus of the last part of this book).

Second, this book focuses on relationships that exist between human beings and computers. In the first half of the book, our concern is with the functional relationships that determine computer-human interactions, and we find that the entitlement phrase *computer-human communication* captures this functional emphasis particularly well. We examine the signs and symbols that pass between human beings and computers, how these signs and symbols control the relationships between humans and computers, and the effects of engaging in such human-machine communication. In the second half of the book, our concern is with the values or moral relationships that characterize computer-human interactions. Using any tool, such as a computer, serves an immediate function, but the decision to use any tool also establishes expectations about when, where, with whom, and how human beings should act. The social norms created by tool using ultimately become, then, an important component of any complete assessment of a technology.

Third, this book focuses on the range of possible uses that exist when a human being operates a computer. While this book does provide a basic survey of computer uses, these uses are isolated because they provide important indications of why and how people respond to computers in the ways that they do.

Fourth, this book focuses on the social consequences of using a computer. Questions have already emerged that are not easily answered: Do computers reduce or even displace face-to-face communication? Or will they dramatically increase the number of face-to-face contacts among people? Moreover, if a computer is used to communicate with other people, will the computer affect how human beings talk to others and how they respond? Computers have already affected and will increasingly affect many other dimensions of the personal life. Not the least of these changes will involve how and where people work, what type of work they do, the social environment in which they work, and the types of friends they have. Furthermore, as computers increasingly make their way into homes, a direct impact upon personal life-styles can be anticipated. We explore these issues because human beings can control the consequences of computers in their personal lives only if they are aware of what the choices and potential consequences of computer use are.

Fifth, this book is designed to offer a critical perspective on the role of computerization within the social system. Not intended to be definitive and reserved for the final chapter of the book, the evaluation is designed to stimulate readers' critical reactions.

This book does not attempt to accomplish other ends. It is not a how-to manual. At last count, some 700 operations manuals are available from bookstores throughout the country (Appelbaum, 1983, June; Porter, 1983), and, depending upon how a computer magazine is defined, some 150 to 400 technical computer magazines are now on the market ("Printing Out," 1984). A clear need simply does not exist for another operations or technical publication, and this book is not such a text. Moreover, this book is not a scientific and technical treatise that explains the mathematical and mechanical principles controlling a personal computer. Human beings can operate any number of machines without knowing what scientific and technical principles control them. Finally, this book is not a programming textbook. Computer programming is an extremely specialized skill which few people need to develop, given the rich variety of readily available, prepackaged programs that now serve the needs of the vast majority of home-computer users.

We hope that the reader finds this book informative and useful. We hope most of all that this book functions as a stimulus and guide to the reader's critical approach and assessment of the ways in which our society should evolve as computers become more and more a part of our personal and public environments.

I.
Computers in a Human Environment

Part 1 provides an introduction to computing. We assume that the reader has no formal exposure to computers or to the terminologies and concepts of computer scientists and computer specialists. We outline a basic but complete overview of the fundamentals related to the role of computers in society and to the ways in which computers and human beings differ as information and language users.

In chapter 1, "The Information Society," we trace the growth of the Information Society from an agricultural economy to an industrial and service-based economy to the emerging postindustrial or communication era in which we now live. Changing employment patterns and trends in media technologies are examined to illustrate the social reality in which computers now function. Given this context, computers are treated as communication technologies that facilitate the already dramatic increase in the power of the Information Society. Because the revolutionary developments of this Information Society have so deeply affected human beings, we end chapter 1 with a list of central questions relating to the Information Society and the computer. We believe that these questions can be answered as subsequent chapters are read.

Chapter 2, "Humans and Computers: A Comparison of Systems and Processes," identifies the structural features that distinguish human beings and computers as information processors and compares their uses of memory, sensory, and interfacing systems. The chapter also compares the ways in which face-to-face and computer-mediated human communication differ.

In chapter 3, "Humans and Computers: A Comparison of Language Systems," we examine several of the expectations and ideals people should realistically have when dealing with computers, and we specify the factors that are currently blocking understanding and use of computers. From this base, we examine the foundation for machine communication and contrast machine with human communication. A description of the levels and functions of computer languages concludes chapter 3.

Part 1 thus provides an introduction to the role of the computer in society and to communication principles that can be used in describing and contrasting computers and humans as information-processing systems. These considerations provide a strong foundation for dealing with the social uses and social consequences of computer use, which are examined in part 2.

1

The Information Society

We today confront an unending stream of diverse messages that continually compete for our attention. We encounter a multitude of face-to-face verbal and nonverbal communications when dealing with other human beings. We also confront an almost overwhelming number of messages emanating from paper and electronic sources: televisions, radios, newspapers, magazines, records, business notices and reports, mail, telephones, government forms, scientific reports, advertisements, watches and clocks, menus and recipes, billboards, and books. For some, the new technologies—video games, videodiscs, video- and cassette-recording systems, pay television systems, and office and home computers—function as yet another set of information sources. Whether at work or at home, we are now constantly dealing with information. We engage in an ongoing cycle of initiating, processing, patterning or arranging, preparing, transmitting, disseminating, retrieving, receiving, or reprocessing information. We live in an Information Society.

We are in fact so accustomed to this Information Society that we now automatically process, in an almost unconscious fashion, communication of every kind. Information processing has now become second nature to us. Consider how rapidly one might, for example, pass through a daily newspaper. Titles of articles can be scanned in seconds, and irrelevant advertisements can be dismissed with a glance. If seeking only immediately relevant information, one can generally examine a daily newspaper within minutes. An amazingly large number of our behaviors are similarly directed toward surviving in what otherwise might be an ocean of human, paper, and electronic messages. We are now skilled information manipulators.

Nonetheless, the scope of this Information Society must be underscored. The amount of information directed toward and processed by Americans is enormous (see table 1.1). The measurement of media use and the determination of media consequences are now full-time businesses, but regardless of what kinds of measurements are employed, the conclusions are the same: Information systems clearly dominate the life of the average American. Given the experiences of previous generations, this information explosion is nothing less than a revolution in the culture and life of the typical American.

The Information Revolution

We are frequently (probably too frequently) told that cultural revolutions are underway. Such forecasts seldom seem to materialize. In dealing with information, however, the term *revolution* aptly characterizes the kind of quantitative and qualitative transformation that has already occurred in the United States.

The revolutionary nature of the information explosion can be appropriately marked in several different ways. In 1968, for example, Don Fabun noted in *The Dynamics of Change* that the amount of technical information was doubling every 10 years (p. 5). Fifteen years later, John Naisbitt noted in *Megatrends* (1982) that the amount of technical information was doubling every 5.5 years, and he predicted that "by 1985 the volume of information will be somewhere between four and seven times what it was only a few years earlier" (p. 24). Insofar as this information is and must be used to determine "what is," such major modifications in information imply that the nature of reality itself is rapidly and constantly changing.

In yet another exciting, albeit slightly more elaborate, scheme, Frederick Williams (1982, pp. 27–39) has conceived of the development of all media technologies in terms of a 24-hour clock. During the first 8 hours of the existence of *Homo sapiens*, from 34,000 B.C. until 22,000 B.C., no permanent and enduring mode of communication technology unified human beings. Although cave painting emerged about 22,000 B.C., it was not until 12 hours later that writing emerged, in 4000 B.C. By the year 1000 B.C., the alphabet came into existence, roughly 20 hours after the birth of *Homo sapiens*. Printing was developed in A.D. 1453, at approximately 23 hours and 38 minutes after the birth of the intelligent human being. Williams concluded that "the last few minutes explode with new communication technologies. We are on an acceleration curve of communication inventions" (p. 31). In even more direct terms, all of the technological changes we are presently encountering have occurred during the last 1/10 of 1 percent of human history.

Perhaps the simplest measure provides the most vivid indication of the nature of the contemporary information revolution. Employing the quantitative measures of media use introduced in table 1.1, we can develop a profile of the typical American's information experiences in a given year: He or she will read or complete 3,000 notices and forms, read 100 newspapers and 36 magazines for a total of 645 hours, watch television for 2,463 hours and rented and purchased VCR tapes for 468 hours, listen to radio for 730 hours, read almost 5 books, buy 20 records, talk on the telephone for almost 122 hours, and encounter 21,170 advertisements. Interestingly enough, of all of these activities, the combined hours devoted just to watching television, reading, and talking on the telephone constitute 39 percent of all of the available hours within an entire year. If the time devoted to sleep is discounted, we spend 58 percent of our waking hours engaged in these media activities. Although these averages can certainly distort our perception of the life-style of any given individual, they do reveal central tendencies and provide an overall image of our cultural system. We are left with the unavoidable conclusion that we are in the midst of an information explosion of revolutionary proportions. Although its future may be difficult to predict with certainty, the information explosion does possess certain outstanding characteristics that can be pointed out.

First, the emerging media are predominantly electronic. Virtually all of the new information technologies introduced within the last 50 years have relied upon electricity as a central component in their design, and all of the new technologies are therefore potentially compatible.

Second, the new technologies are becoming increasingly integrated. Beyond the combination stereo-and-radio systems, new technologies are increasingly being designed for linkages with other technologies. Several of the new television models, for example, provide for television-telephone as well as television-telephone-computer interconnections. We anticipate that more activities both at work and at home will occur before one screen that integrates human efforts. As Tannenbaum (1988, January) has already reported, " 'media rooms' for the home" are "seen by some manufacturers and retailers as a way to get more money out of people who are flocking to any one blockbuster product. So they team up and try to get consumers to buy a total package [of media systems]" (p. 29). Correspondingly, such programmable control devices as General Electric's HomeMinder (Greer, 1986) and Audio Design Associates' Integrated Media Controller (Tannenbaum,

Table 1.1 The Information Society: A Media Profile of the United States

*Forms and Notices:** The Stanford Research Institute (cited in Dizard, 1985, p. 71; also see Panko, 1977, p. 32) reported that the volume of formal notices and forms used in business, government, and other organizations equals 800 billion pieces of paper annually, or roughly 3,000 notices and forms for every man, woman, and child in the U.S. Paperwork costs American businesses more than $100 billion a year. The Office of Management and Budget (cited in "Administration Says," 1984) estimated that individuals and businesses spend 2 billion hours a year reading and filling out only the forms required by the federal government. Thus, on the average, every person in the U.S. spends 8.5 hours a year completing just federal government forms.

*Technical Journals and Scientific Reports:** Fabun (1968, p. I5) estimated that some 100,000 technical journals were published in 1968. In 1982, Naisbitt (p. 24; also see W. Sullivan, 1981) reported that between 6,000 and 7,000 scientific articles were written each day. By 1988, Broad reported that "at least 40,000 scientific journals are now estimated to roll off the presses around the world, flooding libraries and laboratories with more than a million new articles a year" (p. C1). Employing a more precise numeric base and set of measurements (Machlup & Leeson, 1978–80), Kranzberg (1988) noted that, "by the beginning of the 1980s, some 8000 journals were being published in biology and medicine alone—and the same phenomenon was repeated in other fields" (p. 36).

*Magazines:** Some 11,000 magazines are published in the U.S., with 90% of Americans 18 years and older reading at least 1 magazine a month and with 65% of Americans reporting that they read 3 or more magazines a month (Fiske, 1983).

*Newspapers:** Some 1,700 daily newspapers are distributed with a circulation of almost 70 million newspapers a day (De Fleur & Ball-Rokeach, 1983, pp. 29–33). Two out of 3 Americans read 1 newspaper a day (Fiske, 1983).

*Television:** Since 1963, television has been the dominant source of information for Americans, with 64% of Americans using it as their primary source of information and with 53% reporting that television is the most believable source of information (Roper Organizaton, 1985, pp. 3, 5; also see Chesebro, 1984a; Roper Organization, 1983, pp. 5, 6). In fact, in 1987, the television set was on in the average American household for 7 hours and 7 minutes a day (Nielsen Media Research, 1987b, p. 10). Moreover, on an average evening between 8:00 PM and 11:00 PM, almost 60% of Americans, or 135 million people, are watching television (Nielsen Media Research, 1987a, p. 5). It should also be noted that more Americans are reporting dissatisfaction with television programming. Indeed, some now question the value of extensive television viewing. One Gallup poll (1982, p. 36) indicated that 66% of Americans believe that violence on television is related to the rising crime rate in the U.S.

*Videocassette Recorders:** Supplementing the programming offered by network and cable television, videocassette recorders (VCRs) constitute yet another important mode of communication for Americans. While only

Table 1.1 (Continued)

introduced in 1975, VCRs are now in almost 50% of the nation's homes (Nielsen Media Research, 1987b, p. 86). VCR sales have continued to increase each year, and the Electronic Industries Association (cited in "Look and Listen," 1985) has reported that almost 1 million VCRs are sold a month. Similarly, videotape sales and rentals have increased dramatically. In 1985, Lindsey reported that some 304 million VCR tapes were rented, while some 20 million VCR tapes were sold. By 1986, Americans rented 1.4 billion tapes (Video Marketing Newsletter, cited in "Cassette Use," 1987). And, by 1988, Kleinfield reported that number of rented VCR tapes had increased to 2.5 billion per year. In addition, in 1987, the average VCR household recorded broadcast television programs via VCR for 29 minutes a day, or 3 hours and 23 minutes a week (Nielsen Media Research, 1987b, p. 88). These rented, purchased, and recorded tapes were watched for an average of 44 minutes a day, or 5 hours and 8 minutes a week, beyond the time spent watching broadcast television (Nielsen Media Research, 1987b, p. 91). M. R. Levy (1980a, 1980b, 1981; also see Gunter & Levy, 1987; Levy & Fink, 1985) initiated the primary research framework for the study of the social uses and consequences of VCR utilization. Other significant and subsequent contributions (Boyd, 1987; Cohen, 1987; Greenberg & Heeter, 1987; Roe, 1987; Rubin & Bantz, 1987; Schoenbach & Hackforth, 1987) have also been published under Levy's editorship.

*Radio: Radio is a central feature of life for many people driving to and from work and for many teenagers, and some 9,000 radio stations fill the airwaves with every type of audio stimulation. The average American household has 5.3 radios if all portable, car, built-in, and freestanding radios are counted (De Fleur & Ball-Rokeach, 1983, p. 93).

*Books: The 14,000 book publishers in the U.S. release 50,000 titles a year (Fiske, 1983, p. A1; Appelbaum, 1983, January; Appelbaum, 1983, September). The Association of American Publishers (cited in McDowell, 1983, June) reported that Americans paid $647 million for 425 million mass-market paperbacks and purchased 10.9 million best-selling hardcover fiction and general books, 27 million best-selling paperbacks, and 8.4 million trade books. Indeed, for those of reading age, book sales per capita have been increasing. In 1970, those of reading age read 2.75 books per year; in 1980, they read 4.89 books per year (Book Industry Study Group, cited in McDowell, 1985). On the average, Americans read for 113 minutes a day (Fiske, 1983, p. B12). Similarly, the number of bookstores in the U.S. has increased from 11,786 in 1973 to 19,850 in 1984 (Jones, 1984). In total, Americans spend $11 billion to purchase nearly 2 billion books (Book Industry Trends, cited in Jones, 1984). Yet the Book Industry Study Group (cited in McDowell, 1985) has also reported that reading among Americans under the age of 21 has dropped sharply since 1978, from 75% to 63%. It should also be noted that since 1983, a growing number of Americans are reading books more for pleasure and less to find out about a specific topic, as measured by the increase in fiction (from 39% to 44%) and decrease in nonfiction (from 43% to 40%) (L. Williams, 1988).

*Films: While the weekly film attendance per household has consistently de-

Table 1.1 (Continued)

clined since 1936, almost 20 million Americans see a film once a week (De Fleur & Ball-Rokeach, 1983, pp. 59–60). Moreover, some films—such as *E.T.* and *Ghostbusters* or series like those begun by *Starwars, Jaws, Rambo, Rocky,* and *Aliens*—appear to constitute major cultural and apparently unifying experiences in the U.S. ("All Time Film Rental Champs," 1986).

***Records:** While VCR tapes and video games have recently affected record sales, Americans spent over $4.6 billion in 1986 to purchase 618 million singles, LPS/EPS, CDS, cassettes, and 8-track tapes (Recording Industry Association, 1987, p. 4). Rock continues to constitute America's favorite type of music, generating 46.8% of all record sales as measured in total dollar volume, followed by pop at 14.2%, black urban music at 10.1%, and country music at 9.7% (Recording Industry Association, 1987, p. 7; for an analysis of long-term trends in the content of popular music, see Chesebro, Foulger, Nachman & Yannelli, 1985).

***Telephone:** The telephone is now a common mode of communication; 95% to 96% of American households have their own telephone (Dizard, 1985, p. 28; F. Williams, 1987, p. 79); by the end of this decade, there will be 1 billion telephones worldwide (F. Williams, 1987, p. 79). In fact, the average American household now has 3 telephones. Moreover, people use the telephone for an average of 20 minutes a day (Pacific Telephone, 1981; also see Rice & Bair, 1984, p. 207; Tydeman, Lipinski, Adler, Nyhan & Zwimpfer, 1982, p. 114). However, there are reasons to believe that the telephone, rather than being a "mere" mode or channel of communication, influences the substance of communication. Several studies, for example, found that people detected lies more readily over the phone than in face-to-face communication; one explanation is that the telephone blocks out the nonverbal cues that frequently mask the verbal irregularities (increases in pitch level) that people employ to detect lies (see, e.g., Muson, 1982).

***Advertisements:** The typical American encounters some 1,600 ads a day from all sources of advertising. By the age of 17, the average American will have seen over a third of a million ads. By the age of 25, this figure increases to half a million (Comstock, 1980b, p. 109).

1988, June) are able to fully complete the integration process by consolidating all media systems within the home. O'Connor (1981) has coined the phrase "home entertainment center" to characterize these integrated technologies within the home, and Deken (1982) has proposed that the most appropriate metaphor for the emerging American household is "the electronic cottage."

Third, media are becoming interactive. Media consumers are increasingly able to control their information choices. In an extremely preliminary way, the increasing diversity and specialization of magazines and newspapers have allowed consumers to determine more precisely their content options (Dolnick, 1987). The dramatic increase in the number of television channels available to most people allows for even more effective content control. In this context, 59 percent of American homes can now receive 15 or more television channels, and 31 percent can receive 30 or more (Nielsen Media Research, 1987a, p. 9). More than half of viewing Americans are already "zappers," who rapidly switch from one television program to another. Kneale (1988, p. 29) reported that 17.9 percent of viewers switch channels more than once every 2 minutes and 35.8 percent switch channels one to three times every 6 minutes and 30 seconds. More profound is that, with the ever-increasing number of media technologies, consumers will be able to reformat and redesign content options. The television owner no longer must be only a passive receiver of information. Truly interactive systems, which are increasingly becoming available, allow each media consumer to reformat and redesign content and thereby to create and personalize information. Such interactive systems may have profound effects upon virtually every dimension of the home environment.

Fourth, new technologies are increasingly functioning as intermedia systems. The term *intermedia* was coined by Gary Gumpert and Robert Cathcart (1986) to account for the increasing use of new technologies as communication channels in establishing, maintaining, and regulating interpersonal communication. For example, the telephone can easily be employed to convey an interpersonal message. As already suggested, however, such media introduce into a human relationship other variables that would not exist in face-to-face interactions.

Fifth, the new technologies are creating stockpiles of information. We might previously have discussed communication in terms of the "flow of information," but new information is being produced faster than people can use it, and stockpiles of information are accumulating. Given the influence of electronic modes of storage and the use of computers, these information stockpiles frequently take the form of *data bases. The Directory of Online Databases* indexed 2,225 such data bases in the spring of 1984, up from 300 in the fall of 1979. The immediate implication of such information stockpiles is that virtually any kind of information will shortly be retrievable by computers in the home.

Sixth, the new technologies are becoming increasingly popular. As we have already suggested, virtually every American household now has its own television, telephone, and radio. More than half now have VCRs. And the personal computer is becoming a component of the communication systems of a significant number of American homes. As miniaturization and computerization reduce the physical hard-

Table 1.2 Four-Section Aggregation of the U.S. Labor Force

Year	Agriculture (%)	Industry (%)	Services (%)	Information (%)
1900	37	38	21	4
1920	24	51	15	10
1940	16	57	11	16
1960	8	56	9	27
1980	4	36	10	52

Note: Round off accounts for differences above and below 100%.

ware associated with these new technologies, we expect this popularization to continue. In a larger sense, then, information is becoming democratized.

Last but by no means least, the new technologies are increasingly related to computers. As a result, information technologies are becoming more "intelligent." Minicomputers are increasingly a feature of the new technologies, thereby enhancing coding and decoding processes or providing built-in memory systems. Indeed, by influencing information and communication systems throughout the United States, the computer is the mechanism that allows the six aforementioned trends to occur.

The Economic Transformation of the United States

Information now functions as the core of the American economy. Not only do we use information, we depend upon information for our economic survival. This dependency on information is a product of the evolution of the American economy, which has experienced some rather rapid shifts from an agriculturally based economic system to an industrial and service economy and then to our current information-based economy. This transformation has been subtle in many ways, but its key moments are clearly evident and measurable. As identified by Robert Kalman (1978, p. 228; also see Beniger, 1986, p. 15; Beniger, 1988, pp. 21–24; Ginsberg, 1982), one measure of the transformation is found in the changing labor force in the 20th century: Whereas in 1900 most Americans worked in agriculture and industry, in 1980 most worked in the information fields (see table 1.2). The full impact of this transformation has been quantified by Elizabeth Fowler (1983). She reported that more than 50 percent of the country's gross national product is attributable to the "development of data, exchange of information, manipulation of ideas and the transfer of numbers"; she added that "more than 50 percent" of those employed in the United States are engaged in one way or another in these data-processing activities (p. D20).

This kind of transformation does not occur without a drastic reconception of the nature of work. When the economy was grounded in agriculture, the frame of reference was concrete. Nature, its forces, and its products were the objects of concern. The shift to the industrial and service economy displaced human beings from this "natural" environment. The factory's assembly line and the mass production of human services defined the new employment environment. However, even in this "unnatural" employment environment, the product continued to be tangible—manufactured products and human services are concrete. Today, we are once again experiencing a dislocation as we shift from an industrial to an information-based economy: The information economy offers a very different kind of employment environment—information manipulations are cerebral, not physical, endeavors, and the outcome is knowledge, not a manufactured product. Entirely new ways of measuring self-worth, satisfaction, and productivity must be devised and accepted as the new definition of work.

Moreover, there appears to be no way in which we can revert to an industrial economy. We can expect no new industrial markets to emerge; virtually all possible markets have now been fully industrialized. As Burham P. Beckwith (1967, p. 151) reported over two decades ago, the Industrial Revolution is 60 to 80 percent complete in the advanced Western nations. Indeed, certain firms may be overindustrialized. George Stigler (cited in Silk, 1982), Nobel laureate in economics, noted that capacity utilization in manufacturing appears steady at 70 percent. Even with some 30 percent of plant capacity unused, declines in productivity seem linked to inefficiency rather than to the need for new industrial investment. The Bureau of Labor Statistics ("New Data Explain," 1983) reported that since 1973, two thirds of overall declines in manufacturing productivity resulted from a decline in efficiency, while only one third was the result of a drop in new capital investments in manufacturing. Insofar as we rely upon the industrial sector of the economy, significant developments and improvements are very likely to depend on the introduction of the computer and robotics rather than on human input. Computer-integrated production has become the goal, with computer-aided design, planning, and manufacturing as the means to achieve efficient goods production. Computer-directed robots can work 24 hours a day and be reprogrammed to adapt to new production demands. As James A. Baker (cited in Marcus, 1983, June 2) has put it, American manufacturers must "automate, emigrate or evaporate" (p. D2). Indeed, Gerald Nadler and

Gordon H. Robinson (1983) and Martin L. Ernst (1982) have already outlined the methods by which robots might be employed as the ideal means for achieving what he calls the "art of automation"; Bruce Nussbaum (1983) has predicted that "up to 75 percent of all factory jobs may be replaced by robots by the end of the decade" (p. E19); and artificial-intelligence specialists Edward A. Feigenbaum and Pamela McCorduck (1983) predicted that "industrial operatives will constitute 4 to 5% of the work force" in less than 50 years (p. 22). It would be wise to conclude that the changes brought upon us by the new technologies are now a permanent feature of our economic lives.

The new information-based economy is different in kind from previous economic systems. While some mark the beginning of the information economy with the launching of *Sputnik* in 1957 (see, e.g., Naisbitt, 1982, p. 12), others, such as Daniel Bell (1976), see a postindustrial society emerging after World War II. In any event, by 1979, the clerk became the number one profession in the United States (Naisbitt, 1982, p. 14). Currently, some 28 percent of the labor force is employed in the primary information sector of the economy, with an additional 24 percent working as information processors in the industrial sector (Porat, 1974, 1977; also see Ehrenhalt, 1986). Information processing has indeed become a multibillion-dollar industry in the United States today. Feigenbaum and McCorduck (1983, p. 19) calculated that information processing constitutes an $88-billion industry in the United States today, while a 1978 study conducted by AT&T (cited in Tydeman, Lipinski, Adler, Nyhan & Zwimpfer, 1982, p. 81) noted that all related business expenditures for all types and forms of information total almost $200 billion annually ($104 billion for personnel, $34 billion for telecommunications, $24 billion for word processing and mail, and $16 billion for electronic data processing). We are moving from a system based on transportation and production to one based on communications, in which decisions and their results are becoming simultaneous.

Before leaving this discussion of the nature of the information economy, we should note that this system has produced obvious advantages. First, solely in terms of efficiency, an information-based economy is a mechanism that allows all other sectors of the economy to function. To the extent that a system of mass communication is employed, the nation's production, transportation, and consumption patterns can be efficiently linked. A comprehensive mass-communication system is essential if manufacturers are to know how much to produce, if those in the transportation industries are to know where to send these products, and if consumers are to know both where available products are and how to inform producers of their wants. Communication is the web that links all sectors of the economy into an efficient system. As the development of information systems becomes a more independent objective, this communication system might even eliminate the middlemen or complicated advertising and sales channels that increase the cost of products.

Second, an information-based economy directly affects the quality of products manufactured by the industrial sector. In *The Next Economy*, Paul Hawken (1983) eloquently argued that during the latter part of the 20th century, the Information Society has generated knowledge that has made manufacturing more efficient. He noted that applied information findings have reduced capital, physical resources, and labor-intensive factors in real manufacturing costs while simultaneously ensuring that products are "more useful and functional, longer-lasting, easier to repair, lighter, stronger, and less consumptive of energy" (p. 9; also see Erisman & Neves, 1987).

Third, as the drudgery of physical labor is relegated to computerized robots and as working hours continue to decline (as they have since the turn of the century), human beings can devote more of their attention to those pursuits that generate self-development and self-actualization. Continuing education of all kinds and new social interests offer keys to the development of the individual. In the long run, such a shift toward self-actualization may also reduce the significance of materialism and quantification as central American values or may at least provide a foundation for more efficient uses of resources in personal environments. Moreover, as self-actualization becomes a core value, there may emerge a marked decrease in specialization and an increase in efforts to integrate dimensions and factors affecting the individual. As a study conducted by the New York Stock Exchange (1982; also see Denison, cited in Ginsberg & Vojta, 1981) reminds us, between 20 to 50 percent of productivity increases—depending upon the decade—has been due to increases in the education or knowledge level of the labor force. An information-based economy may serve us well, then, in terms of improvements both in standards of living and in our development as humane individuals. In forecasting such a scenario, we are convinced that the computer will play an important role in achieving such an Information Society.

The Role of the Computer in the Information Society

The role of any technology in human affairs is by no means clear. Traditionally, technologies are perceived as passive instruments, governed and regulated by their inventors and by the people using them. But because technologies appear to exert independent influences over the lives of people, this conventional perspective has lost popularity. Over 10 years ago, in order to discuss the "contemporary ethos," Carolyn R. Miller (1978) found it necessary to distinguish between tools and technologies. In her view, tools serve direct human objectives, are an "immediate extension" of the "biological capacities" of human beings, and are "absorbed into the culture in which they were developed"; in contrast, technologies "take on purposes of their own," "become distant from the original human capability they first extended and advance at the expense of that capacity," and "become a major part of a culture's explanatory system" (pp. 229–30).

Clearly, for some, computers are a technology, not a tool. Advancements in the development of the computer have been viewed as a source of fundamental innovation in what is defined as information and how information is collected, processed, and distributed. Bryan Bunch (1984; also see Broad, 1984, August) has reported, for example, that breakthroughs in the evolutions of the technologies used in astronomy and space, biology, chemistry, medicine, and physics have altered what is reported or viewed as data, stimulated new conceptions, generated new areas of research, and even led to new forms of scholarship and subsequently new journals and associations.

However, among scientists there is disagreement about whether and to what degree computer technologies have affected the objectives and conduct of scientific inquiry. Some have argued that the use of computers is standardizing data systems and promoting remote and decentralized decision making (Abelson, 1986; Cardwell, 1972; Harris & Mattick, 1988; Kranzberg, 1988), while others have maintained that personal, defense, and economic factors are impeding development of the link between computerized technology and the conduct of scientific research (Sterling, 1988; Weingarten & Garcia, 1988).

Among critics, the issues are apparently less controversial. Jennifer Daryl Slack (1984) has argued that a theory of criticism cannot be governed by a solely technological orientation: Instead, human insight and research interact with technological advancements and jointly affect innovation. And although tools and technologies are traditionally viewed as passive instruments, governed and regulated by their inventors and by the people using them, change in one sense can be the result of technological innovations. As Mary S. Mander (1983) noted, "a change in one component" of the communication process, "such as technological innovation, necessarily results in an alteration in other component parts, such as social structure or cultural artifacts" (p. 151). Indeed, she concluded that "the 'contents' of language are mediated by communications technologies" (p. 151).

Such a perspective does provide a way of defining the computer as an evolving data-processing system and ultimately a way of identifying the role of the computer within the Information Society. By tracing the evolution in the development of the computer, the changing and emerging information-processing and communication capabilities of the computer can be isolated. A historical approach, a focus on the origin and development of the computer as a technology, makes it possible to explain how the computer has gained its power. Extensions of this evolution, however tentatively they must be posited, may provide a key to the future of the computer as a communication technology.

The computer has changed radically within the past 40 years. Each of these changes has dramatically modified the computer as an information-processing system and ultimately its potential influence upon human communication. To understand the computer most people experience today, one should consider the changes that computer systems have undergone.

Although the basic theory of contemporary computers was developed between 1834 and 1846, the historical origins of the computer can be traced back some 5,000 years, when the first known calculators were developed. The abacus, frequently identified as the first calculator, was probably developed first by the Chinese and is a device with multiple series of wires or rods strung with beads that can be passed back and forth across each wire or rod. The different levels of the wires and the rules for passing beads back and forth determine the outcomes that can be derived from an abacus. In expert hands, the abacus is an accurate and fast instrument. The abacus, which employs several principles still operative in the contemporary computer, provides a uniform system for representing, manipulating, and storing data, and those skilled in its use can solve virtually all types of arithmetic problems, even geometric ones. Other calculating devices used by different cultures during past ages took the shapes of a tray strewn with sand, a slab, a sideboard, and even a plate with various piles of powders, sticks, or measuring and marking systems. But for massive numerical calculations, such instruments as the abacus are limited by the physical size of the device if not by the enormous energy and potential errors involved in making the calculations.

By the mid-1600s, a series of instruments was devised to facilitate massive and accurate "number crunching." John Napier's slide rule allowed users to complete arithmetic calculations with logarithmic scales. In the early 1600s, Schickad's digital calculator assisted the astronomer Johannes Kepler. Making no known use of either Napier's or Schickad's inventions, Blaise Pascal in 1642 produced the first calculating machine capable of performing arithmetic functions. Pascal's calculating machine involved an elaborate set of dialing mechanisms that moved interlocking cogs and wheels on various axles. It could add, and, with a good deal of effort, it could also subtract, multiply, and divide. Had Pascal's machine been cheaper, easier to maintain, and more readily accepted by his peers, it would have increased the speed and accuracy of calculations in the business world of the 1600s.

It was not, however, until the 1800s that the basic principles for the contemporary computer were concretized. The effort was led by Charles Babbage, an Englishman born in 1792, who labeled his theoretical machine the "analytical engine." The analytical engine used automatically sequenced punch cards for recording data and included a memory and arithmetic capabilities. Babbage produced over some 40 years an extensive series of sketches for an analytical engine involving complex integrations of wheels, levers, and belts. Although never built, the analytical engine would have covered a football field and been run by six steam engines. Nonetheless, in its design the analytical engine possessed the equivalents of a modern logic center, memory, control unit, mathematical center, and operating system that could be changed or reprogrammed at will.

Although none of these pre-20th-century efforts actually produced a computer as we understand it, the principles for contemporary computer systems reside in these early efforts. The first generation of contemporary computers improved on these earlier models and had the vacuum tube as its central defining characteristic. The Electronic Numerical Integrator and Calculator—ENIAC, as it is now known—was unveiled in 1946 by the Moore School of Engineering at the University of Pennsylvania. In 1947, it was installed at the Aberdeen weapons-proving grounds in Maryland. The machine compiled ballistic tables for new guns and missiles and could perform some 5,000 addition and subtraction computations per second. However, the machine was massive and unreliable. ENIAC was composed of 17,000 vacuum tubes, 70,000 resistors, 10,000 capacitors, and 6,000 switches. It filled a huge room, weighed 30 tons, required a tremendous amount of electricity, frequently overheated, required 24-hour maintenance, and had to be rewired to change its program. Nonetheless, the first modern computer had been invented, and it processed information at speeds that were useful to human beings. The system was limited by its core component, the vacuum tube, and related problems, but the limitation was not inherent, for at the very moment of the unveiling of ENIAC, Bell Labs was inventing the replacement for the vacuum tube and paving the way for a second generation of computers.

The second generation of contemporary computers had as its central defining characteristic the transistor, an electronic device that blocks, inhibits, or redirects a flow of electronic current. In this sense, the transistor is a semiconductor that can be interlocked with other semiconductors to create multiple and interacting pathways, thus functioning as a switch. The transistor was one hundredth the size of the vacuum tube, consumed less energy, and required no warm-up. In practice, the first computers employing the transistor were hand-wired, much as early radios were individually wired for operation. Although faster, cheaper, and more reliable, the computers were cumbersome because of the hand-wiring requirements. A more efficient system of production was needed.

The third generation of contemporary computers had the single silicon integrated circuit as its central defining characteristic. Developed independently in the mid-1950s by two firms—Texas Instruments and Fairchild Semiconductor—the single silicon integrated circuit eliminated hand-wiring by "printing" circuits on a board. Production of these integrated circuits involves etching any number of transistors on a single piece of silicon and connecting them to produce the basic logic circuit of the computer. In 1971, Intel Corporation produced the first integrated circuit on a tiny silicon chip, thereby establishing the procedure for the mass production of the microprocessors found in the current personal computer: A simple but complete computer has been put on a chip the size of a postage stamp. By 1975, Altair produced for mass-market distribution a computer kit for under $700, using the principles embodied in the integrated circuit. In 1977, Steven Wozniak and Steven Jobs introduced the Apple II, the first preassembled desktop personal computer.

The fourth generation of computers had very large scale integration (VLSI) as its central defining characteristic. First introduced in 1975 and expected to continue through the 1980s, very large scale integration involves etching tens of thousands of interlocking integrated circuits on a single silicon chip. As the end of this generation of computers approaches in the late 1980s, the first million-unit circuit chips, now developed under laboratory conditions, may become a standard component in computers.

A fifth generation of computers has been many times predicted, but what its explicit foundation will be has produced less agreement. This generation may manifest itself in one or more of the following five forms.

Computers may become symbol-processing systems, capable of comprehending human language and therefore functioning, by most definitions of the phrase, as intelligent agents. Artificial-intelligence specialists Edward A. Feigenbaum and Pamela McCorduck (1983) predicted that the computer of the 1990s will contain knowledge information processing systems (KIPS) as its central defining characteristic and that it will not only process information but also function as an intelligent knowledge specialist, engaging in symbolic manipulation and symbolic inference. Underscoring the seriousness of this endeavor, Bunch (1984) reported that "the Japanese ministry of international trade and industry announced on April 14, 1982, that it was committing one billion dollars to the development of a new artificial intelligence system, which would have, among other abilities, the ability to translate between Japanese and English, to read, and to talk to people in ordinary language" (p. 372). While not currently capable of such symbolic inferences, computers identified as "expert systems" are nonetheless already being sold by some computer manufacturers. These systems are altering human understandings and tasks, for they add a new layer of digital interpretation and functions between human apprehension and action (see, e.g., Zuboff, 1988, pp. 79–96).

Others predict that the fifth generation of computers will shift from the traditional silicon base to an organic, living form. The development of the "molecular computer," with carefully designed and manipulated protein crystal achieved through genetic engineering of the DNA structures, would produce the "biochip" (Fildes & Toffler, 1988; Hartmann, 1984). In this view, a computer is nothing less than a life form, designed to carry out all computing functions in a cell. Some, such as Geoff Simons (1983, pp. 188–95; also see Aborn, 1988, p. 142; Margulis & Sagan, 1986), have speculated that these biochips might be implanted within the human brain to provide full and immediate access to data stored in a computer. Such technological developments would raise intriguing moral and legal questions. Indeed, some might assume that such life forms would possess the basic rights accorded to all living entities. If one made such an assumption, could a computer be shut down if this action "killed" a living and intelligent life form?

Yet another group has speculated that the fifth generation of computers will involve a shift from an electronic to a laser-radiation computer design. Eitan Abraham, Colin T. Seaton, and S. Desmond Smith (1983; also see Broad, 1985) have already argued for the speed and efficiency of the "optical computer." They suggested that a computer powered by beams of light rather than by electric currents might be capable of a trillion operations per second. The crucial component for these systems, an optical analogue of the transistor, has already been built. These computers would employ an intense beam of light that acted upon the properties of certain crystalline materials. If such computers could satisfy mass-production standards and were compatible with other electricity-based technologies, an electronic technology would be displaced by a light technology.

Others believe that the fifth generation of computers will involve the development of computer compatibility. At present, hardware and software developed for one computer model may not function on other models, but some anticipate that computer manufacturers will gradually adopt universal standards in producing personal computers. Such standards have been adopted by Japan's leading computer producers (see, e.g., Pollack, 1983, June 16). Similarly, some major manufacturers of mainframe computers are gradually and informally adopting the communication standards of IBM's computers. In addition, the National Bureau of Standards is establishing standards for the computer hardware on which the federal government spends $2 billion each year. Others believe that interface systems are being developed that would allow each computer to communicate with all other computers (see, e.g., Markoff, 1988, June 1, p. C10). AT&T, for example, used such a focus as one of its major rationales for entry into the computer industry, and American Bell's Net 1000 service is designed to allow for this kind of computer compatibility (see, e.g., Pauly & Foltz, 1983). In the manufacturing sector of the United States, some 50 companies, using more than 100 high-technology operations and support systems, have sought—with some indications of initial success—to establish an international compatibility standard (known as the Manufacturing Automation Protocol, or MAP, and Technical and Office Protocol, or TOP) for high-tech manufacturing (see, e.g., Feder, 1988).

Finally, one group proposes that the brains and nervous systems of animals and human beings will be the models for a fifth generation of computers characterized by "biological computation." David W. Tank and John J. Hopfield (1987) have argued that "modern digital computers are latecomers to the world of computation," whereas "biological computers" in human beings and animals "have existed for millions of years, and they are marvelously effective in processing sensory information and controlling the interactions of animals with their environment" (p. 104). Noting that "the 1980's have seen an extraordinary growth of interest in neural models and their computational properties" (p. 104), Tank and Hopfield proposed that artificial computers be based upon the "collective-decision" or "neural-network circuit" of human beings and animals (p. 105; also see Peled, 1987, p. 64). From this perspective, the multiple and interconnected nature of human and animal nerve cells would constitute the model for future hardware design. Theoretically, this new design would bypass the serial-logic systems and predetermined step-by-step programs now used in computers in favor of a model that seeks to duplicate the parallel processing of the human being: "The overall progress of the computation is determined not by step-by-step instructions but by the rich structure of connections among computing devices" that operate as "one continuous process" (Tank & Hopfield, 1987, p. 105). The fundamental structure of the computer would be designed to duplicate that of the human being, making the computer more like a human being.

Each of these fifth-generation predictions has its advocates, and future developments along one or more of these lines should not surprise us, but how the computer industry will develop in the 1990s is plainly a contested issue. If previous developments are an indication, the needs of computer users will control these innovations. In any event, some four generations of computers have been developed and a future generation is in the making. Each generation represents a qualitative and quantitative advance in the evolution of computers and a marked increase in their effectiveness.

The computer has now emerged as one of the major communication technologies in the world. The scope of computerized communication is difficult to dramatize adequately. Large mainframe computers in American corporations, for example, now perform the work of 3 *trillion* clerical workers every day ("Small Business and the PC," 1984, p. C22). When companies were asked how much they relied on their computer facilities, 19.6 percent of them said they were "totally dependent" and 65.8 percent said they were "heavily dependent," while only 13.9 percent said they were "moderately dependent" and less than 1 percent, or 0.7 percent, could claim they were "slightly dependent" (Center for Research on Information Systems, cited in Wall, 1988). In addition, Americans annually transmit more than 2 billion electronic messages to each other via computer (Markoff, 1988, June 1, p. C10). On a comparative basis, H. Weil (1982) has noted, "there are approximately 100,000 instructions per U.S. citizen being obeyed by computers *every second*" (p. 58). Placed within a global context, computers currently generate, process, and transmit more information in a single day than the combined volume of information produced by every person in the world within a 24-hour period. By these measures, computerized communication is now far more dominant and pervasive than human communication.

When compared to other technologies, the computer is also a unique medium of communication. As communications specialist Frederick Williams (1982) has so pointedly observed, "The computer is the first communications technology to interact intellectually with its users. Most technologies only transform light, sound, or data into electronic impulses for transmission, then reverse the process at the receiving end. Computers, by contrast, can accept or reject our messages, reduce or expand them, file them, index them, or answer back with their own messages" (p. 38). In greater detail, Williams has explained:

Although we often think of modern electronic computers as giant calculation devices, they can also qualify as a *communication technology*. They are capable of taking our messages and giving them back to us or others, as does any communication device. But unlike any other communication device, they are capable of *acting upon* them in a manner defined by an extension of our own human intelligence. While other communications technologies extend the range of our human messages, the computer allows us to extend our human capability for acting upon messages. (1982, p. 108)

What makes the computer a unique communication technology is that it is intentionally designed to process and to alter human messages and to draw new conclusions regarding human messages. Other communication technologies may affect the substantive meaning of a human message, but the alteration is typically an unintended by-product of the medium. The computer, on the other hand, is employed because it will reformat the ideas contained in a human message. The computer processes and manipulates the messages it conveys, and, in terms of its effects upon the receiver, a computer message does not have the same social consequences as a person-to-person exchange.

Computers are now a fact of life in the business world, but our focus is primarily on the desktop personal computer and those situations in which individuals have direct contact with a computer either in their own homes or in their work environments. Although we have already detailed the trend in the Introduction, the numbers bear repeating in this context, for they vividly indicate the trend toward personal computers becoming an important part of many American households. This revolution in home personal computers occurred in the first half of the 1980s. In 1981, some 1/2 of 1 percent of American households had a home computer. By 1982, this number rose to 2 percent; our survey of the recorded sales of personal computers by the 10 largest producers of home computers indicated that 3,362,500 were sold in 1982. By 1983, a Gallup opinion poll indicated that 3 to 5 percent of American households had personal computers and that almost 35 percent of Americans were interested in purchasing a home computer, with 17 percent "very interested." By 1985–86, 20 percent of American households had computers. By 1987, 22 percent of American households owned a computer.

It is clear that more American households have personal computers, but it becomes far more difficult to explain *why* people have purchased home computers. Diverse explanations are possible, although it is unlikely that any one approach to this question will satisfy all. One set of explanations for home-computer adoptions has been provided by innovation and social-diffusion researchers who have compared the characteristics of adopters and nonadopters as well as early versus late adopters (see, e.g., Danko & MacLachlan, 1983; Dickerson & Gentry, 1983; Hardy, 1984). William H. Dutton, Everett M. Rogers, and Suk-ho Jun (1987) have provided "a summary and synthesis of the findings of 11 primary research studies on the diffusion, use, and so-

cial impacts of microcomputers in the home" (p. 222) and have isolated eight factors that "explain the household adoption and use of a
personal computer" (p. 226). Their explanation is derived from their
description of early computer adopters, who are characterized as (a)
having high levels of "formal education," "the single variable most
consistently associated with the adoption of computing" (pp. 228,
231); (b) "middle-aged," which may be "due to the locus of decisional
control with the family being lodged with parents" (p. 231); (c)
"males" (pp. 231–32); (d) having a "greater interest in, and relatively
more favorable attitudes toward, science and technology" (p. 232); (e)
spending "less time with television, in social activities, and in out-
door sports and recreation" (p. 232); (f) "more likely than others" to
"use a computer at work" (p. 233); (g) sharing "a household with a
child" (p. 233); and (h) possessing technical skills likely to be relevant
to computer operation, such as "the ability to type" (p. 235). To these
possible explanations for the diffusion of home computers, we add the
following observations.

First, personal computers became cheap enough for many families
to own one. In 1983, when home-computer adoptions first became
popular, about 60 to 70 percent of those with home computers had
machines that sold for less than $1,000, according to polls conducted
by Yankelovich Skelly White and by National Family Opinion (cited in
"Profile," 1983). The relatively small investment (low risk) required
attracted consumers. Yet it must also be noted that personal-computer prices can change dramatically every year. Any serious decision
to purchase a personal computer requires that the current range of
costs be closely surveyed. The personal-computer market has, in fact,
been one of the most highly volatile of any of the monitored markets.
During certain shakeout periods, when manufacturers are dropping
out of the market, discontinued desktop personal computers may be
very reasonably priced. At one point, for example, the Timex Sinclair
1000 had a suggested manufacturer's list price of $99 but was fre-
quently sold for under $30 by certain discount retailers. Personal com-
puters manufactured by Texas Instruments, Commodore, Atari, and
Osborne have been similarly discounted. When the computer market
has been controlled by fewer firms, however, the prices of personal
computers have increased. In all, then, while the overall prices of personal computers have been generally declining since 1977, the price of
a personal computer during any given year can vary radically, and the
diffusion of personal computers is therefore likely to be affected by
consumers' perception of the comparative cost of purchasing a personal computer.

Second, while the cost of the machines is typically reasonable, the
efficiency of the personal computer consistently improves. Each year,

personal computers are improved technologically and are appropriately advertised as processing material faster, possessing larger memories for storing more information, and increasingly energy efficient. All indications are that even greater efficiency can be expected in the future (Peled, 1987, p. 64).

Third, the personal computer can generally be easily incorporated into the typical American household. If need be, for example, a personal computer can usually be connected to an existing television set. More generally, the portable nature of the home computer allows it to be introduced without making major changes in the physical or social structure of the household.

Fourth, major social institutions have increasingly maintained that computing skills are an educational necessity. Elementary schools, high schools, colleges, and universities frequently maintain that "computer literacy" is a basic feature of a comprehensive education. Several major colleges and universities even provide students with personal computers or require that they own one.

Fifth, as sales of home personal computers have increased, computers have been (and continue to be) cast as somehow linked to an emerging national necessity. For example, the National Science Foundation (cited in Pollack, 1986, September 30; also see Boffey, 1983) has reported that the United States' economic survival may now depend upon the nation's ability to capture the international technology market. Indeed, American high-tech corporations are already asking not only for a governmental policy but for governmental protection from foreign competitors in the area of computer technology. And as a national priority on computer technology emerges, the American labor force is repeatedly cast as a component that must be prepared for such a transformation.

Last but by no means least, home-computer operators seem to find uses for personal computers. In 1983, in a national random sample of home-computer owners' opinions, Gallup reported the following uses for the home computer (owners were allowed to give multiple responses):

51% video games
46% business or office homework
46% child's learning tool
42% adult's learning tool
37% budget or balancing checkbook
27% business-in-home uses
18% word processing
16% mailing lists
14% information retrieval
 9% appointment calendar

9%   recipes file
4%   calorie counter (p. D1)

Four years later, while home computers continued to be devoted to essentially the same ends, respondents reported a dramatic increase in their use of home computers for these same tasks. In 1987, C&S/SRI Research (cited in "A Computer in Every Home?") reported that respondents said they used home computers for the following purposes (again, owners were allowed to give multiple responses):

76%   education
76%   games
63%   word processing
62%   programming
54%   record keeping
51%   finances
46%   business records
19%   remote (p. 49)

Compared to those polled in national random samples, more selective and specific groups of users are likely to use computers in different ways. For example, a survey of subscribers to *Personal Computing* (cited in Lewis, 1986, May) indicated that they used their computers in the following ways:

88%   word processing
81%   spreadsheet calculations
74%   data-base and file management
64%   education
54%   video games (p. C7)

Link Resources Corporation (1988) predicted the following breakdown for software sales among consumers in 1991:

26%   entertainment
25%   home productivity
24%   education
 5%   household management and business
 4%   other (p. 27)

Given the diverse responses consistently provided by computer owners, it is appropriate to note that not only is the personal computer used, it has become a multifunctional technology for its owners.

A profound change has indeed occurred in the United States. In some 50 years, the American economy has changed from an agricultural-manufacturing system to an information-processing system. Stimulated and perhaps dictated by this Information Society, an even more rapid change has occurred in the private lives of a significant portion of Americans. In essentially one decade, a number of American households have become computer centers: Between 1977 and 1987, some 20 to 25 percent of American households adopted and began to extensively use personal computers. Though the reasons for this rapid innovation and diffusion of computers are complex, it is clear that computer usages have decisively altered the behaviors and patterns of interaction within these households. The Information Society and its related technologies, particularly the computer, have transformed the public and private lives of a significant number of Americans.

A Critique of the Information Society

The Information Society and the home personal computer raise some extremely important issues, for change cannot occur without some disruption of social patterns and social institutions. We will examine these issues, but we want first to alert the reader to 10 key questions.

1. *Are we substituting a paper and electronic reality for the world of physical phenomena?* Should the American economy be predominantly an information-processing system, for example, at the expense of goods production? As we manipulate paper and electronic patterns, are we forgetting how much physical circumstances affect us?

2. *Does the Information Society promote the use of isolated facts without a consideration of the political-cultural context in which these facts occur?* Are overall patterns of social meaning lost when isolated facts are readily available? In an even larger context, is the meaning of knowledge itself being fundamentally changed by the computer? Will massive quantities of data, now defined as information, ultimately be defined as knowledge? Can the consumption of mass quantities of information be equated with understanding? Is knowledge itself becoming a corporate product rather than an issue of personal comprehension, utility, and growth?

3. *Are the Information Society and the use of the computer promoting a world of numbers?* Computers promote a numeric nomenclature. Each of us already has a Social Security number, a telephone number, a partly numerical street address, and a host of other numerical references. All of these numerical references have become— whether we like it or not—a part of our self-definition. Should we be promoting such numerical referencing? Is individuality lost when

people are understood as statistical groupings? Can we more easily dehumanize others when they become perceived as numbers? What dangers does an emphasis upon sheer data pose for individual freedom?

4. *Are information and computer relationships replacing human interactions?* Will computers have the same effect on social relationships as television has? George Comstock (1980a, p. 500) noted that television owners spend less time with their friends than nonowners. Frederick Williams (1982) reported that 46 percent of children say they like television "more than daddy" (p. 141). A Gallup poll (1977) found that Americans identified television viewing as the most preferred "way of spending an evening" and one selected 4 times more than being with friends (pp. 14–15). Will a similar pattern occur as computers become a more important part of the American household? Forms of computer obsession have already been reported to have negative effects upon family life. Will those who fear computers be socially isolated? Will the home become a socially isolated island connected only electronically to the world outside? Will machines diminish the need for human contact, or will people always need people?

5. *As people increasingly use computers, will they develop new types of friendships, "computer friendships," which are based solely on the electronic messages transmitted among them?* To what extent are real friendships possible without the immediate presence of another in a person-to-person exchange? If the computer is perceived as one more communication technology that has invaded our personal environment and reduced face-to-face human contact, will loneliness increase? As the number of different technologies in personal life increase, will people report that they are more lonely? Have communication technologies been increased in the hope of eliminating loneliness? Has this technological solution to loneliness been successful? How long can this kind of technological solution to loneliness be employed before people seek a radically different solution?

6. *As home computers become linked to all sectors of the economy, will there be sufficient privacy safeguards?* Are these safeguards reliable? Computer law is already becoming a recognized legal specialization.

7. *Will the computer displace other communication media?* In 1964, Marshall McLuhan (pp. 268–94) predicted that television would destroy interest in books. For most Americans, it so far has not, although, as we noted earlier, significant reductions in reading have occurred among those age 17 and younger. Computer owners are already believed to watch less television than non–computer owners (Rogers, Daley & Wu, 1982). With the advent of extensive and popular com-

puter use, particularly among those under the age of 21, is the death of the book likely? Book publishers are already using computers to produce books and are entering the electronic-publications industry in an attempt to prevent computer companies from gaining a monopoly in that market. As we shift our attention more toward the computer in the years to come, will we pay correspondingly less attention to the printed word and become less sensitive to its power?

8. *Will we rigorously test the information we receive from computers?* When computer programs are employed, information and decision-making systems are easily insulated from the debate and confrontation typically employed to ensure that the best information is obtained and the best decisions are made. Is something "true" simply because a computer says so? Will machine decisions begin to replace human decisions? Should computer intelligence replace human decision making in certain areas? If so, in what areas and why?

9. *Does a "computer society" create new social responsibilities?* When a significant number of Americans have personal computers, will we be able to deny personal computers to those who cannot afford to buy them? Will "technological discrimination" become an issue?

10. *Can we control our futures in a world of computers?* As computers become more "intelligent" and make more decisions, will this new technology be within our control? What kind of future do we seek in terms of the relationships between human beings and machines? Should computers function, for example, as our mentors and teachers? Have sufficient time and energy been given to the kinds of intensive ethical discussions that should precede the decision to employ computers at critical areas of human interaction?

There are no easy answers to any of these questions. We hope, however, that the following chapters provide a foundation for responding to them.

2

Humans and Computers

A Comparison of Systems and Processes

A personal computer system is, first and foremost, machinery, an assemblage of diverse manufactured components powered by electricity and designed to transmit energy in predetermined patterns. Regularity and predictability characterize the computer as a communication system. In contrast, human beings are ever-changing, flagrantly open-ended systems, capable of wildly divergent responses to others and to their environment. Human beings are innovative, emotional, value-oriented creatures; these qualities are as much a part of human beings as their quest for logic, consistency, and stability. Change and ambiguity therefore characterize human communication systems.

In this chapter, human beings and computers are compared and contrasted in two basic ways. First, we focus on the ways in which human beings and computers differ as systems, on the regularly interacting or interdependent physical and organizing elements that distinguish human beings and computers as discrete entities. We examine most closely the cognitive structures that distinguish computers and human beings. Second, we focus on the ways in which these structural features affect the process of communication, suggesting some of the ways in which face-to-face human communication differs from computer-mediated communication. We isolate selective criteria common to all communication systems and then compare the face-to-face human and computer-mediated communication processes in terms of these criteria.

Several objectives guide the discussion. One objective is simply to define the nature of the two basic entities involved in the computer-human communication process, and contrast functions as an extremely useful mode for defining the essential features of human beings and computers. Another objective is to provide an introduction to basic concepts that must be employed in any discussion of the computer-human communication process. A third objective is to provide what Terence Hawkes (1977) identified as a semiotic or structural analysis of face-to-face human and computer-mediated communication. Although poststructuralist and deconstructionist emphases can be extremely useful, the structural analysis offered here is designed to reveal the modes employed by human beings and computers to encode or to create messages and to decode or to understand messages. As Hawkes has stated, a structural analysis reveals the "inherent bias which affects what is perceived" by an entity, the kinds of "relationships" that an entity "creates" with other entities, and what is finally viewed as the "stuff of reality" for an entity (p. 17). In other words, a structural analysis of human and computer systems should reveal the different means used by each of these entities to create meaning in and to respond to an external and often chaotic world.

A Comparison of Structures

Such a discussion appropriately begins with the system-centered features employed to create or encode messages. Specifically, we first compare and contrast the ways in which human beings and computers process information. We then consider the different kinds and functions of memory systems in human beings and computers. The perceptual structure humans employ when perceiving and reacting to external stimuli is then compared to the input and output system of a computer. We conclude this structural analysis by characterizing the interactive systems that distinguish humans and computers.

Processing Information

KNOWLEDGE. Human beings and computers initially differ in terms of what each identifies or processes as knowledge. Human beings react to many different kinds of information, develop different conceptual systems to deal with them, and ultimately generate multiple ways of perceiving and understanding any single event or phenomenon. In contrast, computers possess a unidimensional conception of what reality is and how reality should be examined and understood. This initial difference deserves particular attention.

Human knowledge systems are tremendously complex. Some have defined human knowledge in terms of specific but highly diverse areas of specialization. Others have variously defined human knowledge as the ability to analyze or break down a complex process into its component parts, as the ability to synthesize or find relationships among diverse components, as the ability to rapidly resolve a complex problem through insight, flashes of understanding, or intuition, and as the ability to motivate others through sympathy and encouragement. These definitions do not exhaust common understandings of human knowledge.

Systematic accounts of such a complex process as human knowledge are frequently elaborate. In the late 19th century, William James (1950 [1890]) sought to identify the multiple dimensions involved in human knowledge and understanding. Using a psychological perspective, he set out to describe nothing less than how people come to understand what reality is. He initially reasoned that the origin of reality is subjective, maintaining that what is believed is what is known, that beliefs control the ways in which reality is cognized. In this view, experiences are *believed* to be real, which directly affects what is perceived and what actions are taken. This position ultimately led him to propose the existence of multiple ways of conceiving of reality, and he posited seven "orders of reality" or "sub-worlds": (a) the world of sense or of physical things, (b) the world of science or of physical things as the learned describe them, (c) the world of ideal relations or abstract truths, (d) the world of "idols of the tribe," illusions or prejudices common to the race, (e) the various supernatural worlds, (f) the various worlds of individual opinion, and (g) the worlds of sheer madness and vagary (pp. 296–97). James contended that each of these orders of reality possesses its own distinctive style of existence.

During the 20th century, a similar explanation was posited for the diverse ways in which humans understand. In 1945, Alfred Schultz reaffirmed James's line of thought and argued for the existence of "multiple realities" or "finite provinces of meaning upon each of which we may bestow the accent of reality" (p. 551). Such a perspective has been reinforced by Kenneth Burke (1935, 1962, 1973) and more recently by Peter L. Berger and Thomas Luckmann's (1966) notions of reality as socially constructed.

Perhaps the most comprehensive and insightful conception of human understanding has been provided by social psychologist Howard Gardner in his *Frames of Mind* (1983). Gardner posited that the intellectual structure of the human being may manifest itself in one or more of seven cognitive potentials. Rather than viewing human intelligence in terms of one dimension, he argued for a theory of multiple intelligences, each of which is equally important and constitutes a unique way of viewing the world. These intelligences are (a) linguistic abilities; (b) logical-mathematical skills; (c) spatial intelligence, or the ability to find one's way around in an environment, to form mental images, and to transform them readily; (d) musical intelligence, or the ability to perceive and create pitch patterns and rhythmic patterns; (e) bodily-kinesthetic intelligence, or the ability to understand and perform the fine motor movement required of a surgeon or a dancer; (f) interpersonal knowledge, or the ability to understand others, how they feel, what motivates them, and how they interact with others; and (g) intrapersonal intelligence, or an individual's ability to be acquainted with himself or herself and to have a developed sense of identity.

While Gardner cast these seven modes of understanding as distinctive forms of intelligence, we might also identify them as different types of communication systems. Each of these modes of understanding does require that a different set of concepts be employed to deal with the area involved, that particular grammars be developed to link these concepts into coherent "thoughts," and that different conventions and standards be developed to determine and to measure effectiveness in each of the particular areas. When these systems of intelligence are cast as communication systems, it becomes clear that these systems frequently merge and overlap, creating transformations, change, and ambiguity in social systems. Thus, while each of these seven systems individually constitutes a way of knowing, the overlapping and transforming linkages among these systems may also constitute ways of understanding what exists. Human understandings are therefore likely to be tremendously complex, characterized by ambiguity in terms of perspective, and subject to changes, if not radical transformations.

In vivid contrast, the knowledge or understanding provided by a computer is far more specific and direct and is ultimately narrower in scope. A computer system posits and deals with but one of the kinds of knowledge human beings employ: logical-mathematical intelligence. It may be appreciated for effectively executing this form of intelligence, yet such a mode of intelligence is severely limited from the perspective of a human being, who must function in a complex social arena that requires the use of all forms of intelligence. As we examine the information-processing system of the computer, we will see its power but also its limits.

The processing unit is the heart, the guts, or, more precisely, the brain of any computer system. It can also be referred to as the central processing unit (CPU) or as the microprocessor. Regardless of the label, the processing unit carries out several functions that define what knowledge is for a computer. As these functions are revealed, it becomes evident that a computer system is capable of processing only logical-mathematical information.

The processing unit receives information from the human user and translates the information into a notation system that the computer can use. It then directs the information to appropriate sections of the processing unit (much as a bus drops off passengers at their own stops along a bus route), manipulates the transferred information according to preestablished rules, and then communicates the results of this manipulation to the user. More precisely, the processing unit carries out three functions (see, e.g., Capron & Williams, 1982, pp. 72–75; Sanders, 1985, p. 18): First, it directs and coordinates the electrical signals within a computer system (a control function); second, it manipulates these electrical signals by recombining or repatterning numeric values used to represent certain human concepts (an arithmetic function); third, it manipulates data according to specific procedural rules (a logical function). The control, arithmetic, and logical functions thus formally define the central activities carried out by the processing unit of a computer system.

In the personal computer, the processing unit is typically located directly beneath and behind the keyboard. In appearance, the unit is not unlike a solid-state television's circuit board or replaceable component recreated in miniature. All of the functions of the personal computer are generally executed on one silicon chip, which can fit on the tip of a finger. In the large minicomputers and mainframe computers used by industry, the circuit board is covered with various clusters of interconnected silicon chips, each chip serving a different function in the computer: Some handle control functions, others carry out arithmetic functions, and still others are responsible for logical operations within the computer.

Regardless of the size of the computer or the number of chips that operate it, a coherent computing system is made possible by the marvels of microelectronic technology. The cornerstone of microelectronics is the semiconductor, a mechanism for manipulating and storing electronic charges in an organized fashion. The semiconductor is coated with silicon, whose latticed or gridlike molecular structure provides niches for electrons. Thus, when a user enters data or commands into a computer, the computer transforms this information into electronic charges. Technological developments and innovations have affected how the electronic charges are physically manipulated, but in most personal computers these charges travel along the silicon chips, directed by manufactured phosphorus "fences" in the silicon, until they come to "rest" in their appropriate locations. The path an electron follows is controlled by the fences or pathways stenciled on the chip by the manufacturer and by the computer's control unit, which can manipulate and alter these pathways. Once an electron is appropriately located, each electron charge functions as a signal or "marker" to the computer, and the computer monitors only the presence or the absence of the electronic charge. These markers thus constitute a kind of information for the computer: The presence of an electronic charge is read as a "yes" or "on" statement, and the absence of an electronic charge is understood as a "no" or "off" statement. This yes/no or on/off information can then be added, subtracted, multiplied, or divided in different logical combinations. These arithmetic and logical functions constitute the basic computing functions of every processing unit.

These basic functions do provide a foundation for the computer's execution of extremely powerful logical-mathematical activities, but one should remember that such activities represent only a very small portion of the knowledge possessed by human beings.

DATA STRUCTURES AND DATA. Human beings and computers also differ as information-processing systems in terms of their respective structures for processing data. Human beings, in order to create and to respond to multiple kinds of knowledge, must be capable of linking extremely divergent kinds of information. The pathways linking divergent facts are necessarily multidimensional. In contrast, the pathways linking computer information need not satisfy such complex information requirements, for only one kind of knowledge—logical-mathematical—is being employed. Indeed, the requirements for logical-mathematical knowledge allow, and perhaps are facilitated by, linear and sequential interaction modes. The difference is a profound way of distinguishing human beings from computers as information-processing systems.

In the human being, neurophysiological pathways are multidimensional, simultaneous, and relational. The complexity of the neurons of the brain illustrates the complexity of the process. As the psychologist Harold Hawkins (cited in Goleman, 1986) described it, "The brain contains somewhere between 10 billion and 100 billion neurons, each of which receives information from 1,000 to 100 thousand other neurons, and sends information to a like number. Even the simplest mental act, like reading the letter "A," requires the activity of many millions of neurons spread through many parts of the brain" (p. C7).

To consider the multidimensional and simultaneous networking structure of the brain is to ultimately redefine what a fact is. We may conceive of facts as discrete information units in everyday interactions with others, but for the human brain, a fact is more appropriately understood as a relationship or association of these discrete facts. In

Parallel Distributed Processing, David Rumelhart and John Mc-Clelland (1986) proposed that the brain retains not specific facts or events but rather the relationships among various aspects of those facts or events as they are encoded in groupings of neuronal cells or patterns of cell activity. Indeed, if the human being is to process facts in terms of seven kinds of intelligence, the structure of the facts or events retained within the human brain must be organized to respond to the different kinds of integrated knowledge demands made by the human being.

The way in which the human brain reorganizes facts or events into relationships or associations constitutes the inherently creative, symbolic, or communicative dimension of all human understanding. In this sense, the human brain is an active agent reformulating and reconceiving external stimuli into new interpretative and evaluative modes. As Richard B. Gregg (1984) stated, "The brain is not inert or passive, waiting for the sensory apparatus to come in contact with external stimulation in order to initiate brain activity. The brain is active, is operative prior to birth, and initiates activity by ordering the sensory network to respond to certain structures of information. The neuronal structures of the sensory systems are never activated individually, but always in relation to and coinciding with other neuronal structures" (p. 30). Gregg concluded that perception and knowledge themselves are a function of the neurons' multidimensional, simultaneous, and relation-creating activities, which he viewed as a profound form of symbolic inducement and ultimately as the foundations of rhetoric.

In sharp contrast, the data structure of a computer is linear or sequential, and the data are retained as discrete entities. As we have already noted, the circuits of a computer are linear, and all data are processed within this sequential pattern. Moreover, electronic charges, designed to represent information, can be in only one of two states—present or absent. The representation is binary or either-or in fashion (i.e., yes or no, or 0 or 1) and can function only as discrete information if coherence in the computational process is to be preserved.

It is certainly appropriate to note, as we did in chapter 1 and will again in chapters 7 and 8, that the promised fifth generation of computers may generate new kinds of hardware that minimize this difference between human beings and computers. Breakthroughs cannot be precluded. It is conceivable that combinations of computers might appear to mimic, in sheer volume and speed, the multidimensional, simultaneous, and relational information process of the human being. For example, with parallel processing, a complex task might be separated into several distinct parts, with each part assigned to a different computer in one large set of interconnected computers, so that the work can be done simultaneously, each computer working in tandem with the others. One corporation, Thinking Machines, successfully solved a problem by linking as many as 65,536 individual processors into one complex computer system (Markoff, 1988, June 16, p. D5). Nevertheless, the known state-of-the-art processing systems believed to foreshadow the fifth generation of computers—such as parallel processing or, for that matter, such new technologies as vector processing or multiprocessing—have thus far continued to rely on linear and discrete data conceptions and on sequential and independent programs (Fox & Messina, 1987; Gelernter, 1987, esp. p. 92; Sanger, 1985, September).

Far more critical in this context is the difference between the associational or relational processing of the human brain and the computer's need to hold its charges as discrete in order for them to be meaningful during computation. Rather than creating relationships, as the human brain does, linear processing of discrete information can and must destroy information. Charles H. Bennett and Rolf Landauer (1985) argued, in discussing the "fundamental physical limits of computation," that information destruction may be an inherent feature of all computation and noted that when computation is designed to simplify input, the output necessarily destroys information to accomplish this end: "In fact, any logic gate that has more input than output lines inevitably discards information, because we cannot deduce the input from the output" (p. 48). While they argued that information destruction within a computer may be minimized and that information may be randomly created or destroyed, they concluded that the effects of time, scales of size and time, and universals regarding scales of time and length remain unclear in terms of the inherent information-destruction capabilities of a computer (pp. 55–56). In contrast, the associational or relational processing of the human brain creates new information as an inherent by-product of its structure.

ONTOLOGY. Finally, in terms of their ontological structures, human beings and computers differ as information-processing systems in terms of fundamental questions regarding existence itself. Although ontology may certainly deal with, as Peter Angeles (1981) noted, "the essential characteristics of Being in itself apart from the study of particular existing things," ontological discussions may also focus upon "the order and structure of reality in the broadest sense possible, using categories such as being/becoming, actuality/potentiality," and so forth (p. 198). In this sense, information processing by human beings and that by computers appear to be discrete systems.

For the human being, knowledge is a subjective activity. As James has noted and as neurophysiological descriptions have confirmed, human beings create new relationships among the external stimuli they perceive. Even the concept *free* is in some respects confirmed by such a perspective, for, as Benjamin Libet (cited in Goleman, 1986) stated, appreciable brain activity precedes all voluntary acts. In one sense, then, human beings have no choice in the matter, for the structure of the brain itself and the requirements that humans place upon the brain demand that such creative associations and relationships be constantly formulated.

In contrast, knowledge for a computer is an objective activity. Specific and particular control, arithmetic, and logic functions are literally stamped onto the chip of the microprocessor. These functions are invariant. Moreover, computer programs constitute, by design and structure, predetermined ways for dealing with information. The structure of the computer and its operating programs determine how information is processed. Although certain outcomes may seem unexpected, the information-processing system itself is objective and predictable.

The Memory System

Humans and computers differ not only in the ways they process information but also in the ways they retain and retrieve information. A subject of intensive investigation (Cytowic & Wood, 1982; Gardner, 1985; Martin & Caramazza, 1982; Polich, 1982; Risberg & Ingvar, 1973; Rosenfield, 1988; Wood & McHenry, 1980; Wood, Taylor, Penny & Stump, 1980), human memory retention and retrieval is predominantly selective and creative. When retaining or recalling, a host of choices must be made. The human memory must adjust to and interpret social conditions. Highly critical and selective choices must be made regarding what to retain. Humans deal with a wide range of information, not all of which is appropriate to remember. In addition, retrieving information may occur under conditions that are at best problematic. External stimuli may compete with or hamper a human's ability to recall particular information. Physiological and psychological conditions, such as aphasia and amnesia, may affect human recall. Moreover, what a human being is to retrieve from memory is seldom clearly specified by others; a kind of free choice and creative function influences all human recall processes. In contrast, the memory system of the computer is precise, designed to retrieve only what is asked for and only when it is asked for. These differences deserve particular attention.

HUMAN RECALL. In many respects, the ability to recall information has declined as an important skill within our culture. Print media and a wide variety of other recording systems have diminished the need to remember specific information and the need to develop skills for recalling such information. At one time, a good memory was perceived as an essential skill for effective communication. The first classical Greek rhetoricians identified memory as one of the five major canons, equal in importance to creativity, organizational skills, style, and delivery. Four hundred years later, the Roman teacher Quintilian continued to view memory as one of the five basic skills required for the development of a "good man speaking well." Even as late as the 19th and early 20th centuries, memorization retained a position as a necessary skill and as a basic feature of the educational process. Indeed, in all eras and places where facts were not readily available to all, the ability to recall specific information was prized as a particularly useful communication skill (Baldwin, 1959).

Today, the study of memory frequently falls within the province of medical science. Neurophysiological researchers have provided a great deal of contemporary understandings of the elements that constitute and affect human memory. These neurophysiological conceptions operate within a scientific framework in which conclusions regarding memory require anatomical and social validity and reliability. Accordingly, tremendous efforts and energies have been devoted to understanding memory with reference to the human brain and to generalizations that apply to most people.

Several conclusions regarding human memory appear warranted. First, humans possess multiple types of memory. After tracing changes in regional blood-flow responses within the human brain, for example, neuropsychologists and neurologists Wood, Taylor, Penny, and Stump (1980) concluded that "an anatomical basis" existed for the "distinction between episodic and semantic memory" (p. 113). In other words, our ability to recognize people and events appears to be a different skill than our ability to recall the linguistic class into which these people and events are commonly placed. Second, the ways in which we memorize affect our recall ability. Psychologists Randi Martin and Alfonso Caramazza (1982) reported that short-term memory is affected by the use of a visual and phonological coding mechanism. Third, the speed at which we recall is affected by the way in which a type of information was retained. Neuropsychologist John M. Polich (1982) found that verbally coded items dealing with holistic, gestalt, spatial, and recognition information take longer to recall than nonverbally coded items. These rather technical results suggest that the human memory system is highly complex. Humans possess many ways of memorizing and many different types of information. And the ways in which they memorize information will affect the speed with which it can be recalled.

In contrast, computer memory systems are relatively simple. Verbal and particular, responding to linguistic and semantic classifications of specific items, computer memory systems are not designed to deal with visual, episodic, random, holistic, integrative, spatial, and recognition information. The human being's memory possesses a much larger number of memorization skills, and the computer can assist human recall in only a relatively narrow area.

THE COMPUTER'S MEMORY SYSTEM. In the personal computer, two major types of memory systems exist. One system is known as the *random-access-memory*, or RAM. The other memory system is identified as a *read-only memory*, or ROM. From a technical perspective, each of these memory systems serves a different function, requires different standards of assessment, and therefore requires independent analysis. These technical distinctions not only provide essential definitions of a computer's memory system but also constitute important evidence regarding the nature of its memory system when compared to human recall.

The random-access memory, or RAM, is a temporary holding space within a computer where a user can store information for brief periods. Among computer specialists, the key issue involved in any discussion of RAM is capacity. RAM's ideal size will depend upon what tasks the user plans to perform on the computer. Such activities as writing a book involve storing a great deal of information, while video games can generally be carried out with a small RAM. Different computer models are frequently designed with different functions in mind and accordingly with different built-in RAM sizes.

RAM capacity is measured by the number of information bits that it can store. For all practical purposes, a single letter of the alphabet or single numeric digit equals 8 *bits* of information. Thus, an average word of some 5 or 6 letters will require 40 to 48 bits of storage. Using bits of information as a measure for determining the size of the memory soon becomes unmanageable: One double-spaced, typed manuscript page of words equals almost 12,000 bits of information. Memory is therefore most frequently measured in *bytes*: 8 bits equal 1 byte. Accordingly, one 5-letter word equals 5 bytes. Thus the term *bytes* allows us to scale down the number of units being discussed: Instead of talking about 8,000 bits of information, one can talk about roughly 1,000 bytes of information. However, even when using bytes, the unit of measurement remains unnecessarily large. By convention, bytes are most frequently measured and discussed in thousands of units and designated in KS. Thus, 8,000 bytes equal 8 K. Bytes measured in thousands of KS is the system commonly used to measure the storage capacity of a personal computer. However, computer manufacturers have increasingly expanded RAM size, and it is not unusual to now find RAM size measured in megabytes, or millions of bytes. The introduction of 10- and 20-megabyte RAM computers for all practical purposes resolves any problems most home-computer users might have with regard to sufficient RAM size.

Moreover, while RAM is only a temporary storage system, extremely comprehensive systems have been developed to permanently preserve materials created in RAM. Such storage systems are technically identified as *external archival storage*, or EAS, and function as a user's personal-computer library. A user may store documents created in RAM on floppy disks, cartridges, hard disks, audiocassettes, videodiscs, and videocassettes. Each of these external archival storage systems has advantages and disadvantages, depending upon a user's needs. Regardless of the choice made, each ultimately provides unlimited storage for RAM-created documents.

The read-only memory, or ROM, is the second major type of memory found within the personal computer. ROM provides information that is permanently "written" into the computer by the manufacturer and is retained when the computer is turned off. ROM cannot easily be altered by the user; for all practical purposes, the user can only "read" or use the messages provided by ROM.

ROM serves several important functions. It typically includes at least enough information for a computer to function when it is turned on and to interpret keystrokes entered on the computer's keyboard. ROM will likely also include enough information to display several different program options on the computer's screen. ROM thus contains the information that directs and instructs the computer in all of its operations. As the cost of ROMs has declined, manufacturers have included more and more information within ROMs. Virtually every personal computer now contains at least one complete computer language within its ROM. A computer language allows a user to manipulate all features of a computer and carry out all of the functions within the range of that language.

ROMs are typically associated with the circuits imprinted on the silicon chip of a personal computer, but ROMs can also exist on special secondary-storage devices, such as a cassette tape, disk, or videocassette, which are purchased independently of the main console. These secondary-storage programs are also unchangeable by ordinary means, but they allow the user to carry out more specialized and complex activities than those provided in the ROM of a typical computer. For example, if writing a large number of papers or reports, one might decide that word processing would be an extremely convenient supplement to add to a computer's range of activities. One would purchase a special cassette or disk that provides a computer with special functions for carrying out this activity as well as guiding the user through the techniques necessary to use word processing. Computer manufacturers and retailers are more than eager to describe the range and specific types of secondary ROM systems (identified as *software programs* or *programs*) that they offer to accompany the personal computer. With time, purchased programs can easily exceed the cost of the processing unit itself, but they add flexibility to a computer system and allow the user to adapt the computer to particular requirements.

While the distinction between RAM and ROM has been rather rigidly maintained by computer specialists, new technologies are blurring the distinction. Electronically *erasable programmable read-only memory* chips, or EPROMS, for example, can be altered but retain information without electrical power, unlike the typical RAM. EPROMS allow users to customize their personal computers by reprogramming the functions of a computer key whenever desired. However, such reprogramming requires the use of a special ultraviolet light machine as well as higher voltage than that normally used in computers. Another new technology, *firmware*, transcends the traditional dichotomy between hardware and software. Firmware refers to programs written in a storage system, generally ROM, that prevents the program from being accidentally erased. Though we may be premature, we believe that these technologies will ultimately make the distinction between hardware and software extremely difficult to maintain. We suspect that memory systems, functioning as customized program-storage systems, will increasingly bridge the distinction between hardware and software. Time and technological developments will determine, however, if these forecasts materialize.

While recognizing, then, the technical distinctions that currently occupy the attention of computer specialists, we can say nonetheless that all of these memory systems share certain common features when compared to human recall. Regardless of the specific kind of computer memory system being discussed, all of the systems are verbal and particular, responding to linguistic and semantic classifications of specific items. They are not designed to deal with visual, episodic, random, holistic, integrative, spatial, and recognition information. The human being possesses a much larger number of memorization skills, and the computer can function as an aid to human recall in only a relatively narrow area.

Sensory systems are apparently powerful variables in determining what we experience and how we understand those perceptions.

As sensory media are varied, what is known and understood changes. In this sense, ways of knowing determine what is known.

The link between knowledge and the senses highlights the importance of any examination of sensory input and output systems. If we were to assume that this knowledge-sense link constitutes a highly significant relationship for human beings, we might also assume that the decision to employ computers as either input or output devices would dramatically affect our understandings of what reality is. In this sense, computers are directly altering our world.

These extremely significant issues require consideration. It thus becomes appropriate to consider the nature of human perception and then to compare this perception system to the types of input and output devices employed by computers.

HUMAN PERCEPTION. Rather than functioning as a window to the world or a camera faithfully recording the external environment, human perception is a highly complex process that selectively highlights and processes only certain stimuli, alters and integrates these stimuli, and reforms or restructures the meaning of these external stimuli. Perception is therefore a cognitive rather than an impressionistic system (Ornstein, 1972, pp. 21–24).

Although the selective nature of human perception is commonly recognized, the full scope of this filtering process is frequently understated. The specialized or differentiated nature of human sensory receptors means that only certain energy forms are apprehended. For example, X rays, infrared radiation, and ultrasonics are ignored by the human senses. More important in this context, given the world of constant information bombardment we described in chapter 1, we can attend to only those stimuli that directly affect us, or we would experience disabling information overloads. In a series of classic experiments, Jacobson (1950, 1951a, 1951b; also see Kaufman, 1979) quantified the full impact of the selective nature of human perception, reporting that only 1 percent of available visual and auditory stimuli is detected by the human.

Beyond its selective nature, human perception is also a transformational and coding process. Photic, mechanical, chemical, and thermal energies are transformed into electrochemical impulses by the human sensory mechanism (H. Brown, 1976, p. 86); external stimuli bear little resemblance to the stimuli received by the human brain and central nervous system.

The human perception system also reintegrates and reorders the stimuli received by the brain and central nervous system (H. Brown, 1976, pp. 106–7; McLuhan, 1964, p. 54). Nobel laureate F. H. C. Crick (cited in Blumenfeld, 1982; also see Crick, 1979) has aptly captured the point: "The brain fills in where it hasn't got the information. It's guessing. If it has only partial information, it guesses the rest . . . You tend to fill in what your brain thinks ought to be there" (p. 15).

Finally, it is no longer clear that our senses provide discrete links to environmental stimuli. In fact, growing evidence suggests that it is possible for the senses to affect one another, to merge sensory experiences, and ultimately to create new, vivid, concrete, and therefore apparently real experiences that cannot be had in physical reality. Identified as *synesthesia*, these sensory mergers create, as Brad Lemley (1984) noted, "a condition in which perceptions commonly confined to one sense overlap with two or more senses" (p. 65). As neurologists Richard E. Cytowic and Frank B. Wood (1982) have more carefully explained, "Synesthesia is a cross-modal sensation that is perceived as real" (p. 23). In this context, such a statement as "I see what you are saying" must be taken seriously. Indeed, in 1968, Luria described a vivid and classic case of synesthetic ability: The subject was consistently able to visualize even the words and sounds of languages unintelligible to him. These synesthetic experiences might provide an explanation for such concepts as roundedness, depth, movement, number, rest, size, and length, all of which are difficult to explain by reference to only one sense. Indeed, synesthesia may also offer one explanation for schizophysiology. Some researchers—such as Osgood (1960) and Marks (1974, 1975)—have suggested that language experiences may create among the diverse senses a semantic and connotative link that later allows the different senses to make an immediate, neural, low-level connection within the paroxysmal limbic and sublimbic levels of the brain.

Cross-modal sensory experiences have led some to postulate the existence of and an explanation for extrasensory experiences. Such an argument informs Robert Rivlin and Karen Gravelle's *Deciphering the Senses: The Expanding World of Human Perception* (1984). While leaps of faith seem evident here, such discussions do suggest that human perception and its full functions and powers will remain topics of vigorous debate.

COMPUTER INPUT/OUTPUT DEVICES.   Computer technologies are constantly being altered. We may think of computers as accepting only typewritten material and responding only with typewritten outputs, but that is no longer so. More computers are capable of responding to an audio stimulus, to the human voice, and to such physical sensations as movement, heat, and touch. A more complete list of computer input-output devices includes the alphanumeric keyboard; the numeric keypad; the joystick; the light pen; the voice activator and speech synthesizer; physical sensors that measure position, stress, temperature, magnetism, fluid level and flow, force, and radiation; keypunch cards; the cathode-ray tube (CRT) or television screen; printers; the mouse; and robots. Again, depending upon the uses an operator has for a computer, each of these input-output devices has certain advantages and disadvantages.

When compared to the sensory systems of human beings, the input and output systems employed in computers are at first glance relatively simple receptors and transmission devices. In virtually all personal computers, each input is intentionally and specifically entered into the computer. Computers are typically programmed to receive only one kind of information at a time and only at specified rates; they respond to only such stimuli and no others. Moreover, computer input systems are incapable of selective perception; as long as all technical requirements are satisfied, they will always accept all of the information they are designed to receive. In addition, they typically accept inputs only in discrete, verbal, and linear form. For all practical purposes, a computer cannot create and alter inputs through any kind of cross-modality system. Thus, the creativity associated with human perception does not currently characterize computer reception and transmission; however, even the input and output system of the computer is subject to technological innovation, and some have anticipated that it may be possible to duplicate human perception in a computer. For example, Richard Jay Solomon (1988) has predicted that,

using a number of clever arithmetical techniques and relatively conventional sensor and transducer technologies, the programmable process can be made to store, re-create, modify, and analyze virtually anything that a human can hear, see, touch, smell, and taste—and quite a lot that humans cannot sense! The machine does these things by accepting analogues of external signals and converting these signals to digital form using preprogrammed rules. An example of how digital devices can interface with and manipulate the human world of hearing are the computers that digitize sound, a process called pulse code modulation. These computers were among the first rudimentary expert systems but now have evolved into full-scale stored-program machines for switching and sound enhancement. Extension of this concept to visual systems permits image enhancement and computer animation and in the coming years will greatly improve television systems through manipulation, compression, and anticipation of an image's motion components.

The digital communication lines that can mix voice, pictures, and data indiscriminately are all based on variations of this technology. This is the new dominant mode of all telecommunications installations worldwide—a powerful example of the merging of technologies and the blurring of lines of control by the carrier of communications. (pp. 43–44)

Interface Systems

Precisely defined, an interface may be either a physical surface forming the common boundary of two bodies or a connecting unit that allows independent systems to interact and communicate with each other. Although we seldom employ the term *interface system* to describe how human beings socialize, there are commonalities and differences in the ways human beings and computers interrelate.

HUMAN RELATIONS.   For human beings, relationships differ in kind, each relationship requiring a different style, set of conceptions, and appropriate behaviors. In other words, human behavior is context-dependent. As Kenneth Burke (1973) remarked, " 'Circumstances alter cases' " (p. 23). The ways in which humans communicate depend upon the situations in which they are functioning. From a communication perspective, human activities are frequently classified as intrapersonal, interpersonal, intragroup, intergroup, intracultural, intercultural, mass, and international. Each type of situation contains its own definition of appropriate behavior. Moreover, each type of situation can be distinguished by the use of particular words, unique concepts, degrees of intimacy, forms of feedback, and even the number of people typically involved. Situations can thus determine what is said, how it is said, and even whether anything at all is said. Often unstated, these frames of reference control human behavior and frequently function as operational definitions of societal and cultural systems.

COMPUTER INTERFACING.   Computers operate in a context-free environment and are immune to circumstances, social ordering systems, and the rules that govern cultural systems. Data are treated as data regardless of their source, intended use, or social consequences. In one sense, by ignoring the social boundaries established by human beings, computers create an entirely new frame of reference for understanding information. In another sense, computers are completely insensitive to the subtle yet frequently profound meanings that particular data can have in certain situations.

Defining the word more precisely in the context of computer use, IBM's *Data Processing Glossary* (1977) notes that "an interface might be a hardware component to link two devices or it might be a portion of storage or registers accessed by two or more computer programs" (p. 127). In our discussion of interface systems here, we deal with both of these meanings.

We should first note that interface systems are not essential for all users of personal computers. However, interface systems are useful or even essential for those who want to employ such peripheral devices as printers and disk systems, who want to communicate with other personal-computer owners, who require extensive data bases for research, or who find it desirable—if not necessary—to transmit their work to a place of employment without being physically present at that location. Pregnancy, child rearing, or a physical handicap, for example, may require or encourage workers to use telework interface systems. Interface systems are not currently viewed as a necessity for every personal computer owner, but these systems may ultimately become indispensable elements of a comprehensive personal computer system. For now, however, the hardware involved in establishing an interface system defines these systems. We focus particularly on two types of interface systems that we identify as a *peripheral interface system* and a *data transmission interface.*

A peripheral interface system can serve any of several functions. It can connect such accessory devices as printers and disk systems into the processing unit of a personal computer and regulate the flow of information among these accessory devices. The system can expand the power of a personal computer to include, for example, extended memory or a dual disk system. A peripheral interface system can allow different personal-computer owners to engage in two-way communication through their computers. A peripheral interface system, then, allows a user to connect, regulate, and expand a personal computer and to transform a processing unit into a complex but coherent and potentially socially shared system.

A physical component in most personal computers, a peripheral interface system is incorporated by different models in different ways. In several models, the system is built into the console of the computer and is therefore invisible to the computer operator. In other models, the system is an external component added onto the console as an additional hardware unit.

Regardless of the way in which the peripheral interface system is connected to a personal computer, certain universals define its operations. First, it coordinates or regulates the rate at which information is transferred from one mechanism in the computer system to another device. The number of bits transferred per second, identified as the *baud rate,* is regulated by the peripheral interface system. Baud rates of 110, 300, 1200, and 9600 are common; dividing a baud rate by 10 provides a rough approximation of the number of English words transmitted per minute. Because a processing unit typically transmits much more information per second than a printer can reproduce on paper, the peripheral interface system serves the essential function of preventing overloads on the printer and indeed on any devices connected to the processing unit. Second, it controls the number of bits of data transferred in each character. The amount of data a personal computer conveys with each keyboard stroke can vary. Some personal computers transmit 8 bits of information, while others may convey as many as 16, 32, and even 64 bits of data in each cycle. The peripheral interface system ensures that the same amount of data per cycle is employed by all accessory devices connected to a personal computer. Third, the peripheral interface system introduces *parity* into the operation of all accessory devices. Parity provides a check for errors in electronic transmissions. It tests whether or not the number of binary characters—the language unit of a computer, defined in detail in chapter 3—is consistent with the conventions governing the computer's language system. Finally, the peripheral interface system adds a stop command to each unit of information transferred among accessory devices. Identified as a *stop bit*, this added signal indicates that a character has been successfully transmitted and that a new element or character is about to be transmitted. Thus, while performing essentially technical functions, the peripheral interface system provides the necessary coordination of several different accessory devices added to a personal computer.

The peripheral interface system functions predominantly without the direct control or attention of the user, thereby allowing the user to devote energy to the primary task of entering and manipulating information. In addition, it can be set for default values for its manipulation of baud rate, data bits, parity, and number of stop bits. These default values reflect standardized rates in controlling the interaction of accessory devices. However, the user is provided with a series of commands to adapt these rates to the requirements of any unusual equipment added to the personal-computer system. The manual that accompanies each accessory device typically provides the information needed to alter interaction rates. At this point, we seek only to draw attention to the essential functions carried out by the peripheral interface system. In our view, the existence and functions of the peripheral interface system are among the most neglected areas for consideration in introductions to personal-computer systems.

A personal computer can function as much more than a logic and computing device for only the immediate user. With the aid of a push-button telephone and a special connecting device, the user can establish a link with virtually any other computer user and can gain access to some of the most comprehensive data bases in the world. It is this system that allows a user to transmit work, in the form of information, to a place of employment without being physically present at the employment center. For others, as noted in the Preface, it may function as an important social network.

Among computer users, the device interfacing a personal computer and telephone is identified as a *modem*. The modem has made the personal computer a medium of national and even international communication. At this point, however, we are concerned with its role as hardware in a computing system.

Technically, a modem is a translation device that converts the type of information stored in a computer into human terminology and back again if necessary. A modem modulates and demodulates signals; it enables digital data used in a personal computer to be transmitted over analog transmission facilities, such as a telephone. In more practical terms, a completely interlocking computer-to-computer system allows a user at one end of the connection to enter information into his or her computer, manipulate the information within the computer, then transmit the information through the modem across telephone lines to another computer user. The receiving modem will translate the information into terms the receiver's computer can understand and then display the information in the receiver's native language on his or her CRT screen.

No single physical description of a modem pertains, as they vary in size, shape, and mode of connection. In some models, identified as acoustic modems, the telephone receiver is placed in a cradle, and one of the couplers links the computer at one end with the peripheral device at the other. These models were once the most economical available, but the model is particularly susceptible to transmission interference caused by outside noise from the telephone line. In other models, the modem is a small unit attached to the base of the telephone and equipped with switches to shift back and forth between regular telephone connections and modem use. Identified as a direct-connect modem, this model has become cheaper over the years; it now equals the cost and does not have the technical problems of an acoustic modem.

We began this discussion of computer interface systems by noting that computer systems are immune to the circumstances, social ordering systems, and rules that govern human interactions. Within a computer system, data are processed in predetermined ways as specified by a computer program, regardless of the nature of the source, its intended use, or the social consequences. In this sense, computers ignore the social boundaries established by human beings. In another sense, however, computers' interface systems create their own frame of reference, a new world not previously experienced by human beings. A computer network, for example, is created by the interaction or merger of several computer interface systems, yet such a network interaction does not exist in any specific geographic place. In this regard, Joshua Meyrowitz (1985) noted that the computer, as an electronic medium of communication, provides a user with no sense of place, for the interactions occur through telephone lines and within a centralized computer. Accordingly, the circumstances of the interactions lack any predetermined social customs and rules, and users must create their own sense of what is appropriate for such interactions. A new kind of social system is thus a by-product of a comprehensive computer interface system. In the next section of this chapter, we explore in detail the ways in which this new social system has affected human communication.

We have noted that the cognitive structure and functions of the human being have been described as distinct in nature from the kinds of logical activities executed by a computer. These two entities acquire and process information in different ways. Structural differences determine the ways in which they independently encode information and decode or respond to messages. Some of these decoding differences are aptly illustrated by comparing how face-to-face human communication differs from human interactions that occur through a computer-mediated communication network or a computer bulletin board system.

A Comparison of Processes

Face-to-face and computer-mediated communication systems are dramatically different. The differences we highlight at this point turn solely upon the modes involved in each system, modes so radically different that significant contrasts between the two systems can be noted even before their contents are investigated. Although there are more, five of the variables relating to differences between face-to-face and computer-mediated communication systems are identified here: the channels used, the type of discursive modes used in each system, the unique feedback systems built into each system, the different kinds of social roles involved in each system, and the use of time embedded in each system.

The Channel

In face-to-face exchanges, both verbal and nonverbal channels are employed. Mehrabian (1981) claimed that nonverbal communication accounts for 93 percent of the social meanings conveyed in face-to-face communications. In computer-mediated exchanges, the nonverbal channel is eliminated. All social meanings must be translated into and conveyed by a verbal mode. Users have attempted to introduce a nonverbal mode into these computer exchanges by developing a set of visual signs intended to simulate the nonverbal facial reactions, emotions, and vocalistic patterns that characterize face-to-face communication. As conveniently compiled by Peter H. Lewis (1986, July 8), some of the most common signs include

:)	=	I'm happy.
:(	=	I'm sad.
:s	=	I have mixed feelings.
8)	=	I'm wide awake.
:o	=	I'm surprised.
(:o	=	I'm very surprised.
:p	=	Pffft! (Sticking out the tongue.)
:9	=	Yummy.
:/	=	Humm.
:v	=	I'm chatting.
B)	=	I'm wearing my shades. (p. C5)

Though an efficient and often enjoyable code, such a makeshift sign system clearly does not reveal the unique, personal, and spontaneous nonverbal reactions of each user. In the end, computerized exchanges remain a solely verbal mode of communication, affording the user a higher degree of control precisely because the information conveyed by the nonverbal channel is eliminated.

The Discursive Mode

In a face-to-face exchange, verbal communication is typically oral. In conveying meaning, vocal quality, pitch, and tone are as important as the content or ideas of message itself. These vocalistic features allow face-to-face communicators to convey a great deal of information efficiently and without the kind of commitment involved in solely written messages.

In a computer-mediated exchange, verbal communication must always be in written form. Beyond the typing skills required if messages are to be conveyed at any kind of reasonable rate, messages must always be inputted line by line. Asides are incorporated only by way of parenthetical comments. Modes of response that are typically conveyed only in an oral form must be translated into written forms; for example, a snicker can be included in a transmission only in such a written form as "(*hee hee*)." Needless to say, such asides, parenthetical comments, and transcriptions require greater concentration when one is creating written rather than spoken messages. Accordingly, as Amy Friedman Phillips (1983, p. 844) noted, those who are more literate in the written mode will be more satisfied and confident in a computer-mediated system.

Feedback

In the face-to-face relationship, feedback is synchronistic. While face-to-face exchanges typically involve verbal communication by turns, nonverbal exchanges are constant and immediate. Even the absence of any expressive nonverbal response on the part of one speaker constitutes a form of immediate feedback to the other speaker. In his classic study of human communication, David Berlo (1960) presumed the existence of face-to-face interactions that were "dynamic, on-going, ever-changing, continuous" (p. 24).

In a computer-mediated relationship, the physical structure and physical requirements of the technologies require that all feedback be asynchronistic. In the computer bulletin board system, one user sends a message. The transmission must be completed before the receiver is able to respond to the sender's message. Only one-way transmissions are technically possible at any given moment. Obviously, because nonverbal variables are completely eliminated in such exchanges, only these one-way verbal transmissions define the feedback system. In particular, while most home computer telecommunications allow for both "half-duplex" (only one-way transmissions) and "full-duplex" (two-way transmissions) settings, the full-duplex setting allows for only one-way transmission at any given time.

Computer users do attempt to compensate for this asynchronistic feedback system by following a kind of computer etiquette. A user will typically send a relatively short block of copy dealing with a single issue. Standard abbreviations are used (e.g., "oic" for "Oh, I see!"). In addition, a sender will typically transmit a single message in groups of 40 or so characters, enabling the receiver to read the message line by line rather than in entire blocks of information. Sending a single message in blocks of 40 characters or so also decreases boredom for the receiver, who would otherwise have to sit staring at a blank screen until the sender finishes entering data. The successive transmissions of small units of data also simulate the more rapid information exchanges characteristic of face-to-face interactions. Furthermore, when the entire message is completed, the sender will typically enter several blank lines (by hitting the "enter" key) to let the receiver know that he or she may now respond, thereby eliminating the need for such explicit and formal statements as "message completed." Nonetheless, while all of these compensation strategies may be employed, feedback remains essentially one-way and asynchronistic.

Social Roles of the Participants

In face-to-face exchanges, participants necessarily provide a complete and immediate sociological composite of the self. A face-to-face exchange reveals not only one's age, race, nationality, and gender but also a host of other messages regarding one's place in society. Occupations, income, and even social preferences may be (correctly or incorrectly) inferred from one's appearance and physical features. The decision to convey information regarding all of these sociological variables is simply not possible in face-to-face contacts. Our physical presence automatically conveys these social characteristics to others.

In computer-mediated exchanges, a person exerts discretionary control over what and when sociological information is conveyed to others. In addition, the way in which these sociological factors are to be characterized is determined by the individual. Accordingly, particular attitudes, ideas, and beliefs of a computer user, rather than the apparent sociological class with which the user would normally be associated, can initially establish a definition of that person for other computer users.

The Use of Time

Face-to-face interactions always occur in real time. The moment an utterance or a nonverbal signal is made, it is conveyed to another. Time itself cannot be manipulated in a face-to-face exchange. We may prepare for a social exchange before it occurs, but the exchange itself is defined by what we do at each moment during it. Even a pause during an exchange may convey meanings: Others may, for example, associate a pause in a conversation with slow-wittedness, indecisiveness, or even dishonesty. During a face-to-face exchange, every moment counts, and every moment has a particular quality that affects the social relationship.

In computer-mediated interactions, time can be more directly controlled and manipulated. Preparation time can be employed during message construction. Virtually all computer bulletin board systems allow users to access a system and to read messages at their own pace.

In addition, "private mail" can be directed to anyone on a system, and a "letter" to be sent can be as carefully worded as one desires. The receiver is unaware of the time or effort given to any message he or she receives. Moreover, such mail systems allow two people to stay in contact even if they work at different hours, live in different time zones, or function during different times of the day. However, even if users are engaged in "on-line chatting" in real time, time must be provided for message construction. If nothing else, users must allow for those who type slowly, for transmission problems, for differences in transmission systems, and so forth. Though extensive delays may create boredom during an on-line chat, delayed time is a consistent feature of all computer-mediated interactions, and the user is therefore provided with more time to prepare and to give greater attention to the construction and the accuracy of a message. Time thus becomes a variable that can be controlled and manipulated toward personal ends.

The mode or method employed to create an interaction dramatically affects the kind of relationship established. Face-to-face message constructions are characterized by a complex, spontaneous, simultaneous, and immediate collage of verbal, nonverbal, and oral symbols. In contrast, computer-mediated message constructions are characterized by written, critical, deliberate, and delayed symbols. In terms of the tradition of the discipline, face-to-face messages resemble epideictic discourse, a form of praising and dispraising and a kind of celebration in the complexity of the here and now; in contrast, computer-mediated messages most closely resemble deliberative and forensic discourses, which are characterized by advance preparation and a critical style. In sum, the dominant metaphor of face-to-face communication is the anecdote, with its attendant concern for the dramatic, while the dominant metaphor of computer-mediated communication is science, with its attendant concern for regulation, precision, and delayed response.

Conclusion

In this chapter, we have sought to identify the structural differences that distinguish human beings and computers as information-processing systems and that affect the processes governing face-to-face human and computer-mediated communication systems. Having specified these differences, we will examine in the next chapter how computer-human communication can occur.

3

Humans and Computers

A Comparison of Language Systems

The idea of "communicating with a machine" seems dehumanizing to some, bizarre to others, and literally impossible to still others, yet human beings have found it necessary in everyday life to interact with an ever-increasing variety and number of machines. In our Information Society, human-machine interactions have become routine, if not a natural way of life.

In most cases, human-machine interactions are relatively simple. A television requires only that you know how to turn it on, select channels, and perhaps make minor viewing adjustments. In other cases, human-machine interactions are extremely complex, requiring detailed knowledge of the capabilities and limitations of the machine. Many believe that computers are complex and mysterious machines. Such a view need not exist. Confidence and understanding begin with knowing how computers and people interact.

In this chapter, we explore how it is possible for humans and computers to interact. As a point of departure, we describe both the ideal and the actual relationships that exist when human beings and computers interact. We then detail the language system of a computer, identifying the underlying assumptions of a computer's language system as well as the types or levels, functions, and limitations of this system. Finally, we suggest that the nature of computer language is a direct product of the physical hardware from which a computer is constructed.

Talking to Computers: Ideal and Realistic Expectations

A human being can interact with a computer because of the latter's language system. A computer language allows a human being first to instruct a computer about executing specific activities, then to receive information about the processes being carried out within the computer, and finally to provide responses or feedback to the activities thus carried out by the computer. The language system of a computer not only allows the human being to control the functions carried out by the computer but also allows the computer itself to prompt the human being about the appropriate steps to follow in a given activity. The study of such human-computer interactions falls within the science of *cybernetics*.

A Cybernetic Relationship

As conceived by Norbert Wiener in 1948, cybernetics is "the study of messages as a means of controlling machinery and society" (1950, p. 15). The study of cybernetics can become extremely complex. For example, in Wiener's view, cybernetics necessarily involves the study of the transmission of messages, languages in general, the recognition of imprecision or unpredictability in all human-machine interactions as specified by improbability theory, the impact of interactions upon human psychology and the nervous system, and ultimately the development of a new theory of scientific method. Yet we need not concern ourselves with the theoretical foundations Wiener developed—the theoretical principles have a commonsense dimension that allows us to apply them without detailing the background of their development.

The use of personal computers is one form of applied cybernetics. When so viewed, four major relationships exist between the computer and its user. First, human-machine interactions are two-way interactions. Both the human being and the machine generate information; neither is passive. To achieve this mutually active relationship, the structure of the human being's sensory and intellectual processes must be compatible with or capable of interfacing with the basic functions of the computer. The relationship produced is thus actively defined by both the human being and the computer.

Second, human-machine interactions are neither completely biological nor completely mechanical. In fact, to use either the term *biological* or the term *mechanical* automatically creates confusion when describing how human beings and computers interact. A human-computer interaction is an *informational* exchange. Both the human and the computer expend energy to convey information; both transmit information in order to prevent disorganization or entropy. Information exchanges of this order are commonplace among human beings, and certain machines, such as computers, display a similar information-adjustment capacity. Wayne C. Minnick (1957) has noted, in defining a "cybernetic analysis," that certain machines do not "complete an operation in a rigid, unalterable way" but have within themselves "devices for gathering information about the process it is engaged in, and the capacity to adjust itself as it proceeds, according to the information which it collects" (p. 251). Insofar as a computer will adjust its calculations when it receives new information, a computer can be said to be a purposeful entity. As Howard Gardner (1985) has observed of the early cybernetic theorists, "The authors introduced a then radical notion: that it is legitimate to speak of machines that exhibit feedback as 'striving toward goals,' as calculating the difference between their goals and their actual performance, and as then working to reduce those differences. Machines were purposeful" (p. 20). Given these perspectives, one can make information-based analogies between a human being and a computer to explain how human-computer interactions occur. One might liken the synapses of the human brain to the on/off switches of the computer. We are not attributing human characteristics to a machine or mechanical characteristics to a human. Rather, we use such analogies to describe the process that occurs *between* the human being and the computer and to describe the nature of the relationship that exists between them.

Third, human-computer interactions are never perfectly precise. One must speak of the relative degree of control that one is capable of exercising over a computer. A human being will never be able to control all dimensions involved in human-machine interactions. As machines become increasingly complex, human beings increase the possibility of losing control over the internal operations of the machines. We say this not to create fear in a potential user of computers but to underscore the reality of complex human-computer relationships. We would note particularly that as the language system within a computer becomes more elaborate and sophisticated, the user is less likely to know how the computer executes its functions. However, we seldom have complete knowledge of any complex system in our environment. Few people could explain how and why a telephone works; it is generally enough to know what to do with a telephone even if we do not understand its internal operations.

Fourth, human-computer interactions constitute a form of communication. The decision to identify human-computer interactions as a communicative exchange turns on the criteria employed to define the communication process and how those criteria are applied to the specific case of human-computer interactions. How these criteria are defined and applied are contested issues that cannot be resolved here, for they involve the paradigmatic coherence of the entire discipline of communication. Yet a review of these issues—one guided by questions of syntax, semantics, and pragmatics—is relevant to understanding the computer-human communication process.

From a solely syntactical perspective, computers function as communication systems. Robert L. Benjamin (1970) argued that a syntactical analysis deals solely with the "rules" governing the ways in which units of a language are "organized" (p. 36), while J. A. Cuddon (1984) simply noted that the province of syntax is "sentence construction" (p. 677). In these senses, a communication system exists if it possesses a grammar and consistently employs formal rules for using and manipulating the grammatical units. Computer languages and programs are clearly logical-mathematical systems. Discrete units for analysis are specified within a computer language, and a computer program provides specific, rule-governed criteria for the manipulation of these units. At least in these senses, the operations of a computer satisfy the syntactical requirements of a communication system.

There is less agreement that the operations of a computer satisfy the semantic requirements of communication. John C. Condon, Jr., (1966) defined semantics as the study of how entities "respond to words and other symbols" (p. 1). Karl Beckson and Arthur Ganz (1975) stated that a semantic procedure occurs when relations are established among "signs, their meanings, and the actions—both mental and physical—evoked by them" (pp. 226–27). In Kenneth Burke's (1973) view, "the semantic ideal" occurs when "a vocabulary" is able to provide a specific "name and address" for "every event in the universe" (p. 141). In these senses, communication exists if an entity is able to provide a psychological and historical association with the signs employed within a vocabulary. If these conceptions are interpreted to mean that self-reflective and intentional motivations must exist independently of a computer language and programs, then computers do not function as semantic systems. If computer languages and programs are viewed as sets of procedures that manipulate certain signs, compute or create new linkages or associations among these signs, and generate certain results and recommended behaviors based upon their computations and correlations, then computer languages and computer programs are, by definition, semantic systems.

Finally, communication may be said to exist if an exchange generates pragmatic meanings. Pragmatic meanings convey evaluations, are contingent upon the circumstances in which they occur, and prescribe actions beyond the realm of language. In one sense, of course, computers do evaluate in that they process only information "judged" or "evaluated" to be useful and consistent with the objectives governing their operating systems and programs. Moreover, with certain input and output devices—such as physical sensors and robotic mechanisms—computers can and do alter events and function pragmatically in the real world. There is also a sense in which reprogrammed computers have changed and can therefore evaluate and respond to different circumstances in new ways. Of course, if pragmatics is believed to require a form of self-consciousness and free will, it is virtually impossible to argue that computers, of and by themselves, can voluntarily judge, identify, or respond to social customs and circumstances. In this sense, computer systems are incapable of pragmatic communication. Yet, hoping to avoid intentional and pathetic fallacies, several communication specialists have been unwilling to adopt conceptions that define communicative activity as founded upon self-determination, free will, and introspection. As Paul Watzlawick, Janet Helmick Beavin, and Don D. Jackson (1967) argued in *Pragmatics of Human Communication*, "Neither can we say that 'communication' only takes place when it is intentional, conscious, or successful, that is, when mutual understanding occurs. Whether message sent equals message received is an important but different order of analysis, as it must rest ultimately on evaluations of specific, introspective, subject reported data, which we choose to neglect for the exposition of a behavioral-theory of communication" (p. 49).

In this book, we have opted to employ the phrase *computer-human communication*. In our view, whenever we study situations in which human beings respond, even if they are responding only to computers, we are studying a form of communication. Moreover, the phrase reflects our belief that issues of syntax, semantics, and pragmatics are interrelated and no longer as easily distinguishable as one might wish. Syntax and the logical-mathematical modes of analysis that stem from syntax can function as powerful variables in determining how human beings communicate semantically and pragmatically. Likewise, depending upon how one views the operations of a computer and wishes to argue the case, there is a sense in which computers can be said to function semantically and pragmatically. In any event, these remain open and unresolved issues. If our use of the phrase computer-human communication seems problematic, we see no reason why a reader should not mentally substitute for it the phrase *computer-human interaction*. We do believe, however, that a growing body of research suggesting computer-human interactions possess unique syntactical, semantic, and pragmatic features warrants use of the expression computer-human communication.

The Ideal Relationship

Because the four relationships described above can exist whenever humans and computers interact, it is appropriate to identify the ideals or standards that should govern these interactions and should function as guidelines in the development of any system of human-machine interaction. The most universal of these standards is provided by Wiener (1950): "to develop a language and techniques that will enable us indeed to attack the problem of control and communication in general" (p. 17). Applied to human-computer relationships, such a standard means that every computer should be designed to make information processing as compatible as possible with the processing needs and limitations of the human being: In the jargon of the computer age, the computer should be *user friendly*. The computer's responses on its display screen should adhere to certain presentational prescriptions: Simplicity, naturalness, ease of use, consistency, meaningful feedback, and individualization are all standards for assessing computer responses to the computer user.

The Actual Relationships

Given our earlier discussion of basic cybernetic principles, we would anticipate that such ideals cannot always be realized in practice, but the current human-computer systems seem further than necessary from these ideals.

The observations of several computer reviewers and critics provide an indication of some of the negative factors currently controlling interactions between humans and computers. Some rather pointed remarks include: "they [computer scientists] like even more to give new things names that are as mystifying to an outsider as the secret password of an esoteric cult," and computer manuals are "couched in the vocabulary and language habits of the computer experts" (Friedrich, 1983, "Glork!" p. 39); therefore, "it is fair to say that a pure form of computerese now exists" (Sandberg-Diment, 1982, November, p. C6). As a computer critic aptly concluded, the computer industry is one in which "describing the use of an on-off switch may take six pages or six words, either version rarely making sense to anyone but an engineer, who understands it all by osmosis" (Sandberg-Diment, 1983, July), creating a form of "techno-babble" (Sandberg-Diment, 1983, September, p. C4). Some critics even believe that elaborate computer languages constitute nothing less than an intentional conspiracy to exclude new users: "Much of the jargon of programming and computers exist only to intimidate and exclude nontechnical people" (Crawford, 1983, p. 153).

A good deal of this confusion might be traced to the initial misconceptions, mistaken strategies, and inappropriate methods used by computer manufacturers when they first introduced the computer in their advertising and sales promotions. Indeed, financial reporter John Marcom, Jr., (1985, September) noted that even today "research shows that consumers usually believe they will need a computer someday—but they aren't sure what for" (p. 35). Marcom also pointedly demonstrated how major advertising campaigns for Apple, IBM, Commodore, and Epson have ignored these results. As John Merson (cited in Marcom, 1985, September), who was then marketing vice-president of Ashton-Tate Regis McKenna, has aptly observed, "People are, frankly, bewildered, and bewilderment isn't something you can overcome with flashy advertising," concluding that "the more you advertise, the more you create additional confusion" (p. 35). His claim seems to be sustained. As Bill Kelley (cited in Marcom, 1985, September), who was then vice-president for Keye/Donna/Pearlstein, handling the advertising account for Microsoft software company, recalled that "everyone in the industry convinced themselves the computer was self-evidently some kind of mechanical advantage for the mind. It moved into our-brand-vs.-theirs fast" (p. 35).

Moreover, the way in which computer specialists decided to simplify their language may have created further problems. Acronyms, for example, dominate the language of computer science. Although intended to be mnemonic, acronyms so permeate the discourse of computer scientists that many of the original meanings of the unabbreviated phrases have been lost, and a host of dictionaries, guides, and manuals now exist to define the acronyms. Even the selection of such a manual can be a complicated issue. In *Popular Computing*, Elizabeth Weal (1983) provided nine guidelines for selecting a manual. More profoundly, Patricia Sullivan and Linda Flower (1986) have sought to demonstrate that the linear conception and design of the computer manual itself are inconsistent with the functional character of reading of the users.

Complicating things further, many of the computer-science terms now employed as substitutes for more common terms produce more confusion than clarity. For example, there seems to be no reason why the word *documentation* (which for most people carries a sense of verifying) must be used as a substitute for the more commonly understood *instructions*. This diction is certainly problematic for someone new to computers. As Franklynn Peterson and Judi Turkel (1985) have wryly commented, "If you can't read about computers without feeling as though you're lost in a foreign language, you're far from alone. We think computer sellers learned the trade from snake oil peddlers who wooed folks into buying by giving fancy names to ordinary things" (p. XQ6).

Indeed, all indications are that users have been confused by the strategic and language choices employed by computer specialists. Kevin C. Howe (cited in Lewis, 1986, July 1), then president of DAC Software, reported that 20 percent of their software purchasers must telephone for additional instructions and clarifications before they can use the software they have purchased. Based upon its survey results, *InfoWorld* (Mace & LaPlante, 1986; LaPlante, 1986) reported that the typical software company receives more than 1,000 calls a day, each call averaging 6 to 7 minutes. The survey further indicated that some companies regard an answer rate of 50 percent as quite satisfactory.

These reviews and results suggest that a good deal of the current confusion about computers stems from the language employed by computer scientists and computer specialists. They use a very detailed language system in which at least three major metaphors are used repeatedly in textbooks, articles, scholarly papers, and the manuals that accompany computers. Each of these three controlling or archetypal metaphors deserves special attention.

First, computer scientists employ a *print metaphor* to talk about computers. In a sense, computer scientists have borrowed from the technical vocabularies of other disciplines to explain a new technology. We can sympathize with this effort. One often explains a new experience by drawing parallels to experiences already understood. In the case of computer science, computers are talked about as if they were books or part of the publishing industry. Thus, such terms as *file*, *print*, *print file*, *save file*, *edit*, *recover edit*, and *read* are frequently used as commands in instructing a computer; other terms, such as *file processing* and *word processing*, suggest that paper manipulations are occurring. For those outside computer science, the print metaphors confuse, for none of the physical features of print or paper manipulation is actually involved when dealing with computers.

Second, computer scientists employ a *scientific metaphor* to talk about computers. The manuals that accompany new computer components use the jargons of mathematics, electronics, and other specialized disciplines when offering instructions on the use of new equipment. Consider, for example, this instruction found in one of the most accessible manuals:

Connect the end of the second external drive's cable into the adapter board of the first external drive's cable although all but the last disk drive (if you are using more than one drive) should have their termination packs removed, although the drive farthest from the controller should be the one that is not modified. *Note:* It may be necessary to rotate the adapter board in order to insert it. It goes in easily if you have it positioned correctly.

Such instructions do not reflect the fact that the personal computer must become part of the everyday environment of the computer owner. The scientific metaphor does not clarify; it creates confusion.

Third, computer scientists employ a *passivity metaphor*, which implicitly tells the computer operator that she or he must conform to the requirements of the computer. We say that the ideal computer is user friendly, but the term *user* creates the image of someone who functions in a less than creative role. *Webster's New Collegiate Dictionary* (1981), for example, defines a user as "one who consumes, expends, or takes" (p. 1279). Such a term, when combined with the fact that a person new to the world of computers is described as *computer illiterate*, may contribute to a negative self-image for a new operator of a personal computer. The new user may say to himself, "I use a computer—I don't create it, design it, or change it. I'm not the computer creator. I'm not the computer designer. I'm not the computer innovator. Of all of these active roles, I am only the recipient of the final product—I am only the user." For those new to the world of computers, computer scientists do seem to exist in an enclave, in a world apart from others. If one is not a member of this club, the closest affiliated membership that can be achieved is that of user. Only within the last few years have a few had the courage to suggest that the products of computer science create powerful social issues potentially affecting the life-styles of all citizens.

We perceive the irregular diction of computer language as a symptom of a much more profound set of issues, which stem from the inherent nature of any effort to develop a language usable by both humans and computers. Humans and computers do share common characteristics from an informational perspective, but they are structurally discrete entities. The attempt to create a link between the two entities must necessarily be incomplete. The type of language structure necessary for a machine to process information differs in kind from the symbolizing processing that characterizes human communication. Accordingly, the language built into a computer must necessarily be a compromise between two different processing systems. In our view, one of the tremendous breakthroughs of the 20th century has been the creation of a mode of communication that links—albeit in a complex and partial fashion—human beings and machines. In order to detail the nature of this breakthrough and reveal both the potentialities and the limitations of this system, we must first examine the language system within a computer.

Computer Language: The Basic Unit of Machine Communication

A personal computer manipulates and stores electrons on a silicon chip. The presence or absence of an electron at any particular location on a chip is the technological foundation for a personal-computer language. Yet knowing whether electrons are present or not does not explain how we can communicate with a machine. We need to explain how and why a computer's pattern of electrons conveys messages to or has meaning for people.

People use certain analogies to give meaning to the presence or absence of electrons as a communication system. An analogy to a light switch has been employed: The presence or absence of an electron has been likened to the on/off actions possible when "communicating" with a light switch. Similarly, the human vocal response of either "yes" or "no" has also been used as an analogy: The existence of an electron signifies "yes," its absence "no."

Yet these on/off and yes/no analogies do not describe the physical or constitutive essence of the electron itself. If an electron is present, its charge is there—it cannot be turned on or off; an absent electron is simply nonexistent—it is not off. Neither does an electron's presence or absence reflect the way people use the words *yes* and *no*. Human beings impose these analogies upon the electrons, and the imposition is arbitrary and conventional. The presence or absence of a pattern of electrons has social meaning only because human beings agree that these meanings exist and will have certain social or human interpretations.

The basic unit of machine communication is thus a human creation, not an element naturally found within the machine itself, and it is appropriate to consider the various ways in which people perceive the basic unit of machine communication. In identifying these conventional meanings assigned to machines, we also contrast these machine descriptions to the ways in which humans actually communicate, a contrast that highlights the unique characteristics of machine language as well as underscores the potentials and limits of any such communicative devices. Four frameworks are especially useful in understanding the nature of the basic unit of machine communication.

Digital versus Analogic Communication

Communication systems are frequently classified as either digital or analogic. In practice, few systems are solely digital or analogic, but for descriptive purposes it is useful to cast systems as opposites or to employ dichotomies when one wants to highlight differences between systems. As one might suspect, the terms *digital* and *analogic* can be defined in several different ways, depending upon one's objective and circumstances. Because we want to characterize computer-human communication, our exploration, conception, and use of these two terms are intended only to reveal this relationship and no other.

DIGITAL COMMUNICATION. Originating with the use of the fingers and toes as counting devices, digital communication involves all of those systems in which discrete units or elements are employed to convey information. Numeric designations are typically digital communication systems; even Social Security numbers are used by many to represent certain identifying facts. Besides employing discrete units, digital communication is generally content-free. The units or elements employed to represent an entity typically have no relationship to the physical characteristics of the entity itself. The numbers on a Social Security card, for example, convey nothing about the designee's physical appearance; the relationship between a Social Security number and its designee is purely formal, arbitrary, and conventional. Beyond using content-free, discrete units, digital communication also emphasizes the pattern or form of an information exchange. The pattern or form of the discrete units can convey as much information as the particular units or elements employed in constructing a message: A Social Security number identifies its designee only if the correct nine numbers are in the proper order. Moreover, in order to promote readability, to reduce errors, and to promote recall, the first three numbers of a Social Security number are grouped together and are followed by two numbers, which in turn are followed by the last four numbers; the three groups of numbers are separated by hyphens. The pattern or order of numbers is thus as important as the numbers themselves. In sum, digitally constructed messages employ precise arrangements or patterns of content-free discrete units.

Digital communication systems are associated with logic in that they are conventional and rule governed. They are tremendously reliable in practice, can be employed by others to consistently produce identical outcomes once the system is understood, and can undergo different applications by different people at different times and places. Elements of the systems can be easily combined to accumulate new and more complex banks of information. Thus, while the term *logic* is appropriately applied to digital communication systems, the logic is of a very special type: It is based upon the repetition or replication of the same formulas. Other, equally useful forms of logic also exist, but the logic embedded in digital communication systems is profoundly useful.

For all practical purposes, all computers are digital communication systems. In fact, the expression *digital computer*—once so popular—is now perceived as redundant. The word *digital* has been dropped from references to computers, for to speak of a computer today is to speak of a digital system. From this view, the notion of the *present* or *absent* electron is cast as a minimum, mutually exclusive, dichotomous state essential to a computer. The presence or absence of an electron is equivalent to the use of a numeric expression that we can designate with the numeral one (*1* for presence) or with zero (*0* for absence). In addition, remembering that in digital systems the pattern or arrangement of such numeric units is as important as the numbers themselves, we could use any number of 0s and 1s to represent the letters and even the numbers of any human language. We might, for example, represent the alphabetical letter *A* as 1100 0001, the letter *B* as 1100 0010, the letter *C* as 1100 0011, and so forth. Such a system—if the 0s and 1s are properly regulated—could represent all letters of the alphabet in terms a computer could understand. A digital system is, of course, being used to represent the alphabet, for discrete units are employed to represent each letter of the alphabet. These units are relatively content-free (few of us make value judgments about the numbers 0 and 1 of and by themselves), and the pattern of the units becomes as important as the units used.

DIALOGIC COMMUNICATION.   Analogies permeate human languages. A president may compare his or her role to that of a captain of a ship. We might wish for a more creative use of language, but the analogy conveys information about the particular kind of role the person wishes to enact as a president. Other analogies may be less than evident to us even when we are using them. We speak, for example, of the "leg of a table," knowing full well that the table's support apparatus—if we think about it—bears little resemblance to a human's or animal's leg. Such language constructions employ associations that were initially viewed as obvious analogies but that with time become viewed as literal statements. If we were to search our native language for all such uses of these "literal analogies," we would find that virtually every human utterance contains an analogic feature. Moreover, if we expand our notion of a human language to include nonverbal communication, the use of analogy again dominates human action. A smile, a tear, or a frown is equivalent or analogous to a verbal statement or an internal emotional condition. In this sense, all nonverbal communication involves the use of an analogy of one kind or another.

However—and almost paradoxically—the extensive use of analogies makes the concept of an *analogy* even more difficult to define. It is difficult to specify the unique characteristics of an object, for example, if those characteristics are found in all other objects. Nonetheless, some rough approximations about the nature of analogic communication are needed if computers and humans are to be distinguished as communicators. Three defining features of analogic communication stand out.

First, an analogy creates an association or resemblance between two or more objects even though these objects are dissimilar in one or more major respects. This association is created and exists because human beings use linguistic and nonverbal constructions; an analogy is a communication construction. An analogy is a product of language manipulation and can exist only within a language system. These analogies are thus uniquely human constructions, for the analogy asserts that different kinds of entities are similar even though their linkages are not to be found in the real world. The ability to create such analogies among elements generally perceived as members of different classes is frequently, in fact, a measure of human creativity. In addition, analogies have often altered the ways in which humans perceive and therefore act upon the world, ultimately creating philosophical, scientific, political, economic, or religious breakthroughs for a cultural system.

Second, an analogy creates a substantive relationship between two or more objects generally held to be different. The physical existence, physical functions, and physical characteristics of different classes of objects are the foundation for analogies. Thus, for example, a president is like a captain of a ship because both the president and the captain can be expected to carry out similar functions. Although an analogy can be based upon solely visual rather than functional characteristics ("Batman looks like a nun"), such an analogy fails to satisfy the requirements for a logical argument. Accordingly, only analogies based upon commonly shared substantive characteristics are classified as "strong" or "powerful" analogies. Analogies employing solely formal (nonfunctional) relationships are "weak" or "meaningless" analogies.

Third, an analogy attains its meaning within a social context. The situation in which an analogy is employed determines its utility and its acceptance. Analogies implicitly suggest that there is a "tendency toward" a relationship or a "trend toward" a certain outcome. Because the elements involved in the analogous relationship are not actually linked in physical reality, the power of the analogy necessarily turns upon the resemblance's satisfying the expectations and gains of the people employing the analogy. Particular analogies are acceptable to some groups of people while remaining meaningless to others. Because analogies are solely human constructions, we should not be surprised that social context determines an analogy's meaningfulness.

Only human beings employ an analogic communication system. The language of the computer is grounded in the significance of precise arrangements or patterns of content-free discrete units; the language of the human being is grounded in the significance of substantive associations in social contexts. In this sense also, the language system of the computer is profoundly different from the language system of the human being.

DIGITAL AND ANALOGIC COMMUNICATION AS OVERLAPPING SYSTEMS. The dichotomy between digital and analogic communication has thus far been overstated. The two systems of communication actually overlap in important ways. Insofar as it is possible for digital and analogic communication to overlap, the overlap provides a foundation for computer-human communication. Analogic and digital modes overlap in three different ways.

First, humans employ both analogic and digital modes of communication. While humans may constitute a distinct class of animal by virtue of their use of analogic communication, and while the major advances in human development may be associated with the use of analogic communication, humans do not use only analogic modes. Human beings are also proficient digital communicators. Their use of digital communication links the human species to other species, but more important for our purposes, it allows computer-human communication to occur even if it is only a digital relationship. We should recognize that computer-human communication must always be incomplete from the point of view of humans, for the full range of human expression is unlikely to occur during computer-human interactions. Computer-human communication will always be an insufficient method of human interaction.

Second, new computer developments have come extremely close to simulating human analogic modes of communication. We detail these new computer developments in chapters 7 and 8, but at this point we note that recent integrations of multiple high-speed computers are designed to create a sense of human analogic communication. In the popular press and in industrial advertising these new systems have been referred to as *expert computers* and have frequently been advertised as equivalents to an expert human consultant. While we may deny that true human analogic communication and reasoning have been achieved by these interlocking computers, efforts can be made so that computers adapt more completely to the human use of analogic communication. The efforts may never be completely satisfying, but as we move toward more comprehensive computer-human systems, we expect that both humans and computers will adjust to the anticipated requirements of the computer-human interaction.

Third, a significant number of human analogies can be expressed digitally. Not all human analogies can be reduced to digital terms, but analogies involving particular behaviors, analogies expressing trends or developments, and analogies involving different measures of frequency all seem capable of digital expression. In other words, common modes of human expression can be transformed as computer-human interactions become more important. Anticipating a computer-human interaction, people may gradually adjust and begin translating analogic expressions into digital modes whenever possible. With time, we believe that, if computer interactions are expected, the nature of human expressions will undergo a change whereby highly dramatic, poetic, and philosophical dimensions will be reduced to more behavioral and operational conceptions. This is not to say that computers will not also become more user friendly. We are simply noting that human beings themselves are likely to adjust if extensive computer-human interactions occur. It is commonplace in our culture for humans to create technologies that thereafter control them.

The digital-analogic dichotomy begins to reveal the basic unit of machine communication. A basic dimension of machine communication is its digital nature, its being predominantly grounded in pattern-recognition and the use of content-free discrete units. Though human beings are more likely to be analogic communicators, they have a capacity to employ digital modes. The use of a digital mode is a limitation for a human being, but the degree to which the shared mode of digital communication is employed allows humans and computers to interact in a multitude of beneficial ways. At the same time, this shared digital mode reduces the scope of potential exchanges which can occur between computers and human beings.

The digital-analogic perspective helps to explain the general nature of machine communication and how humans can respond to this system, but a more precise description of human-computer interaction is made possible by specifying the type of digital system not used by a computer. Computers now employ only one subtype of digital communication, a subform identified as *binary communication*. Our second framework for describing computer-human communication thus focuses upon forms of digital communication and the social consequences of using only binary communication within a computer.

Binary versus Relativistic Communication

BINARY COMMUNICATION.   Binary communication deals with all issues and questions in terms of two categories, such as yes or no. In a binary system, maybes, ambiguities, and contradictions do not exist as fundamental and substantive entities. Every concept examined in a binary system is treated as one of two things.

Binary communication, in the world of computers, is most frequently described in mathematical terminologies as one of several different systems of numbers. As a form of mathematics, a binary system has the number 2 as its base, which means that only the digits 0 and 1 are combined to express all concepts. Each of the letters, punctuation marks, and symbols that make up the human language must be translated into different strings of 0s and 1s when a binary system is employed. Even the decimal numbers humans use, which belong to a base-10 number system, must be transformed into the binary system or into different sets of 0s and 1s. The number 3 might be expressed as 0011, the number 4 as 0100, 5 as 0101, 6 as 0110, and so forth.

Binary values can be assigned to any class or group of items that are placed in a consecutive sequence. Accordingly, the letters of the English alphabet can be converted into binary notation by conceiving of *a* as the first in a sequence of 26 items, with *b* as the second, *c* as the third, *d* as fourth, and so on. Once each of the letters of the alphabet is assigned a decimal value from 1 to 26, each of these decimal values can be converted into the binary system. Even punctuation marks can be so converted. All punctuation marks can be arbitrarily ordered or sequenced; each punctuation mark can then be assigned a decimal value based upon its place in this sequence and finally converted to its binary equivalent. Virtually every human concept represented in letters, numbers, punctuation marks, or other kinds of symbols can be placed into a sequence (regardless of how arbitrary, formal, or conventional the sequence), assigned a decimal value, and then converted into a binary numeral.

As one might guess, if each of us sequenced alpha letters and punctuation marks as he or she wished, we would shortly have a chaos of systems. A universal system is needed so that no two symbols have the same binary value and to ensure that everyone consistently employs the same binary value for each symbol. The standard most universally used is the American Standard Code for Information Interchange, referred to by its acronym, ASCII (pronounced *as-key*). The ASCII code runs from the decimal numeric value of 0 to 127, with all of the corresponding decimal numbers ultimately expressed as 7-digit binary numbers. Accordingly, a particular and constant numeric value is given to each lowercase and uppercase letter of the English alphabet, punctuation mark, and decimal number and to some mathematical symbols. For example, if the lowercase letter *a* is typed on a computer keyboard, the decimal 99 is arbitrarily and conventionally transmitted in binary form to the processing unit of the computer. ASCII thus functions as a nearly universal code that assigns a decimal value for virtually every semantic character used by human beings.

Once all human signs and symbols are translated into decimal and then into binary numerals, a computer can receive, store, order, and process all verbal human communication. The binary mode is a method particularly well suited for representing concepts in a computer because, as we have repeatedly noted, computer circuitry operates in one of two states, on or off, indicating the presence or absence of voltage or electrons. In this sense, the binary system is the basic "alphabet" of the computer.

RELATIVISTIC COMMUNICATION. The contemporary computer now employs only one digital system, the binary mode, but when human beings use digital communication, they use relativistic or multioption digital systems. The ability to use relativistic communication highlights several major differences between computer and human communication. Three of these differences are worthy of special note because they so vividly draw attention to important issues involved when human beings interact with computers.

First, humans use more than one kind of digital system. The English alphabet, solely from a digital perspective, is a base-26 system. The Arabic numeric system is a base-10 system, and weight and measurement systems can vary from base 3 to base 10. A human being can simultaneously employ all of these diverse systems in communicative exchanges.

Second, not all of the digital systems employed by human beings are mathematical in nature. The digital system of the computer is always mathematical. The binary system used by computers assigns meanings to all entities placed into a sequence in the sense that the items can be manipulated by the computer. In contrast, English is not a purely mathematical system; for example, not all possible combinations of alpha letters are socially recognized as meaningful. The word *cqcvyhe* can be theoretically created in English, but such a combination of alpha letters possesses no social meaning. Humans employ English in a highly selective, highly conventional, and situation-bound fashion. Words only refer to something or convey meanings to other people if there are prior, perhaps informal social contracts that assign particular denotations or connotations to particular words.

Third, humans use relativistic digital systems because these systems reflect and convey the ambiguity and paradox inherent to human communication and human thought. Machines differ sharply from humans in this respect; the clarity and precision of the yes/no switch in the computer reflect the structure of the computer's processing system. In contrast, humans must frequently act when they do not have all of the facts or when not all of the issues involved in acting are resolved. They must frequently formulate ambiguous policies in order to compromise differences if any kind of progress is to be made. In addition, people frequently believe that they must say what is not. Consciously or unconsciously used, a lie may protect a person from acknowledgments that could be detrimental to the self, or a lie may be a stratagem to gain a secret advantage over others. We may wish it otherwise, but conscious and unconscious lies exist in human exchanges. Once more, ambiguity and paradoxes are central features of human use of language.

The use of ambiguity and paradox is viewed by many as a creative and essential dimension of being human (Chesebro, 1984b). Paul Watzlawick, Janet Helmick Beavin, and Don D. Jackson (1967) have argued: "In fact, some of this country's most important achievements in the areas of logic, mathematics, and epistemology deal, or are intimately linked, with paradox, notably the development of metamathematics or the theory of proof, the theory of logical types, and problems of consistency, computability, decidability, and the like" (p. 187). Adopting a different perspective, Carl Jung (1968) argued that paradox permeates daily life: "The sad truth is that man's real life consists of a complex of inexorable opposites—day and night, birth and death, happiness and misery, good and evil. We are not even sure that one will prevail against the other, that good will overcome evil, or joy defeat pain. Life is a battleground. It always has been, and always will be and if it were not so, existence would come to an end" (p. 75). Employing a more comic mode, which reflects part of the enjoyment involved in employing ambiguities and paradoxes, literary and social critic Kenneth Burke (1965) recommended the use of "planner incongruity" and a "perspective by incongruity" for its "heuristic value"; he suggested that we should

found a mathematics—or an ethic!—by outraging the law of the excluded middle whereby, instead of saying "*A* is *A*; *A* is not non-*A*," we may say, "*A* is either *A* or non-*A*." Let us say with Lawrence that the earth's crops make the sun shine, or with James and Lange that we're sad because we cry.

Let us contrive not merely the flat merger of contradictions recommended by Bergson, but also the multitude of imperfect matchings, giving scientific terms for words usually treated sentimentally, or poetic terms for the concepts of science, or discussing disease as an accomplishment, or great structures of thought as an oversight, or considering intense ambition or mighty planetary movements as mere following of the line of least resistance, a kind of glorified laziness; or using noble epithets for ignoble categories, and borrowing terms for the ephemeral to describe events for which we habitually reserve terms for the enduring. (p. 122)

In sum, when humans use computers, a dimension of their social condition is ignored. While a large number of human expressions can be conveyed in binary notations, the binary system itself reflects only one feature of human consciousness. It gives one an incomplete mode of communication; nonetheless, when creatively employed by human beings, many of the rich and varied meanings of human thought are amazingly reflected in digital form.

Insofar as we recognize a valuative dimension as part of all human communication, a dimension not generally treated in computers as a level of abstraction distinct from the use of words themselves, we can appropriately consider a third way in which computer and human communication are different.

Signal and Symbolic Communication

Human beings use both signal and symbolic communication. The computer is structurally capable of dealing only with signal communication. If human beings are to communicate with a computer, they must use only signal communication, abandon the use of symbolic communication, or attempt to translate all symbolic expressions into signal form. Regardless of which choice is made, human expression is profoundly affected. The consequences of these choices are best identified by defining signal and symbolic communication.

SIGNAL COMMUNICATION. Signal communication includes all of those uses of verbal and nonverbal concepts that specify a referent. Particularly, signs are verbal and nonverbal concepts that identify the physical existence, physical characteristics, and physical functions of an entity. Signs are thus used to deal with the realm of things, phenomena, or the concrete. The word *dog* functions as a sign, for example, when the word is used to refer to the physical existence, physical characteristics, and/or physical functions of the particular animal or class of animals.

Signal communication was undoubtedly most important to human beings when the primary object of attention was nature and when biological survival was the primary human need. In a world in which physical forces directly and constantly affected the human being, the properly selected word or the precise gesture could determine whether or not one lived. Under such circumstances, the vast majority of human communication signifies what is, what something can do, and how it is done. In an era of signals, human language and gestures must reflect the nature of reality as closely as possible.

The communication system of the computer parallels the human use of signal communication. The binary concepts of the computer are designed to reflect as accurately as possible the exact words, numbers, and punctuation system used by human beings. Moreover, the binary concepts of the computer manipulate information only according to the predetermined instructions the computer has received. Even more fundamentally, as we previously observed, computers respond only to the presence or absence of voltage or electrons and only in terms of whether or not an electron is physically present.

SYMBOLIC COMMUNICATION.   Symbolic communication includes all of those verbal and nonverbal concepts that posit a value judgment (see, e.g., Blankenship, 1966, pp. 104–19). The value judgments are not an intrinsic feature of the object in question but are a statement about its morality (good/bad), potential potency (strong/weak), or range of activity (still/lively) as the human being perceives it in the context created by human beings. In this regard, the White House in Washington, DC, is more than a building or a residence; it is a symbol because it represents the moral commitments as well as the power and action associated with a democratic way of life and with chief executives. Symbolic communication functions as the primary vehicle by which self-actualization and a humane society can be created, for symbols ultimately express value or moral judgments regarding the events, persons, and experiences that people encounter.

As we have noted, human beings have gradually evolved to become more and more symbolic. We now live in a society in which our verbal and nonverbal concepts are largely responses to the verbal and nonverbal concepts of others. Fewer and fewer of our actions are direct responses to physical forces within our environment, partly because information manipulation has displaced agricultural and industrial production as the primary activity of the majority of Americans.

At the same time, humans are extremely creative users of verbal and nonverbal concepts. For example, humans may use language in a purely signifying fashion, in both a signifying and a symbolic fashion, or in a solely symbolic fashion. Situations determine which meaning is to be associated with any particular language choice. The central point is that great variety in meaning is possible when a human being communicates. His or her verbal or nonverbal concept can signify, can signify and be symbolic at the same time, or can be symbolic. In sharp contrast, computers can function only as signal communicators. The difference between a human being and a computer turns on the ability of the human being to render value judgments about data, whereas computers can merely process data. When human beings communicate with computers, only a signal relationship is established; if humans want to vent their emotions, only relationships with other human beings will do.

This signal-symbolic difference suggests another perspective for viewing the ways in which humans and computers interact. It is often observed that computers are necessarily aligned with scientific thought and action. Human beings can enter this realm, but to remain human they must also participate in other arenas, using modes of expression and discourse other than the scientific.

Scientific versus Anecdotal Communication

In contrasting computer and human communication up to this point, we have assumed that these differences function as choice items for the human being. We have suggested that the range of the human's communication choices is greater than the computer's and that the human must choose to employ the communication system of the computer at the expense of other modes of human expression. This view implies that communication choices are equivalent to merely selecting the best tool for accomplishing a job. But communication choices involve more pragmatic considerations. Ways of talking also reflect what is to be done and why it is to be done. In other words, communication styles reflect ways of knowing, cognitive systems, or perceptions of reality. As we conclude our discussion here, it is appropriate to recognize that many of the differences between computers and human beings stem from profoundly unique conceptions of the nature of reality. Let us first secure a historical context for the philosophical difference between computers and human beings as information processors.

As we noted in chapter 2, William James (1950 [1890]) reasoned that the origin of reality is subjective. He maintained that what is believed is what is known, that human beliefs control the ways in which reality is cognized. Beliefs about what is real or unreal determine how experiences are understood, and this directly affects perceptions, apprehension, and action. The position ultimately led James to propose the existence of multiple ways of conceiving of reality; more precisely, he posited the existence of seven "orders of reality" or "subworlds": (a) "the world of sense, or of physical things"; (b) "the world of science, or of physical things as the learned conceive them"; (c) "the world of ideal relations, or abstract truths"; (d) "the world of 'idols of the tribe,' illusions of prejudices common to the race"; (e) "the various supernatural worlds"; (f) "the various worlds of individual opinion"; and (g) "the worlds of sheer madness and vagary" (pp. 296–97). Moreover, James allowed that "some similar list" of equal validity might be devised.

James's list of realities is provocative. We would add to his list the world of media and information as a newly formulated reality to which we now respond. But we think it important to note that there are many instances when the world of science and the world of everyday experience function independently. Hanna Adoni, Akiba A. Cohen, and Sherrill Mane (1985) have recently offered confirmation for this multiworld conception. In our view, the kind of information processing carried out by the computer draws us into the world of science, whereas everyday experiences and the way in which we talk in everyday environments are profoundly different. More pointedly, computers employ the discourse or communication pattern as well as the mode of reasoning of the scientist, in direct contrast to the anecdotal communication pattern that characterizes everyday human interactions. Scientific and anecdotal communication styles and the relationship of each to computer-human interaction deserve special attention.

SCIENTIFIC COMMUNICATION.   Scientific communication possesses several central characteristics. In terms of computer usage, several observations are relevant to our concerns here.

We should note initially that the computer is an information processor and producer. Artificial-intelligence specialists Edward A. Feigenbaum and Pamela McCorduck (1983) have insisted that the computer "is a different kind of machine" because it "processes information": "To understand the essential function of computers—as machines—we have to shake the old metaphors from our heads and begin thinking in a new way. The computer is the main artifact of the age of information. Its purpose is certainly to process information—to transform, amplify, distribute, and otherwise modify it. But more important, the computer *produces* information" (p. 40).

The information processing and production of the computer is carried out according to scientific principles. As I. D. Hill (1983) has demonstrated, a comparison of natural and computer languages vividly illustrates the scientific bias of computer processing and production. Moreover, two of the built-in structural features of the computer place it within the realm of scientific procedures.

First, a computer employs the notion of the *operational definition* in all of its processing procedures and outcomes. In *Communication Theory*, Ernest G. Bormann (1980) points out that the use of an operational definition "provides one of the best methods" for understanding "the intersubjective nature of the scientific enterprise" (p. 112). In practice, say Gustav Bergmann and Kenneth Spence (1951) in their landmark essay, "Operationalism and Theory Construction," the use of operational definitions provides "a description of the actual steps, in sequence, that taken together describe the phenomenon in question at a lower level of abstraction" (pp. 56–57). In other words, an operational definition is employed when all of the procedures involved in generating data can be specifically identified. As we have noted, the procedures involved in translating human data into a computer fulfill the requirement of the operational definition. The formula employed to translate human data into the binary system has been detailed. Virtually every step in this process can be specified, and these steps are always employed whenever a computer receives data.

Second, the computer employs clear and consistently applied rules of deduction. For the scientist, says Jack D. Douglas (1969), the decision to manipulate data according to predetermined and operationally defined procedures is typically identified as the use of a "hypothetico-deductive-statistical paradigm." The control and logic-arithmetic systems in the central processing unit of the computer guarantee that such a paradigm will be employed.

Given these characteristics, a computer functions as an extension of the scientific method. Experiences become real in this system only if they can be operationally defined and only if conclusions are reached through clearly and consistently applied rules of inference. While scientific ways of knowing are important, they are also extremely narrow in scope. The human condition includes more than what is immediately measurable and subject to impartial controls and manipulations. We know many things based upon very informal and selective points of view, and not everything known is quantifiable or subject to experimentation. Science may challenge intuitive knowledge, but we continue to believe in our intuitions until (and sometimes after) science proves them wrong. We gain understanding in everyday encounters in ways other than a scientific mode. Our everyday method of knowing is, in fact, anecdotal rather than scientific.

ANECDOTAL COMMUNICATION.   In its purest form, an anecdote is simply a narrative or a dramatic story. It deals with a specific incident and is organized by a plot that includes conflict, competing agents, a climax, and perhaps a denouement; it has a beginning, middle, and end. Anecdotes are intended to invoke suspense or to surprise a listener. In everyday interactions, anecdotes are the specific but dramatic encounters we experience day after day. They are concrete and familiar activities that we cast as major incidents from which we draw a conclusion regarding "what is."

Anecdotal understandings occur when we string together concrete and familiar activities from a variety of very diverse contexts or situations. In a precise sense, these diverse contexts have little in common. However, the contexts are cast or perceived as similar because they share perhaps as few as one common feature, which is extracted and constructed as a controlling and operational principle or explanation of all of these diverse situations. We might, for example, draw a conclusion regarding the nature of interpersonal relationships today or the roles of men and women today based upon our personal experiences with very different people in very different situations. Such a conclusion is derived from and represents an anecdotal way of knowing.

When we reason anecdotally, the criteria for drawing a conclusion or inference are often suppressed, if not illogical. In this sense, the inferences derived are seldom scientific. As Herbert W. Simons (1978) noted, " 'good' anecdotalism has a justificatory logic of its own" which "cannot be 'reduced' to the language of orthodox empiricism without great loss" (p. 22). Simons added that anecdotalists "do not offer 'proofs' in the strict scientific sense of the term" (p. 23). Yet the anecdotal mode allows us to give coherence to what might otherwise be a very chaotic set of experiences. Simons has noted that anecdotalism provides an alternative to the "rather unimaginative theories" of the empirical or scientific school, "insightful crosscultural generalizations," and "holistic" understandings of "person-person relations."

For the human being, anecdotalism constitutes an informal but powerful way of drawing conclusions and provides a means for formulating generalizations and principles of behavior regarding many different situations. Hardly scientific in its mode of defining or drawing inferences, anecdotalism nevertheless provides the kind of insight we associate with the thinking human being. It is by no means insignificant that anecdotalism is precluded in the processing system of a computer. For diverse kinds of experiences to be merged in a computer, a common way must exist for reducing these experiences to one class. Anecdotalism, by its very nature, defies such reductionistic action. This is not to say that all forms of anecdotalism are good; indeed, some have led to patently absurd conclusions. Nonetheless, the anecdotal mode has also generated profound observations regarding the human condition.

While humans may reason in both scientific and anecdotal ways, then, computers employ only the scientific. For computer-human communication to occur, the human being must temporarily suspect and abjure the anecdotal perspective, adapt her or his thinking to a scientific frame of reference, and reserve the anecdotal for everyday person-to-person relationships.

We began this section by attempting to account for how human beings and computers can communicate with each other. In so doing, we have specified the communication features unique to human beings and those features used by the computer and concluded that human beings are far more flexible and creative communicators than computers. Humans employ both analogic and digital communication modes, use a variety of digital systems, are comfortable as both signal and symbolic communicators, and can be at home with both scientific and anecdotal conceptions of reality. Computers, on the other hand, operate within a narrower sphere of action: The computer is a solely digital, binary, signal communication system that deals only with the precise kinds of questions suitable within a scientific frame of reference.

Human beings can communicate with computers insofar as they adopt the mode of operation controlling the computer's skills as a communication device. Yet we need to recognize some limits to the conclusion we have drawn here. The fifth generation of computers and major advancements in artificial intelligence (discussed in chapter 8) may allow computers to increasingly function as symbolic manipulators adapting to the range of communication skills used by human beings. We believe that such advancements will occur and that the differences between computers and human beings as communicators will gradually dissolve. At this time, however, we see major differences and conclude that it is the adaptability of the human being that explains how computers and human beings can exchange and produce information.

Our discussion of the communication system of the computer has focused solely upon the most fundamental features of a computer's language system. At best, we have described the figurative alphabet of the computer; we have yet to describe how words are formulated within a computer, how these words create sentences, and how computers can function as specialized language systems. Our discussion of the levels of language abstraction within the computer reveals how these processes occur.

Levels of Language Abstraction in the Computer

When processing information, a computer can engage in a vast range of actions. It may simply respond to the on/off switches of the electric current, or it may respond to and manipulate a host of English phrases. In order to sort out the degrees of complexity associated with different activities carried out in a computer, we have found it useful to conceive of processing activities in terms of *levels* of complexity.

Machine Language

Machine language is the lowest level of language that exists within a computer. As we have explained, this language responds only to the presence or absence of electricity and translates this electrical activity into a set of binary signals. All human communication with a computer at this level must therefore be done through a series of 1s and 0s. Machine language is the most direct way of controlling a computer, but it is also extremely time-consuming, boring, and subject to untold errors. However, because every computer ultimately must respond to the presence or absence of electricity, every computer contains machine language. No matter what language a human being inputs via a computer's keyboard, all data and programs must ultimately be translated within a computer into machine language before the computer can use the data or execute any instructions. Machine language is thus the most immediate intermediate system of the computer, and it is found in every computer.

Assembly Language

The assembly language of a computer can be distinguished from machine language in several ways.

First, assembly language employs some form of mnemonic system. A mnemonic system, like an acronym, summarizes complex information by reducing it to a more compact notation. A mnemonic system should also enable the user to easily remember binary expressions.

Second, assembly language typically introduces alpha letters into the human-computer interaction. The alpha letters function as the base for the mnemonic system, for they provide an easy-to-remember system for inputting data and instructions into a computer in language symbols native to the computer user. Thus, one might use a series of three letters to represent an entire string of 1s and 0s.

Third, the use of an assembly language requires the use of an assembler or compiler, a program that translates assembly-language instructions into machine-language instructions. The value of an assembly language is probably self-evident. It provides a method of computer control that is only one step removed from the kind of direct control that machine language provides, yet it is more efficient, less time-consuming, and less susceptible to error. In assembly language, an entire sequence of instructions can be called up by a name, yet each operation is specified before it is processed. Assembly language also provides a socially shared set of statements regarding the use of the computer because assembly language comes closer to the verbal communication system used by most people. This is true despite the fact that assembly languages are typically machine-specific, that is, designed for a specific model of computer; assembly languages are generally not wholly interchangeable. Even given these restrictions, assembly language is still more user friendly than machine language.

We should note, finally, that an assembly language functions—in the terminology of computer scientists and computer specialists—as a "symbolic language." An assembly language is symbolic only in the most superficial senses of that word: Alpha letters are used to present binary notations. An assembly language is not symbolic in that it does not impose a value judgment upon the data or instruction manipulated by the computer. We avoid the term *symbolic* when referring to assembly language because it diminishes the clarity of the distinctions between signal and symbolic communication; nonetheless, we include notice of that usage because the term is frequently employed by computer scientists and computer specialists when referring to assembly language.

High-Level Languages

When high-level languages are used, entire groupings of assembly-language statements are merged and executed by a word or set of words that approximate the language the user speaks every day. High-level languages are powerful modes of communication, for they convey more instructions more rapidly to the computer. Being fairly universal in formulation, high-level languages also function independently of any one computer or class of computers. However, even high-level languages must be translated into machine language before a computer can process data or instructions. Although high-level languages do not approach the flexibility of everyday person-to-person conversations, they do allow a human being to communicate with a computer in many of the phrases of the user's native language.

A cluster of high-level languages now exists. These specialized high-level languages have been developed to satisfy particular needs of users. Thus, for example, one might communicate with a computer through FORTRAN (Formula Translator) if engaged in scientific endeavors, through COBOL (Common Business-Oriented Language) if computer applications are related to business, or through Pascal if needing structured programming in education, computer science, or scientific efforts. Most personal computers now come equipped with BASIC (Beginners' All-Purpose Symbolic Instruction Code), although Pascal is rapidly becoming the dominant high-level language.

We will not survey all of the types of high-level languages that exist today. In a survey conducted by *Popular Computing* (cited in B. Cole, 1983), some 200 distinct languages were recognized. As computers evolved, the rush to adapt them to the particular needs of particular groups of users created chaos in computer-language compatibility. Nonetheless, we can safely say that a language now exists for virtually every specialized use.

We avoid a detailed discussion of the nature of any particular high-level language simply because such background is important only to those who plan to create their own computer programs. Unlike the computer enthusiast, most home-computer operators will use the programs provided by manufacturers. In fact, some 15,500 different program titles and some 40,000 different versions of these titles have already been produced (Seneker & Pearl, 1983, p. 94). Currently, the number of new titles produced has been running at about 1,000 per month. These programs are designed for technical, business, entertainment, education, science, engineering, word-processing, data-base management, spreadsheet, and multifunction uses. This complex software business increased from $2.2 billion in 1983 to $11.7 billion in 1988. In this context, we find Peter McWilliams's (1983) observations particularly appropriate:

You do not, however, need to write a computer program to use your computer, any more than you need to write a TV program to use your television.

You see, there are professionals who write both computer programs and television programs. There are well-written computer programs and poorly written computer programs, just as there are well-written and poorly written television programs. But your problem, as a consumer, is one of selection, not authorship. (sec. P, p. 10)

As for learning a high-level language, McWilliams argues

Learning BASIC, like learning any language, is something some people take to and some people don't.

It's unnecessary to the successful operation of a computer, and has nothing to do with the goal of computer literacy. Teaching BASIC is a holdover from several years ago when there were no programs for personal computers. If you wanted a computer program, you had to write it yourself. That time is past, but the habit of teaching the language of programming remains. (sec. P, p. 10)

Some, however, argue that there are benefits to learning programming; they reason that developing programming skills (a) allows users to develop software not available to them or to customize existing software, (b) can be fun, (c) constitutes an important intellectual exercise, particularly in the development of logical skills, (d) allows users to learn algorithms or the formulas and procedural steps involved in computer information, and (e) allows users to learn the importance of precise communication. One might wonder whether more direct routes could be employed to achieve these ends and whether evidence exists suggesting that such gains do, in fact, emerge from learning programming. Douglas Noble (1985) argued that "we really know very little about the cognitive processes involved in programming, and still less about the transfer of these processes to other areas of intellectual activity" (p. 595). Indeed, the existing evidence does not indicate that programming benefits most users. As Erik Sandberg-Diment (1985, August) has observed, "For maybe five percent of the people involved in personal computing, programming remains a tentative goal, and for probably less than one percent the art becomes an actual, and pleasurable, activity" (p. C5).

Functions of Computer Languages

The functions carried out by the language within a computer will always depend upon the purpose the language is developed to achieve. As we have noted, some languages are structured to deal with business objectives, while others are designed to facilitate scientific, educational, or computer-science outcomes. Other languages, such as BASIC, are created to satisfy the needs of computer novices.

Regardless of the language structure built into a computer, all computer languages carry out some commonly shared processes. The ways in which these shared functions of computer languages are perceived, however, depend upon the perspectives one employs.

A Technical Perspective

For the computer specialist, every computer language carries out but one central function. It adds. Based upon the addition principle, other processes, such as subtraction, multiplication, and division, can be executed. These basic arithmetic functions can lead to some rather esoteric technical manipulations and to advances in computer science and programming. A somewhat limited perspective for a home-computer user, the technical perspective nevertheless underscores the primary process of any computer language.

A User's Perspective

For a user, a computer language carries out several major functions. The Institute for the Future (cited in Tydeman et al., 1982) has provided a fivefold perspective of the basic functions of a computer language. First, a computer language can retrieve information. Using a modem, the computer can tap into virtually every electronic data base in the world. Second, it allows a user to carry out such financial transactions as teleshopping and telebanking. Third, it provides a means for person-to-person communication. Fourth, it carries out computing functions for a user. Data can be formatted, restructured, and/or processed. Fifth, it allows a user to establish telemonitoring systems within the home. Used as a control device, a computer can monitor emergency, fire, medical, and crime conditions in the home and automatically report these conditions to the proper authorities. In part 2 of this book, we detail and extend this list of uses.

A Communication Perspective

Communication specialists examine the ways in which a computer's language affects users' establishing and regulating social connections. The language of the computer cannot be formally distinguished from a human language system if the same functions are carried out. Frank E. X. Dance and Carl E. Larson's (1976) views are especially instructive: They argue that a communication system has three functions: to link individuals with their environment, to develop higher mental processes, and to regulate human behavior. We have already suggested the ways in which the communication system of the computer carries out these functions.

More precisely, a computer serves five specific communicative ends. It serves as (a) a transmission device, (b) an expressive mode, (c) a correlational device, (d) a method for determining causal analyses, and (e) a creative instrument. In part 2 of this book, we treat the ways in which a computer carries out each of these communicative functions.

Conclusion

In this chapter, we have identified the standards by which computer-human communication can be evaluated. In our view, human-computer interactions still fall far short of satisfying these objectives, but we suggested how computer-human communication is possible within these limits. We noted that human communication involves analogic and digital modes, diverse kinds of digital systems, and symbolic and signal as well as scientific and anecdotal communication skills. We emphasized that the digital, binary, signal, and scientific modes of the computer require that human beings restrict their own range of communication skills if they are to communicate with a computer. We concluded by identifying levels of language abstraction in a computer and several perspectives for viewing the functions of the language system of a computer.

II.
Types of Computer-Human Communication

In part 2, uses of the personal computer are identified and their social consequences assessed. In this sense, part 2 emphasizes the means-ends relationships involved in computer-human communication. The focus upon uses serves a pragmatic purpose of particular value to the personal computer operator, while the attention given to the effects of such uses explores the equally important issue of the social consequences of computer-human communication.

A theoretical perspective also controls part 2. A generic conception of computer-human communication is posited, and five types of computer-human communication are identified. Systematic, functional, effects, and critical methods guided the formulation of each of these five genres of computer-human communication.

Chapters are progressively organized. The first of the five chapters, chapter 4, deals with those interactions in which the human conceptions dominate the computer-human relationship. By chapter 8, the last chapter of part 2, the focus is solely upon the ways in which computer programming and computer languages can dominate computer-human relationships. The table at the end of chapter 8 summarizes the generic criteria distinguishing these five modes of computer-human communication.

4

Communicating by Computer Transmission

A personal computer system can function as a communication link with others. When so used, the system functions as a transmission device. Personal messages, social and task-group messaging, and commercial exchanges with banks and stores can be executed through a personal computer, telephone, and modem. All of these transmission functions could be carried out through other means—person-to-person contacts, the telephone, or formal letters. Even if the personal computer system is used for transmission of messages, alternative media can be used as confirmation devices ensuring that the correct message has been received by the right person and within the desired period of time.

When a computer is used only to convey messages, human beings dominate the computer system. The computer does not directly manipulate the content of the user's message. The user's inputs and choices dominate the computer's transmissions, and the user is confident about what message is received or what the outcome of using a computer will be. Accordingly, the transmission function of a personal computer system seldom creates a computer-dependent relationship for a user. For all practical purposes, the human being controls the computer's functions, and the computer is merely a kind of elaborate typewriter and delivery system. The computer may be more efficient in terms of time, convenience, and cost, but other systems can be used as substitutes when a computer system is inoperative. A dispassionate attitude typically characterizes the user's psychological state when he or she is using only the transmission function of a computer.

Social Uses

In this chapter, various computer transmissions capabilities of a personal computer are examined. The transmission functions most frequently employed by users are emphasized.

Electronic Mail

Electronic mail is a generic term referring to a class of messages transmitted and distributed through any computerized system used as a kind of postal service. These exchanges range from person-to-person and group communications, to transactions with a commercial institution, such as a bank or a shopping center, to information requests from a data-base system. In a typical case, a user generates and enters a message on his or her personal computer and transmits this message through a telephone-modem connection; the message is received and stored in a centralized computer facility and is subsequently received by the addressee through his or her own modem link to the centralized computer facility. If the addressee lacks a telecommunications system, the message is typically delivered in paper form by a special courier from the centralized computer facility. Because electronic mail uses computers only as a transmission system, alternative modes of communication can be employed at almost any stage in the transmission process. Electronic mail is typically faster and more reliable than the U.S. Postal Service, but the computer is functioning merely as a vehicle or channel of communication. It only conveys human thoughts; it does not function as a source of ideas.

Regardless of the user's reasons for employing an electronic mail system, the procedures for computer communications are the same. First, certain equipment is required: a personal computer, a telephone, a modem, a telecommunications program, and, for some uses, an extended memory system. Second, once all of the equipment is in place, essentially the same connection procedure is employed: The computer is turned on, and the telecommunications programming requirements and instructions for the particular computer are followed; the desired telephone number is dialed, and a telephone connection is established; a modem connection is made; and then whatever communication is desired is transmitted and received. Virtually any home computer can be transformed into a telecommunications system capable of initiating and receiving electronic mail.

Electronic mail services are available in several forms. Direct person-to-person electronic mail connections may be established without using a centralized computer facility. If an addressee has a home computer, the sender can telephone the addressee and orally indicate that a message is to be transmitted, and then both the sender and the addressee can shift from a voice to a modem connection. The sender can then transmit the message. Such direct systems have rather severe limitations. The addressee must have a personal computer and must be at home at the time of the transmission. Moreover, social conventions control these direct systems. A transmission would only be interpersonally appropriate if material in large quantities, or technical or detailed material, has to be transmitted. Otherwise, vocal communication would be sufficiently reliable and efficient.

A person-to-institution connection may be established. McGraw-Hill Books, for example, has dedicated a telephone line to computer-modem mail (Kleinfield, 1986). Any personal-computer user can call in, review available books by topic, and leave an order (with appropriate mailing and credit-card information) for any book desired. Because electronic order systems reduce personnel and overhead costs, many corporations now offer electronic mail services. To encourage use of this system, many corporations also provide a general "board" for public announcements and the means for users to send and receive personal mail.

Commercial electronic mail services are also available for no subscription fee, or a minimal one-time subscription fee, and a monthly on-line, usage fee. The first system was offered in 1972 by On Tyme of Cupertino, California. Management and technology consultant Kenneth Bosomworth (cited in Edersheim, 1985) reported that some 750 million electronic messages were sent through these commercial systems in 1985. In 1988, Markoff (June 1, p. C10) reported that the number of electronic messages transmitted annually in the United States had increased to 2 billion, and he anticipated that this figure would rise to 60 billion by the year 2000. International Resource Development (cited in Hollie, 1984) reported that commercial electronic mail services generated $148 million in 1984 and predicted that revenues for such services will increase to $4.3 billion by 1990. MCI is probably best known for competing with AT&T in the long-distance telephone market, but a branch of the corporation identified as MCI Mail is also available and is relatively typical of the kind of electronic mail service provided by a commercial enterprise. Some 100,000 people have subscribed to MCI Mail. Roughly 35 percent of these subscribers use the service once a month, paying $1 to send a five-page (7,500-character) letter. Such use generates some $6 million annually for MCI Mail (Inman, 1984). Competing with other firms, such as GTE Telenet's Telemail, CompuServe Information Service, Western Union's Easylink, Federal Express's Zapmail, and The Source's Source Mail, MCI Mail plans to broaden its operations by including full electronic banking services and to offer its services to American Express cardholders.

When personal-computer users were given a range of electronic mail options, marketing research revealed that personal "messaging" was the most popular choice of the personal computer owner. In fact, Jay Fitzgerald (1984), then of The Source, has reported that of all the services available through their system, electronic mail was the "heaviest used." In virtually every test, home-computer owners seem to enjoy communication with other users more than any other computer-using activity.

In a style reminiscent of ham-radio customs, messages can be posted for other computer operators. These messages can include a poem, a "political letter to the editor," a recipe, whatever. With the proper command provided by the service, the messages can be stored electronically in a "bulletin board" or central computer memory. At any time thereafter, others on the system may tap into the memory, scan its contents, type in responses, and return the amended entries to the bulletin board. Using this format, electronic mail systems have emerged locally, often as a community service. The systems are typically designed to deal with a relatively small number of people interested in a fairly specific topic. These systems can evolve into electronic bulletin board systems with full networking and chatting capabilities.

Networking, Electronic Bulletin Boards, and Chatting

Beyond person-to-person exchanges, electronic mail can also be used for group exchanges. These are typically identified as *networking*, using an *electronic bulletin board*, or *chatting*. The first such system was established in Chicago in 1978. Local computer-club members could call in and leave simple messages for one another. The systems developed to allow groups of individuals to exchange various kinds of information. Group discussions can now be conducted through formal channels established by commercial organizations, user groups, or special networks established by any personal-computer user. Because electronic bulletin boards are so easy to establish, the number of such systems is for all practical purposes unknown. Some have estimated that 265 systems exist in the United States, while others have more realistically noted that the number of formal and informal systems must exceed at least 1,000. In September 1982, Steven Sieck (cited in Kerr), then of the Link Resources Corporation, a market-research firm, reported that more than 20,000 owners of personal computers regularly used bulletin boards. Within the next 2 years, the number of local computer bulletin boards in Los Angeles alone grew to 200, CompuServe Information Service reported that its own subscribers had increased to 85,000, and the Pirate's Cove, which claims to be the "largest electronic bulletin board in the world," had "nearly 1,000 regular users," who used the "general message board with 61 subboards devoted to subjects ranging from martial arts to legal affairs and computer adventure games" (Goncharoff, 1984; also see Lindsey, 1983). By 1986, the number of CompuServe subscribers had risen to 300,000, and the number of known local computer bulletin board systems had increased to 2,500 ("Computer Clubs," 1986; also see Lasden, 1985).

Technologically, amazing breakthroughs are occurring in the speed at which information can be transmitted through these networks. Scientific Computer Systems Corporation has developed a network that passes information between computers at 1.4 billion bits per second (see, e.g., Markoff, 1988, June 6; also see Wilford, 1987). In other words, the contents of an entire encyclopedia could be transferred from one computer to another in less than 3 seconds.

Interest in electronic bulletin boards turns upon the functions they serve. Networking systems satisfy particular and specialized interests shared by limited groups of individuals, and an electronic bulletin board can be established for any information exchange one can imagine. Topics range from specialized programming for a particular model of computer to recipe exchanges and various systems for dating and sexual contacts (see, e.g., Haight & Rubinyi, 1983; Lasden, 1985; S. Levy, 1984; Lindsey, 1983). *Log On* magazine and J. A. Cambron Company's publication, the *On-Line Computer Telephone Directory*, provide a relatively complete and regularly updated listing of available networks. Together, these publications list over 600 telephone network numbers throughout the United States and Canada.

One reason why local bulletin board systems have increased so rapidly is that the requirements for initiating these systems are basic. Besides a computer, necessary components are an automatic answering modem, a two-disk-drive memory system, a separate telephone line, and a bulletin board program. Ranging in price from under $50 to $300, bulletin board programs are designed for particular computer models and must therefore be purchased from the computer manufacturer or a third-party software manufacturer specializing in software for the computer model. Once the system is put together and appropriately advertised, a computer network is created.

It is also possible to engage with others in chatting. By selecting what is generally identified as a full-duplex option on the telecommunications program, a user can receive responses to messages as soon as they are transmitted if someone else is on the network at that time. Although a message must be transmitted, received, and then responded to in independent steps, thereby precluding a truly simultaneous and immediate exchange of information, this mode of exchange nevertheless approaches the character of real-life conversation and is therefore called "chatting." For those who wish to play computer games with others or who appreciate spontaneous interactions with others, chatting gives speed and enjoyment to an interaction (see, e.g., La Rosa, 1984), despite the fact that chatting exchanges occur via typewritten messages that must be formulated, transmitted, and then received before the other person can respond. The exchange does not, then, duplicate the continuous and immediate exchange of verbal and nonverbal information encountered in person-to-person verbal interactions.

With time, friendships have been formed as a result of these contacts (Lindsey, 1983; E. Brown, 1984, p. 190). What is most interesting about these friendships is that they are not based upon appearance, nationality, race, geographic proximity, age, or even gender. Because code names or pseudonyms are generally employed in exchanges, "computer friendships" may be formed without the parties ever knowing even each others' real names. As one typical user (cited in Kerr, 1982, September) reported, "I have talked to some people for years without knowing where they live or their real names. Yet they are as much a presence in my life as if they were right in the room. They are my friends" (p. C7). Others view these contacts as an "extended family" (see, e.g., Carpenter, 1983; Norman, 1983). Indeed, as we noted earlier, Chesebro (1985) has reported that, in a random sample of computerized bulletin board systems throughout the United States, some 30 percent of all messages were interpersonal in content.

In terms of interpersonal communication, these computer-mediated interactions generate a host of intriguing issues. The definition of friendship itself becomes an issue. What must friends know about each other before they can say that they are friends? What do friends have to disclose? Regarding the physical nature of another, is there a minimum of information that we must know if we are to call another a friend? The questions are not easily resolved at this point. According to communication specialists James C. McCroskey and Thomas A. McCain (1974), an interpersonal relationship must always involve some kind of judgment about the physical attractiveness of the other. For others, this physical dimension is apparently not a feature of an interpersonal relationship. Joseph A. DeVito, in *The Interpersonal Com-*

munication Book (1983), defines a friendship only in terms of the kind of psychological support the relationship provides: "Friendship may be defined as an interpersonal relationship between two persons that is mutually productive, established and maintained through perceived mutual free choice, and characterized by mutual positive regard" (p. 373). If we take his definition literally, friendships can exist without a response to—or even an awareness of—the physical characteristics of the other. We can only guess how these and other authors would characterize the notion of computer friendships. With few exceptions (Cushman & Cahn, 1985), the subject of computer friendships is slighted, although it deserves speculative and empirical study by specialists on interpersonal relations.

We suspect that when such questions are investigated a good deal of the discussion will turn on whether a friendship can truly exist if it is created and sustained only through an electronic medium and never involves face-to-face contact. It seems to us that most theories of friendship presume face-to-face encounters among friends. As described in the relevant literature, the development of a close and intimate friendship typically includes physical intimacy as one of its most important features. Thus, an interesting problem arises. If computer users claim that they have developed friendships solely through electronic connections, how must interpersonal specialists readjust their conceptions of friendships? Will they need to make distinctions among types of friendships, or will they deny that computer relationships exist as friendships? We anticipate that scholarly energy will ultimately be devoted to the study of computer relationships as friendships equal in power and quality to face-to-face friendships (see, e.g., Dullea, 1985; Eckholm, 1984; Gratz & Salem, 1984).

It would be a mistake to assume that electronic mail will only be employed to create and maintain interpersonal friendships. Electronic mail can also be initiated with groups of other computer users, with commercial institutions, and with data banks. At least for the present, however, most computer users use networking systems primarily as a medium for establishing interpersonal associative relationships.

Electronic Newspapers and Encyclopedias

Daily newspapers can be "delivered" to homes and full encyclopedic services are also available via personal computers. Together, these two services provide information on the ever-changing events occurring daily throughout the world as well as on more enduring conceptual knowledge. A personal computer can be the owner's personal electronic news service and library.

Of the available newspaper services, the New York Times Company's three information services are probably the most comprehensive and best known. The New York Times On-Line provides the complete text of all articles appearing in the *New York Times* since June 1, 1980. The Information Bank, the second service, provides abstracts of articles that have appeared in the *New York Times* and several other major publications since January 1969. The third service, the Advertising and Marketing Intelligence system, contains abstracts from specialized publications appearing since September 1979. The New York Times Company continues to update these libraries, but the system is now distributed and sold through the Media Corporation of Dayton, Ohio. Beyond the Times services, Reader's Digest Association provides immediate access to the UPI (United Press International) News Service through its information utility, The Source, located in Mc-Lean, Virginia. In providing complete news services, both the Times services and The Source allow topical selection of news: Specialized key-concept searches can be made on sports, business, national news, and other topics. Other newspaper companies are planning to enter the electronic newspaper-delivery system. Knight-Ridder Newspapers, publisher of the *Miami Herald* and other newspapers, and the Times Mirror Company, best known for publishing the *Los Angeles Times*, are conducting market research to determine the most effective method for providing their newspapers directly to home computers. Their delivery systems are likely to include other services, such as banking and retail-shopping systems.

To date, preliminary market-test results suggest that computer technology has outstripped consumers' interest. In one experiment conducted through CompuServe, home-computer users were provided with access to 11 of the major U.S. newspapers and to the Associated Press wire service. The study found that interest in electronic newspapers decreased as the experiment progressed. At the end of the 8th and final month of the study, the average customer looked at the electronic newspapers for only 5-minute periods. Users complained about the lack of pictures, the difficulty in locating what they wanted, and the need to tie up their telephones when using the system. In addition, about 10 percent of the users accounted for half of the total use of these news sources. These users tended to be young men in high-salary, white-collar jobs. When the experiment ended, only a third of the users chose to keep the service and pay for it (Friendly, 1982). Subsequent market-test findings have found more reliable, widespread, and extended use by customers (Smith, 1984).

Full encyclopedia services are also available for the personal-computer operator. The task of entering the entire contents of an encyclopedia into digital and electronic form is extremely time-consuming and expensive, which has delayed the entry of some encyclopedias into available information-retrieval systems. Nonetheless, the 21-volume *Academic American Encyclopedia* is now available on-line. This encyclopedia contains some 28,000 articles and nine million words. The service, provided by Dow Jones News/Retrieval or BRS, allows a user to call up full-length articles by topic or, using a series of two or three words, to search for sentences containing certain ideas and concepts (called a string search). To receive the photos, graphs, and charts in the encyclopedia, a videodisc system is essential. Nonetheless, in small-scale market testing, most users have found the encyclopedia "genuinely useful" ("First Complete On-line Encyclopedia," 1983, p. 27). As other encyclopedias adopt computerized typesetting (a process that reduces printing costs in the long run), the electronic foundation will exist for offering all encyclopedias to personal-computer owners. In a related vein, the 500,000 entries contained in the 13 volumes and 3 supplementary volumes of the *Oxford English Dictionary* are now available in machine-readable formats in data bases (Sanger, 1984, July).

An intermediate news service exists to fill the gap between the immediate but general coverage provided by newspapers and the seldom current but in-depth information provided by encyclopedias. An example of this kind of intermediate service is NewsNet. Functioning as a kind of electronic clearinghouse or warehouse, NewsNet provides to its subscribers access to over 150 newsletters ranging from the *Agricultural Pollution Report* to the *Media Science Newsletter* to the *World Environment Report*, newsletters that provide analyses of the topics they explore. Because most are provided directly by the producers, they can be updated as circumstances and events require. In addition, these newsletters can be searched by general topic or by key words. It should be underscored that these newsletters do not provide the kind of general survey of the news offered by electronic newspaper services, nor do thay offer the range of topics or the depth of coverage available in encyclopedias. However, as specialized yet current information reports, they provide data that many find very useful.

Electronic Yellow Pages

The Electronic Yellow Pages is now a reality, at least in such limited test-market areas as Ridgewood, New Jersey, Coral Gables, Florida, and Los Angeles, California. In a joint effort with CBS, AT&T has provided a range of product and service advertisements through Bellsupplied two-way terminal systems. To use the Electronic Yellow Pages, which is essentially an advertising and transactional service, consumers connect a personal computer to their television set and telephone. They then select the advertising they wish to receive and are offered an opportunity to order desired products and services. Orders are placed through a keyboard-modem system that even allows payment for the products and services through an interrelated bank and credit-card system.

All financial projections suggest that the Electronic Yellow Pages will become a lucrative economic venture. As a mass-market service, consumers are required to lease a computer terminal (if they do not own one) for $20 to $25 a month and to pay an additional $25 a month for use of the advertising data base. It is reasoned that the cost of the system to the consumer will be offset by the convenience of the system and the financial savings enjoyed by the consumer. Indeed, during its initial experiences with electronic sales, Dow Jones Company reported increases in such electronic sales from 20,000 to 41,000 (cited in Turner, 1982). As Charles L. Brown, who was then Bell's chairperson, has noted, "Our Yellow Page directory [users] might someday become electronic shoppers" (cited in Turner, 1982, p. A26). Thus, while we anticipate that AT&T's Electronic Yellow Pages will become a consumer option simply because of the knowledge AT&T has gained through its test-market undertakings, we believe that broader electronic catalogs will be developed and employed by a variety of firms.

Because electronic yellow pages are only experimental in the United States, it is appropriate to examine more fully operative systems in other countries. France's Teletel system indicates the relative importance electronic yellow pages can have as a national system. France's system operated experimentally for six years in only one region, but subscriptions to the service were offered nationwide in 1984. Surveys of its users suggest several important conclusions. First, a significant number of subscribers, 46 percent, prefer Teletel over telephone books. Second, subscribers use the service. On the average, subscribers use the system twice a week, or 100 times a year. Third, subscribers are willing to pay a reasonable service fee—$8 per month—for the service (Prial, 1984).

In a similar service initiated by Pacific Northwest Bell, subscribers were willing to pay for "dial-up yellow pages." Precise information could be requested through this system, and callers were willing to pay $1.55 for each call. In all, then, a significant number of people apparently find electronic yellow pages a useful service that they are willing to pay for (Pollack, 1984, April). Such findings also suggest the types of electronic yellow pages likely to be established in the United States.

All that we have said above suggests that personal-computer owners can expect to shop regularly at home, using their computers. In a 1981 survey compiled by Benton and Bowles, an advertising agency, 32 percent of Americans were "very interested" or "somewhat interested" in electronic shopping (cited in Tydeman et al., pp. 61–62). In interpreting this statistic, it should be noted that most people are probably unaware of electronic shopping as a consumer's alternative. Even if only one third of Americans shopped electronically, they would constitute a more than sufficient base to make electronic shopping economically viable, perhaps powerful.

Beyond the obvious advantages of using an electronic yellow pages, electronic shopping would provide at least two major conveniences for its users. First, the system would allow a consumer to compare prices and qualities of products and services at home. A computer-modem system would allow a consumer to survey an array of product/service advertisements and to thereby save the time, energy, and transportation costs involved in visiting various retail centers. Comparison pricing is thus tremendously facilitated by shopping from a computer keyboard in the home. Moreover, with the proper programming, a computer could automatically and constantly scan available advertisements, select the lowest-priced items that meet the consumer's quality expectations, and then periodically display these products and services to the consumer. The system would allow a consumer to scan a larger number and variety of products and services before he or she decides which items to order. Such systems do not offer photographic quality in ads, but as introduced by the Videotex Frame Creation Terminal, graphic artists can draw detailed pictures and use as many as 13 colors to portray products. The images can be as detailed and bold as the graphics displayed on most advanced video games. A second convenience is that a home computer might be employed for what we call "preprogrammed purchases." We are all, to some degree, creatures of habit with regular consumption needs and patterns, for most of us purchase certain goods and services fairly regularly. A home computer could have many of these products and services ordered automatically. Consumers might, for example, list in their computers those items that are consumed on a regular basis within a household. The computer would then be instructed to order these products and services at the most reasonable prices and to automatically pay for the products by credit card or by cash transfers from the user's bank accounts. To retain an adequate cash flow for daily use, a consumer would set limits and priorities to guide the computer in making purchases and payments. Such a system would eliminate repetitive purchasing and paying activities.

Prospects for this electronic mode of shopping appear good. Technology specialist Thomas J. Lueck (1983) has noted that

> in more than 40 cities, marketing tests have begun over the past three years in which consumers receive video displays of merchandise on terminals in their homes and can make purchase orders electronically.
>
> More than $500 million has been spent in research and development in these tests . . . and a full-blown investment in commercial development of the home shopping market is expected during the next two years. (p. D2)

By mid-1985, Chemical Bank, Bank of America, AT&T, and Time had initiated a joint service offering computerized banking, discount stock brokerage, and merchandise shopping to 38,500 subscribers and using Chemical Bank's and Bank of America's computerized systems for home banking service. We doubt, however, that electronic shopping will eliminate personal visits to shopping centers; too many people seem to enjoy shopping sprees for this American pastime to be completely replaced. In fact, we anticipate that shopping centers, to ensure the pastime's continuing popularity, will be increasingly designed to provide consumers with various forms of sensory stimulation.

Electronic shopping may become a valuable adjunct to direct-mail marketing. In 1979, the Direct Mail Marketing Association reported that consumers spent some $36 billion on products sold through all forms of direct-mail marketing; by 1983, the association reported that sales through catalogs totaled $44.5 billion, and sales have grown at a rate of 10 to 12 percent annually since then (cited in Belkin, 1986). In 1983, the Directory of Mail Order Catalogues noted that some 6,500 different catalogs were published, an increase from the 4,000 separate consumer catalogs published in 1981 (cited in Hollie, 1983). In 1983, some 5 billion copies of these catalogs were distributed to American consumers, an average of 40 catalogs for each household (Hollie, 1983). By 1985, 10 billion catalogs were mailed. Moreover, sales from catalogs have been growing by some 15 percent each year, twice as fast as over-the-counter purchases (Hardie, 1986). By 1990, mail-order sales are expected to account for 20 percent of all general merchandise sold in America (Hollie, 1983).

We conclude that electronic shopping can enhance nonstore, retail sales. In addition, as an information service electronic shopping devices can alert consumers to stores and sales where products and services of particular interest are available. When time is scarce, electronic shopping can function as a useful, if not a necessary, convenience. While we doubt that electronic shopping will displace personal visits to retail stores, we do expect that such services will function as useful alternatives for consumers.

Storefront Medicine and First Aid

As we have already suggested, a home computer can offer essential services to many of the disabled. For the deaf and the blind, a personal computer's voice activator and speech synthesizer can create invaluable links between the home and external environments. For quadriplegics and those crippled by arthritis, robotic devices linked to home computers can provide a control over the personal environment greater than previously imagined (see, e.g., Semler, 1988). In addition, results obtained from working with aphasics and stroke victims at the New York University Medical Center Augmentative Communication Program indicate that with proper programs even primary language disorders may be susceptible to treatment by use of a personal computer ("From behind the Silence," 1982). Moreover, Wright State University's scientific laboratories in Dayton, Ohio, have reported that for the severely paralyzed, a properly programmed home-computer system can provide controlled electronic stimulations that mobilize otherwise motionless muscles ("Computerized System," 1982).

While these rather dramatic uses of personal computers deserve to be noted, home computers can also function as important tools in more routine health care. Indications of the potentialities of personal computers in general health care emerged during Viewtron's market testing for Knight-Ridder Newspapers and AT&T in 1980. Viewtron reported users' positive responses to inclusion of health tips in its educational programming. In a similar connection, a study completed for the National Science Foundation by the Institute for the Future recommended inclusion of medical emergency information in home information systems (cited in Tydeman et al., 1982, p. 67). The institute particularly underscored the importance of providing at least the numbers of hot lines at poison control centers.

A full medical-information system can now be introduced into the American home by way of a personal computer. In October 1982, the American Medical Association ("A New Medical Network," 1982) unveiled what it called "the largest and most extensive medical information network ever devised" (p. C2). Amidst the variety of useful medical information provided by this system are flashing alerts indicating that the Food and Drug Administration has recalled certain drugs and medical announcements requiring immediate public attention. We suspect that most personal-computer users are unlikely to tap into this data base regularly, but personal computers could be programmed to notify users that medical emergencies are being posted through this network. During a medical crisis, virtually any user would find it convenient to consult such a network. Moreover, although the network cannot replace direct medical attention, it does respond to the users' right to know and to understand medical issues. "A little information can be a dangerous thing," but no information can be disastrous.

Electronic Banking

The banking community and its customers were first introduced to computerized bank tellers in 1967. By 1982, some 25,000 automatic tellers dispensed cash, transferred funds between accounts, and provided account balances throughout the United States; 130 million bank cards had been issued, and they were used in 1.5 billion transactions totaling $65 billion (Sloane, 1983). By 1985, some 65,000 of these devices were in operation at more than 7,000 institutions, and a large percentage of the automatic tellers were connected to one of the more than 100 statewide, regional, national, or international networks that allow cardholders to use machines at banks other than their own (Sloane, 1985). By the end of 1986, some 68,000 automatic teller machines were used to complete 4.4 billion transactions (Berg, 1987). Half of all banks also offer some form of semiautomatic bill-paying service for customers to pay via voice-activated or touch-tone telephones regular monthly bills such as home mortgages, utilities and home telephone bills, and credit-card payments.

Such services are offered to reduce the costs of banking transactions. Some 40 billion handwritten checks are processed each year in the United States at an estimated cost of $8 billion; bank customers pay only 25 percent of these costs (Bronstein, 1985; Ernst, 1985, p. 339; Shapiro, 1984). In addition, the average operating cost of an automatic-teller transaction is 27 to 45 percent less expensive than a transaction completed with a human teller (Berg, 1987). For banks, then, computerized financial transactions are an economic necessity. Robert I. Lipp (cited in Bennett, 1983), who was then one of Chemical Bank's three presidents, estimated that electronic banking would reduce bank costs by one third. The only question that remains is how and when these systems will be established nationwide.

Little resistance appears to exist among the banks' customers. In a Cablevision survey ("Cable Gets the Word," 1981), 52 percent of Americans said they were "very interested" or "somewhat interested" in participating in a fully automated telebanking system. Accordingly, virtually every major banking firm in the United States has instituted marketing surveys over the last several years to determine how these systems can function most effectively. Others, such as Citibank, have already initiated home banking systems. Calling its system Direct Access, during its trial program Citibank provided users with a home computer and a modem at no charge. Similarly, Chemical Bank (undated) has argued that its electronic home banking system, PRONTO, provides "complete information on all your Chemical accounts" and allows the customer to pay "over 400 local and national merchants," to do it "all electronically, without addressing envelopes or writing checks," and to "reconcile your checkbook automatically every single day." Thus, for banking firms, the issue is not if but when such telebanking systems will be established nationwide.

Although electronic home banking was introduced to the public in 1983, as of June 1985, less than 43,000 people nationwide, or 5 percent of the banking population, were banking at home. Links Resources, a market-research firm, has predicted that number will grow to 2 million by 1990 (cited in Updegrave, 1985). As Citibank's Direct Access business manager, Richard Kennedy reported that "by 1990, if 20 percent of the banking population were to use it, we should be very happy" (cited in Updegrave, 1985, p. F9).

While telebanking systems will undoubtedly vary, to date all of them have certain common characteristics. All presume that banking customers will have a personal computer and a modem in their homes. The systems attempt to provide as many automatic services as possible for the home-based customer. Customers can shift money between accounts, "write" electronic checks at home for all bills (if the bank cannot transfer funds electronically, it will print and mail a check for the customer), and receive stock and bond quotations as well as money-market and insurance rates through an electronic service such as Dow Jones. The ideal is to provide the bank customer with full banking services in the home.

A complete nationwide telebanking system has not been established because some hindrances have yet to be overcome. First, the personal computer and its various technologies have not yet stabilized, nor are all computers sufficiently interactive to allow a national telebanking system. Further, in the view of some, only those who are born and raised with the computer, so to speak, will ever fully accept a completely automated banking system. As William R. Moroney ("Home Banking," 1983), who was then president of Electronic Funds Transfer Association, commented, "The market will not mature until the kids who have been growing up with computers go to college and start earning enough money to make it worthwhile" (p. D1). A fully automated banking system will drastically reduce our reliance upon cash. Cash provides flexibility in personal financing, and to many this is important. Moreover, people seem to like cash; currency appears to generate certain psychological responses that a telebanking system would destroy. In addition, telebanking requires a sufficient and perhaps even an elaborate security system for its customers. Customers must be assured that confidentiality concerning their electronic transactions is observed within the bank and that computer deciphering by agents outside of the bank is highly unlikely. Finally, the emergence of other electronic transfer systems may affect the spread of home telebanking systems. For example, debit-card transactions at some 13,500 terminal locations nationwide, used primarily at gas stations and convenience stores ("Statewide Debit Card," 1984), and the use of "smart" credit cards embedded with microprocessors may substitute for use of home banking systems (Sanger, 1985, April).

Despite these reservations, telebanking is now fully functional and is a service available to the personal-computer owner.

Home Security

The awareness and fear of crime has made automatic home security increasingly important to Americans. In 1980, $400 million was spent on home-security systems. The Institute for the Future anticipates that by 1990 Americans will spend some $2.5 billion on home security (cited in Tydeman et al., 1982, pp. 77–78). When listed among the topics of an information-retrieval system, fire/burglar protection devices garner the "highest level of consumer interest" (Tydeman et al., 1982, p. 78).

Two different computerized home-security systems can be tied into a personal computer. One system requires that an autodialer be attached to a home computer. The autodialer automatically signals fire, medical, and police departments when an emergency occurs. If the personal computer has a speech synthesizer, a verbal message providing the home address and a particular message can also be transmitted to the appropriate agency. A second system is part of a more complex information package offered by several different kinds of information providers. A cable television system can be utilized; in fact, some 70 percent of cable companies provide such automatic home-security systems. Other devices, such as remote controllers, allow a user who is away from home to regulate a variety of home appliances, including alarm and security systems. One such device, General Electric's HomeMinder, provides comprehensive remote control and sells for $1,500 to $2,000.

These systems require a relatively high investment compared to the total cost of the home computer. For example, a cable system requires a $500 to $1,000 installation charge and a $5 to $20 monthly charge. Cable companies, however, often offer discounts, as much as 15 to 35 percent, on a home-security system if the home-security subscription and installation are purchased when the cable is installed. Even with such discounts, however, the systems can be expensive. Moreover, for a home-security system to be truly complete, the cost can be much greater: A comprehensive system might easily include an array of such physical sensors as door and window contacts, motion detectors, pressure pads, odor and smoke detectors, and strobe and infrared beams.

Though a theoretical option, in practice a home-security system is apt to be viewed as prohibitively expensive. As we noted at the outset of this discussion, Americans are greatly concerned about rising crime rates; yet, on the average, they spend only $2 per person for home security. This may increase to $10 per person by 1990, but that expenditure will still fall far short of the projected costs of computerized home-security systems (Tydeman et al., 1982, p. 78). Given this reality, we anticipate computerized security systems will use *dedicated*, or small, compact, single-purpose, computers. We surmise further that residents will purchase security-system components one at a time as they are needed. Those making personal computers a programming and expansionist hobby may seek to integrate these security systems, but most will view computerized security as a costly investment.

Travel and Entertainment Reservations

Computer-to-computer communication is not always possible, desirable, or appropriate. We frequently need or want to travel for business or for pleasure, yet travel itself can be unnerving given all of the arrangements that must be made and coordinated: Transportation and hotel arrangements are required, and one may also want to secure special restaurant reservations or means for visiting famous landmarks or other sites. Making these arrangements can be time-consuming, costly, and even risky when entrusted to a travel agent. If greater personal control is sought when making such arrangements, a personal computer can be useful.

Several information providers offer travel and entertainment reservation systems as part of their package of available services. The travel and entertainment services offered by The Source are a typical example of what a user might expect. The Source offers eight major classes of services to its subscribers; one of them, called "Home and Leisure," contains the category "Travel, Dining, and Entertainment."

The travel category offers a variety of useful services. A subscriber can link into airline schedules (domestic, international, and inter-city); airlines' toll-free telephone numbers; air travel updates; travel bargains; toll-free numbers for car rental agencies; climatic descriptions; customs and tariff rates; recommendations for dining out in New York, Washington, DC, and the rest of the United States; schedules of computer fairs and festivals; flight reservations; hotel reservations; national park information; toll-free numbers for ski resorts; the exhibit schedules of the Smithsonian Institution; available tour packages; vacation specials; national temperatures and weather reports; and weekend-getaway plans.

A Source subscriber can explore in equal detail the category "Dining." The Source uses the Mobil restaurant guide, which lists over 5,000 restaurants in cities and towns across North America and which offers a separate guide for New York City and Washington, DC. Both guides rate restaurants and describe their hours of service, prices, specialties, types of entertainment, and accepted credit cards.

The Source's entertainment category ranges from "Absurdity" and "Aces on Bridge" through "Music" (bulletin board notices, news, information on ordering records) to "Words, Wit, Wisdom" and "Wry Comment." Depending upon one's entertainment preferences, any 1 or more of the 32 entertainment subcategories might be relevant; the service lists toll-free numbers for these entertainment possibilities.

A personal-computer owner can thus make travel arrangements in any number of ways. For some, the system allows one to browse through all sorts of possibilities and to weigh and evaluate options. A leisurely approach can be taken. For others, certain services can be quickly examined and appropriate reservations made right away.

Real Estate: An Eye to the Future

A personal computer can be hooked into a real-estate data base if one is planning to move to another house or apartment and wishes to survey the market. For example, RELS (Real Estate Listing Service) contains descriptions of resort property available for rent or sale, including resort time-sharing, resort condominiums, and hotels and motels. This national network allows one to search for the right home in virtually any city as well as to contact owners or landlords. In both *A Nation of Strangers* (1972) and *Lonely in America* (1980), Vance Packard noted that some 20 percent of the population moves from one neighborhood to another every year. Given the disruptive effects of changing neighborhoods, a computer search might ease matters by allowing a family to make a wise housing choice in less time and with fewer headaches.

A national real-estate network would greatly enhance the efforts of those in the real-estate business itself. The Real Estate Investing Letter data base, an on-line service provided by NewsNet, is a major step in this direction. If all real-estate agents throughout the nation were connected through a national network bulletin board, a greater range of far more precise information would be provided to each client. In addition, a real-estate network would provide multiple listings of a home, thereby increasing the possibility that it would be sold quickly.

In our view, use of personal computers in either business or the home would be made easier if real-estate developers considered the needs of personal computers during planning and construction. Installation and use of personal computers could be tremendously facilitated if real-estate planners and developers presumed that personal computers were an essential feature of the environment of every human being. For example, microwave transmission and fiber-optic cables might replace traditional telephone lines now automatically included in real-estate developments. In addition, both community and business planners might consider immediately incorporating satellite communications networks as a means of uniting both local communities and office buildings. If nothing else, builders could anticipate the wiring requirements for a complete personal-computer system in the home. Others may require, of course, that real-estate planning provide for the possibility of being linked to everything that is linkable.

Such real-estate planning has become a reality in some areas of the country. In New York, project Teleport has considered these options in planning a new office building in a 350-acre office park on Staten Island. The project is being undertaken by the Port Authority (an agency of New York and New Jersey), Western Union Telegraph Company, and Merrill Lynch. Communications satellites and a fiber-optic cable will link all of the companies involved, in both New York and New Jersey, with Western Union handling operations and Merrill Lynch providing business-information services to the firms. Similar projects are being undertaken by the Canadian firm Olympia and York, by Brooklyn's Polytechnic Institute of New York, and by one of New York City's largest developers, Tishman Speyer Properties.

We raise the topic of real estate to underscore the fact that personal-computer users must recognize the inevitability of change and the possibility of controlling change even in planning personal and business construction. To date, personal computers have been basically perceived as desktop devices that must be fit into existing physical and social structures. We hold that personal computers will become fully used components in the personal environment only if they can be easily incorporated into current structures. If we are to shape the future, personal-computer users should plan how they want the real estate they own and occupy to interface with their computer systems. We see no reason why new constructions cannot incorporate the latest technological developments facilitating the use of personal computers. Besides satellite and fiber-optic facilities, built-in phone modems and a host of other technologies should be options considered in all future real-estate developments. If personal-computer transmission functions are to be improved and made truly more user friendly, these possibilities must be actualized in the architectural structures in which we live.

Social Consequences

If we use technologies, the technologies will affect us. A decision to employ a personal computer as solely a transmission device may minimize these effects. Nonetheless, even if they view a computer as a mode of communication that could be replaced by other media, people react to the fact that they are communicating by way of a computer. Use of personal computers as transmitters *does* affect the users. The real question is *how*. If we are to control the computer and not vice versa, we need to be aware of the social consequences of its use.

Even though the social consequences stemming from computer use are critical, researchers have not explored these issues in depth. Existing research has been preoccupied with the economics and concerns of the computer industry. N. R. Kleinfield (1986) reported that the "market" for "electronically delivered facts" is "$10 billion to $12 billion a year," with the "sale of electronically delivered information growing at 20 percent a year, while printed information moves along at 11 percent" (p. F1). Research has focused upon the productivity and effectiveness of computer transmissions rather than the human consequences of employing computer transmissions. As Sara Kiesler, Jane Siegel, and Timothy W. McGuire (1984) have noted, "With few exceptions, research on, and analyses of, computer communication technologies evaluate the efficiency of these technologies based on their cost and technical capabilities. Representative of this orientation are discussions of how computer communications can work in organizations such as libraries and engineering firms, surveys of the introduction of computer networks in organizations, and also experimental studies comparing the effects of various communication channels" (p. 5).

In general, research on the technical capabilities of computers has addressed such questions as how organizational efficiency or effectiveness is related to particular technical, economic, or ergonomic characteristics of the technology. The speed of information exchange provided by electronic mail, for example, might allow task completion regardless of geographic dispersion, time zones, access to secretaries, energy costs, and workers' schedules. Increased efficiency might result if computer mail discourages chatting and "off-task" interaction or if people read more efficiently than they listen.

Detailed examinations of the efficiency of computer transmissions can be useful to computer users. Increasingly efficient computer-mediated communication directly affects how human beings feel about themselves and how they interact with others; increased efficiency may also create options for other forms of human contact. Attention is therefore appropriately devoted to the study of the efficiency of computer transmissions. At the same time, however, subjective reactions to computer use cannot be ignored. As Donald P. Cushman and Dudley D. Cahn, Jr., (1985) have observed, "If telecommunications is to retain its importance and popularity, it must incorporate a view of science that treats *persons as persons* and it must study human communication as a process going on between *people*" (p. 150). Yet current examinations still emphasize objective measures of computer use and outstrip the study of the social consequences of computer use. When detailed analyses of the social consequences of computer use are desired, research is frequently not available. These limitations necessarily affect any discussion of the social consequences of computer use. The gap means that exploratory analyses must often substitute for firm conclusions regarding the social effects of human beings using computers to transmit information.

Given the available research, we can identify nine issues regarding the social effects of using personal computers as transmission devices. Each warrants special consideration.

1. *A Highly Selective Communicative Medium:* When teletype-written computer connections are used to establish social interactions with others, all nonverbal cues are eliminated. Beyond eliminating facial expressions and other aspects of physical appearance, computer connections also eliminate the personality clues people can derive from epistolary communications—handwriting, choice of stationery, and so forth. Teletyping also precludes using vocalics (vocal pitch and quality) to understand social meanings. In Mehrabian and Wiener's classic 1966 study, nonverbal and vocal cues accounted for 93 percent of the social meanings people conveyed in communication processes where words and nonverbal behaviors seemed in conflict. Accordingly, the teletype contact provided by personal computers must be viewed as an incomplete mode of commu-

nication when compared to face-to-face communication. On the other hand, there are communicative gains. Computerized communication possesses the advantage of focusing attention upon the written word, inviting extraction of as much as possible from this source of communication. The mode also allows or forces users to employ words concretely, vividly, and meaningfully. Computer-mediated, teletype-written connections transmit only information that can be conveyed in a written mode, and it selectively filters out the clues that are present in other modes of communication and that can be critical for social understandings.

2. *A Social and Antisocial Technology:* People have responded variously to computerized communication and the social relationships they create. For some, a teletype connection is impersonal. One research team found that, as computerization increases, the sense of a "social presence" declines: When Amy Phillips (1982) asked students to evaluate seven different communication media in terms of the "personalness" they experienced when dealing with the media, they ranked computers as the most impersonal of all. For other people, the mode produces the kind of politeness that creates a sense of coolness toward and distance from others.

Others, of course, overcompensate for the incompleteness of the computer contact. In the initial stages of chatting, for example, overly familiar slang expressions are frequently used to diminish the indifferent social relationship created by a computer connection. Lee Sproull (cited in Edersheim, 1985) has reported that conversations via a computer can involve language more informal and expressive than that used when communicating in person, by telephone, or by memo. In corporate computer exchanges, positive responses greatly outnumbered negative emotional expressions. On local computer bulletin boards, the messages sent use "language normally heard only in locker rooms"; Sproull has specifically estimated "that 60 percent of the messages sent by electronic mail wouldn't have been ventured otherwise" (cited in Edersheim, 1985, p. 35). These emotional outpourings can be perceived as methods for overcompensating for the incompleteness of a computer contact. It should also be noted that these emotional responses may not be behaviorally measurable or perceived by users as self-destructive, but they apparently do establish a negative context for assessing others. Sara Kiesler, David Zubrow, Anne Marie Moses, and Valerie Geller (1984) have reported that "communicating by computer did not influence physiological arousal; and it did not affect emotions or self-evaluations. However, pairs who communicated by computer evaluated each other less well than did subjects who communicated face-to-face, and their behavior was more uninhibited" (p. 1).

As we suggested earlier, other users have attempted to overcome the limitations of computer use by forming what they call "computer friendships." In this connection, Eric Brown (1984) reported that "in the last five years" computerized communication systems have generated "close friendships and even marriages" (p. 190). Frederick Williams, Amy Friedman Phillips, and Patricia Lum (1984) more moderately reported that "people are very active in their socio-emotional use of computers for working out problems and in using face-saving tactics or stream-of-consciousness thinking, even when the conference they are involved in is task-oriented," that "face-to-face communication" was "rated" as more "satisfying" than computer-mediated communication, and that "people may use computer bulletin board services to meet new friends." Susan A. Hellweg, Kevin L. Freiberg, and Anthony F. Smith (1984) reported that 63 percent of their respondents believed that "electronic communication technologies" have not reduced their "reliance on face-to-face meetings."

As these various reports and responses suggest, the social value and consequences of computerized communication are subjects of debate, even among communication researchers. For many, computerized communication constitutes, according to Robert Gratz and Philip Salem (1984), a potentially serious threat to human relationships. Several lines of argument have been initiated in defense of this position. Gratz and Salem argued that the time a user spends with a computer is nonsocial experience that promotes an undue emphasis upon "self-reflective" rather than social and cultural conceptions and extensions of the self (p. 100). As they put it, the "interaction between a person and a computer is essentially a narcissistic act" (p. 102). Gratz and Salem do not indicate, however, that such experiences are necessarily harmful to all, and they outline several social experiences that might compensate for any undue self-reflectiveness.

As we noted earlier, computer-human interactions restrict access to the full range of communicative insights possible in face-to-face communication. The technology of the computer scarcely allows analogic, relativistic, symbolic, and anecdotal communication. Gratz and Salem noted further that computer-human communication is "heavily content-oriented," which "limits" the development of "truly human relational behavior," and they stressed that the "kinds of multiple levels of social abstraction that are present in a paradox is beyond the capacity of a computer" (p. 101). One cannot tell at this time whether or not these limitations are only temporary technological limitations of current computers. Some mitigating possibilities of fifth-generation computers were discussed in chapter 1. In any event, exclusively computer-human interactions certainly seem, under current conditions, to preclude exploration and use of modes of communication essential to creative human symbol using.

Critics also contend that the time devoted to computer-human communication distracts from face-to-face contacts. As Case and Daley (1983) reported, an activity such as word processing can consume as much as 2 hours a day of an ordinary user's time. Computer obsessions can emerge, too. Extending the concept of "football widows," Lisanne Renner (1984) coined the phrase "computer widowhood" to describe the situations of wives who feel that their husbands devote more time to computers than to them. Linda C. Lederman (1984) concluded that "social skills" are "replaced by technological skills" when people "gather the information they need, or do the jobs they do, or enjoy the recreations they enjoy, interfacing with machines rather than humans." It seems clear that computerized communication detracts from human contact; the issues for these critics appear to be what satisfaction is derived from computerized communication and what balance needs to be maintained between human and human-machine activities.

Others claim that human contact through a computerized system can also promote deception. As we noted earlier, human contact achieved through a computer bulletin board allows great discretion regarding what to reveal and what not to reveal about the self. As Paul La Rosa (1984) has shown, such computerized contacts easily allow a user to shift from discretionary to deceptive self-disclosure. Computerized interaction certainly has the potential for reducing one's sense of personal responsibility, for all one knows about another person is found in words appearing on a television screen.

Finally, critics argue that computerized interactions displace the uniqueness and humanity of more traditional modes of communication. Samuel Gulino (1982) has forcefully stated the issue: "We ought to recognize that computers have the capacity to virtually dehumanize society" (sec. 11, p. 22). Bob Greene (1983), in discussing traditional versus electronic mail, has underscored some of the dehumanizing aspects of computerized communication:

There is something about the look and feel of the mail—the different handwritings, the different typewriters, the way different people address envelopes—that is, for want of a better word, fun. A stack of mail is like a human variety store—it makes you feel like wandering through, taking your time to see what each item is all about. . . .

Which brings us to the new electronic delivery service. . . . It's no fun. All the personality and humanity that show up in letters disappear on computer screens. There's no such thing as handwriting; it doesn't matter who sent you the message—it always comes out in those efficient bright green letters on the black background. . . . All the warmth and wisdom are translated into those frigid, uniform green characters. Reading messages on your computer screen is not like strolling through a sunlit and dusty variety store; it's like being trapped in an endless, spotless corridor inside the Pentagon. (p. 29)

Needless to say, when unique and personal communicative media are desired, a computer connection is highly inappropriate. But for some people, computerized mail is nevertheless a source of excitement. Donald Norman (1983) argued that computerized mail creates a sense of "eagerness" and also allows one to be in contact with "colleagues, students, friends all around the country" (p. 46).

Indeed, for some, the computer functions as a welcomed and highly social medium of communication. As Frederick Williams and Ronald Rice (1983) noted, "The new technologies are not, in an overall sense, inherently impersonal or personal. Our main challenge is to understand better their distinguishing qualities and, even more so, to develop our stylistic and persuasive strategies for their most effective use" (p. 204). Both Chesebro (1985) and Eric Brown (1984) further noted that computerized bulletin boards frequently create friendships among those who would otherwise never have met. Sherry Turkle (1984) concluded that computer-human communication may even enhance one's self-image and promote a previously unexperienced sense of self-control. Norman (1983) claimed, "It's easy to send messages to anyone who has access to the networks, and popular democracy rules" (p. 48); this form of "computer-network democracy," he added, "is democracy in its purest form, where each citizen has an equal voice and vote" (p. 49). Teresa Carpenter (1983) has pointed out that "when you build a computer system, you're building a social system," a "place where thoughts are exchanged easily and democratically, and intellect affords one more personal power than a pleasing appearance does" (p. 11). We should add to these comments that computer-human communication creates a new type of social arena, one in which the personal and the impersonal merge. As Williams and Rice (1983) noted, these computerized systems blur the "lines between interpersonal and mass-mediated contexts" (p. 201). In their view, "We must increasingly account for the coalescence of personal, organizational, and public contexts of human communication" (p. 220).

Advocates can make plausible claims for unlimited and novel social contacts on certain types of computer networks, but other claims may frighten rather than soothe. Robert Cathcart and Gary Gumpert (1985), for example, have explored the possibility that excessive computer contact may lead a user to treat the computer itself as a "*proxy for another person*" (p. 115). In this regard, Neil Frude (1983) has suggested that a computer can be perceived not as a "passive participant" but as an "ideal companion," as an entity that possesses "a personality of its own" (p. 23). Computer anthropomorphism, moreover, appears to have the potential of both facilitating computer manipulation and substituting machines for human contact.

Socially, computerized communication is clearly a double-edged sword. It can function as either a social or an antisocial force. The strategies we develop to deal with computerized communication need to be our own and to promote our own ends. As Gerald Phillips (1983, September) aptly put it, the computer must become our "slave" (p. 17).

3. *Task and Social Relationship:* Particularly in business environments, computer connections are structured to facilitate an exchange of information, and they are successful in achieving this objective (Steinfield, 1986). Moreover, in task environments, computer networks foster innovation, flexibility, and increased participation in organizations (Allen & Hauptman, 1987; Keen, 1987; Markus, 1987; Rice, 1987; Trevino, Lengel & Daft, 1987). Yet these connections do not provide "automatic" methods for recognizing and establishing personal contact. In fact, one study concludes that computer connections promote efficiency at the expense of the "face" or public image and feelings of the other. Glen Hiemstra (1982) has concluded that "the key feature of the interactive technologies is that they are intended to supplement or supplant communication that is now conducted by face-to-face, telephone, or hard-copy written interaction" (p. 875).

In the less task-oriented world of computer chatting, the computer structure itself initially creates a sense of belonging to an isolated clique. However, with time, this isolation generally gives way as an increasing number of external references are introduced into the computer relationship. Chesebro (1985) identified in local computer bulletin board system participation three phases or stages, which progressed from an initial stage of self-consciousness in operating the computer system, to a stage in which participation within a particular computer bulletin board system is governed by the parameters of the specific system, to a final stage in which the "constraints of the system can be transcended," "communication no longer needs to be governed by the stated purposes of the computer bulletin board system," "more information is gained about other users on the system," and the system "begins to function as a vehicle for new explorations" and "leads to the exploration of other systems devoted to other kinds of topics" (pp. 211–12).

Thus, as we might expect, a computer relationship can be a task-oriented and isolating experience, but under other circumstances, a computer-human relationship can introduce us to new people and expand our experiences. We need to be aware of these different possibilities. In business environments, the computer helps us to accomplish tasks. In social environments, with time, the computer broadens our social experiences.

4. *An Ineffective Conflict-Resolution Device:* The evidence gener-

ated to date suggests that computer-mediated conferences are less effective than more traditional conferences as a means for resolving problems and conflicts. More time and more words must be employed during teleconferencing to eliminate problems and conflicts: As Williams and Rice (1983) concluded, "computer-mediated groups take longer to make research decisions" (p. 209). Apparently, the ability to survey and to react to nonverbal and vocal cues helps us to resolve problems and conflicts more easily: Kiesler, Siegel, and McGuire (1984) have observed that "computer-mediated groups" are more "task-oriented" and take "longer to reach consensus than did face-to-face groups and they exchanged fewer remarks in the time allowed them" (p. 15).

5. *An Efficient Verbal Communication Channel:* If measured by the number of sentences and words used, teletypewriting is a far less wordy way of communicating than are alternative media. For example, voice-only exchanges use 8 times more sentences and 5 times more words than teletypewritten computer-human communication (Chapanis, 1975). When interacting through a teletypewritten mode, users clip their sentences, frequently using only sentence fragments, abbreviations, and computer slang, to reduce word usage. These shortcuts facilitate the speed of an exchange, but they also eliminate details and possibly the valuable time devoted to others during face-to-face verbal exchanges (Chapanis, 1976). Moreover, if disagreements must be resolved during computer conferences, these shorter exchanges may actually hamper conflict resolution (Rice, 1984, pp. 140–41). Nevertheless, computer networks provide access to information that would not otherwise be available to certain groups (Hawkins, Gustafson, Chewning, Bosworth & Day, 1987).

6. *A Time-Saving Device:* With long-term use, teleconference meetings are 30 to 35 percent shorter than face-to-face meetings (Kohl, Newman & Tomey, 1975). Because people are more task oriented, use fewer sentences and words, and may avoid interpersonal issues, teleconferencing meetings are more efficient in terms of time. Accordingly, people report that teleconferencing is more concise, direct, and businesslike; face-to-face meetings are viewed as more personal, relaxed, and spontaneous. Moreover, if messages are transmitted to a central memory and retrieved later, this method of "downloading" eliminates "real-time" exchanges and promotes an even more efficient exchange. Furthermore, when messages are preceded by "headers," which resemble newspaper headlines, exchange becomes even more efficient. There can be no doubt that computerized communication saves time. This is its almost unqualified virtue.

7. *A New Cultural System:* Teleconferencing, electronic bulletin boards, and networking require that users enter a new cultural sys-

tem, a new environment. Computer interactions occur in nonspatial and nontemporal environments, for the exchanges are processed electronically through telephone lines and microprocessors, and, as Joshua Meyrowitz (1985) concluded, these exchanges afford their participants "no sense of place." In solely physical terms, networks are unique places unlike any other kinds of spatially and temporally defined social environments. Moreover, people must create the social norms and rules that govern these new social contexts. In this sense, computer-human communication creates a new "reality" for those using such systems. Focusing upon the reactions of novice computer-science students, Lee S. Sproull, Sara Kiesler, and David Zubrow (1984) argued that new users face "reality shock and confusion" when initially dealing with computers (p. 2). They suggested that the novice experience is equivalent to that of "encountering an alien culture" and noted that

novices must learn how to learn as well as what to learn. They must develop new ways of assimilating information and a new framework for it. They must learn how to recognize and interpret cues, and whom to rely upon as informants. They must learn how to organize new bits and pieces of knowledge into coherent theories of behavior. In these processes the novices bring capabilities, prior experiences, and expectations to the new setting.

It is the interaction between the novice and the setting that provides the occasion for socialization into the culture. . . . There is nothing in the way electrons flow, operating systems work, or PASCAL procedures are written that explains the reactions to computing and computer science courses we discovered. We believe that they are explained, instead, by novice attempts to operate in and make sense of an alien culture. (pp. 6, 26)

Given the technologies involved, where and how the interactions occur, and the unique rules and norms that govern computer interactions, it seems appropriate to view computer-mediated communication as a novel cultural experience.

8. *As a Stimulus to Alternative Media Communication:* Beyond altering the ways in which people interact, extensive use of computers also affects how other communication media are used. In social contexts, on the one hand, other media are employed more extensively when computers are used as a communication medium, perhaps because of the incompleteness of a computer-human exchange. Most prominently, the quantity of written correspondence increases when computer exchanges are used: As a means of confirming computer exchanges and as a way of developing ideas originally transmitted through a computer-human communication, written transmissions increase to compensate for the stark efficiency of teletypewritten messages. In task contexts, on the other hand, the use of alternative media may decline as computer conferencing increases, although the

evidence for this is indirect. Ronald E. Rice and James H. Bair (1984) reported that "shadow functions" decline with extensive office automation (p. 211). They define "shadow functions" as "unforeseen, unpredictable, time-consuming activities that are associated with accomplishing any task, but do not contribute to productivity, including telephone lag and unsuccessful attempts to retrieve information from a personal file" (p. 189). Rice and Bair mentioned some eight studies that confirm the reduction in shadow functions as computer-mediation increases (p. 211).

9. *Decreases Leader-Centered Communication:* As examined in business settings, computer-human communication reduces the role of a single leader as a coordinator, agenda setter, and regulator. Kiesler, Siegel, and McGuire (1984) reported that three studies focusing "on group processes showed that role differentiation was diminished and more unstable in the computer-mediated cases." Moreover, frequency of participation was most equal in the teletypewriting mode, less equal with audio only, and least equal when subjects were face-to-face. Communication by teletype was both " 'egalitarian' and 'disorganized' " (p. 12). Rice and Bair (1984) similarly reported that "electronic mail capabilities increased synchronous communication activity within functional groups and in superior-subordinate relations" (p. 211). Cushman and Cahn (1985) concluded: "Networking describes people sharing information with each other. This new management style is lateral, diagonal, bottom up, and interdisciplinary. In contrast to bureaucracies, networks provide the horizontal link. . . . Whether one is in business for oneself, stays at home and works for someone else, or is employed by some information industries, one may find oneself embedded in a network where everyone serves everyone else. Networking captures the essence of the post-industrial society, which is based on services and is a transaction between people" (p. 154). As we described earlier, computer users have also consistently reported a sense of equality during computer interactions in social contexts. In this sense, a computer-human network might reasonably be established to more effectively utilize the resources of all participants.

Computer-human exchanges do generate identifiable and unique social consequences. For some, these exchanges seem to promote dehumanizing relationships because human exchanges are reduced to a purely verbal level, become more task oriented, are highly efficient, and are shorter in duration. For others, computer-human communication creates a new psychology and sociology involving new time and space relationships, new vocabularies, and more organized human relationships.

These findings suggest that computer-human communication is a new medium of communication that creates new patterns of human relationships. The structure of the computer-human relationship defines these new relationships. As is true of all media and the relationships they allow and create, the style embedded in the medium and its use must be viewed as alternatives among which we must choose. A computer-human exchange, like an exchange via telephone, can be inappropriate for some types of interactions. In other situations, the organized, logically conceived, and dispassionate mode of computer-human communication can satisfy important human needs and objectives. In a fully humane world, human beings must select the medium of communication that most effectively conveys their message. Computer-human communication is simply another option open to us.

In our view, human beings should control the technologies they employ. Such control can be achieved in part by understanding the consequences of using one medium of communication rather than another. While many environmental variables cannot be directly controlled, we can at least be judicious about why, when, and with whom we initiate computer-human exchanges.

Conclusion

In this chapter we have focused upon the personal computer as a transmission device. We identified distinct advantages derived from the use of personal computers as a channel of communication. A personal computer used as an electronic mail system allows new friendships and new patterns and styles among communications; personal computers also provide access to a richer variety of information, to new shopping techniques, to important medical and first-aid information, to more efficient financial and security systems, and to services enabling personal control over national and international travel. However, using a computer has social consequences: The structural features of the computer shape the nature of human relationships and, under certain circumstances, computer-human communication can dehumanize. Under other circumstances, the system facilitates human relationships. As is true with any medium of communication, we must decide when and when not to use personal computers as transmission devices.

5

Human Communication in a Computer Context

In this chapter, we explore uses of personal computers that give expression to human objectives and ideas. We also consider the social consequences of employing personal computers to execute expressive functions.

For those new to computer technology and communication theory, such a notion as expressive communication requires explanation. Expressive communication is a multifaceted mode of communication. At its most basic level, expressive communication is merely a kind of celebration or enjoyment of the present moment and is without ulterior objectives; it depicts moods and sentiments indicative of feelings. On a slightly more sophisticated level, expressive communication can involve a public style, the style of communication that we associate with a person's characteristic public presentation of self. It can convey an image of the artist as an eccentric or the celebrity as a media personality. Such expressive communication can also be linked to what Daniel J. Boorstin (1961) called the "pseudo-event" (pp. 11–12). Pseudoevents are contrived experiences, and the celebrities who participate in them are usually famous (p. 57). Expressive communication can also serve far more profound purposes.

Expressive communication is fundamental to all communication. Ideas must be given socially shared form if they are to become public statements. The form, structure, or format in which an idea is placed necessarily carries an attitude or makes a statement in and of itself. In these senses, communication is always an expressive process that manifests, gives shape to, characterizes, and embodies ideas. As *Webster's New Collegiate Dictionary* (1981) so pointedly notes, the expressive function of communication is "an act of representing in a medium" (p. 401).

A personal computer can be employed to convey human expressions. In practice, some of the expressions carried out by a home computer become habitual, for a computer can be programmed to carry out certain functions not easily duplicated by other media or technological tools.

Computers can function as expressive technologies because they can structure or format materials in ways that give human ideas manifest expression. Some computer programs establish the entire context into which all human inputs will be placed. A video game is an example, for the game's program generates the rules of the game, accepts only certain kinds of human actions as appropriate in the game, and determines what is a scoring or meaningful act in the game. Under such conditions, human input functions as a variable affecting what the computer will do and how it will do it, but the structure of the computer program controls the way in which human inputs are perceived and given meaning. Moving a joystick is a meaningless act without the context provided by the computer program. In other computer programs, the human determines the type of information sought but has no direct control over what the computer system generates as information relevant to the objective he or she specified. In the information-retrieval systems known as *teletext* and *videotex*, for example, the information received by the user depends upon how the computer processes requests for information and upon what information has been stored in the memory system. Thus, while the user determines what is requested, the computer determines what is an appropriate response. In these ways, the computers give expression to human inputs.

In carrying out these expressive functions, computers do introduce other noteworthy implications for users. First, users cannot confidently predict the outcomes of expressive computer programs. While users might anticipate the basic parameters or general patterns of the informational outcomes, these systems do generate new information, and, by definition, *new* information is not known to users. If computers generated only what is already known, there would be little interest in what they produce. Part of the appeal of the video game is its unpredictability, and the value of teletext and videotex systems is that they provide information previously unknown to users. In this sense, the outcome of computers designed to process human inputs within the confines of their programs will always be to some degree unknown.

Furthermore, the outcomes of these programs are more difficult to verify. It is unclear, for example, what might be used to duplicate the excitement or to confirm the eye-hand coordination measurements of video games. These games and what they produce seem almost unique. Is there really a substitute for a video-game experience? Similarly, a videotex search can quickly generate a host of valuable information. While a user might seek through library research to confirm all computer findings, the confirmation process would consume hundreds of hours. Though theoretically possible, such verification processes are extremely time-consuming and unlikely to be carried out in practice.

Those employing computers to carry out such expressive functions therefore operate, in many ways, on faith. At best, the results can be weighed against common sense. If the proper outcomes seem to occur repeatedly, the computer system can be judged to operate usefully. But the user is essentially assuming that the operating system of the computer is wisely conceived, comprehensive, and reliable. Accordingly, such a computer user can easily be viewed as a computer enthusiast. These users have psychologically made a commitment to the processing system of the computer: Without knowing the precise outcome of every interaction, they believe that the computer-human relationship will be a valuable experience, and they trust the machine. The computer is perceived as a useful, if not necessary, expressive technology.

Social Uses

In this chapter, we examine five expressive uses of personal computers: video games, word processing, teletext, videotex, and telework. We begin with the most common use of a home computer—playing video games.

Video Games

Since their inception, personal computers have been used to create and play video games. Video games now possess different levels of difficulty and can be extremely elaborate. They can involve sophisticated video displays, including three-dimensional presentations. The first games offered now seem simple in conception and in operation. They called for "hitting" a white "ball" back and forth across a screen, with each player receiving a point if the opponent or the machine failed to successfully return the ball. The first such commercial game, Computer Space, was developed in 1969 by Nutting Associates.

Their unsuccessful venture sold only 2,000 games. The first commercial success was Pong, manufactured by Atari in 1972: 100,000 games were sold (Surrey, 1982, p. 72). Shortly thereafter, the first video-game blockbuster, King Pong, was developed and marketed. By 1976, some games involved complicated scenarios that included attacking "aliens" or breaking out of "cells."

Video games have developed into a major entertainment industry in the United States. In 1981, $10.5 billion was spent on all features of video games, 3 times the amount spent on movie tickets that year (Surrey, 1982, p. 74). Who plays these games, the types of games, and the known impact of these games on personal computer use deserve our attention.

The majority of video-game players are teenagers, especially teenage boys. In a Gallup poll conducted in 1982, when video games were particularly popular (cited in Rosemond, 1982), 93 percent of those polled, or 22 million teenagers, said they played or had played video games. Some 16 percent played the games 1 to 2 hours a day, while another 11 percent played the games 2 or more hours a day. Eighty percent of all players are teenagers, and 90 percent of these are boys. Some 11.2 billion games are played annually in the United States, or an average of 50 games for every person in the United States. Teenage boys play 8 billion games a year, or an average of 685 video games for each teenage boy per year.

Video games can be roughly classified into three groups. First, there are coin-operated video games in arcades. At their peak, these machines grossed $5 billion in 1981 (Kerr, 1982, June, p. C1). The popularity of video arcades surged between 1977 and 1981 but diminished between 1981 and 1982. According to *Playmeter Magazine*'s 1982 report on the state of the industry, the average video-arcade machine took in $109 a week in quarters in 1982, compared with $140 a week in 1981; the sales of video-arcade machines likewise declined, from $1 billion in 1981 to $700 million in 1982; and overall revenues from the arcades' coin-operated video games declined from $7 billion in 1981 to $5 billion in 1982 (cited in "Stores Reassess," 1983, p. D6). Moreover, while arcades doubled between 1980 and 1982 to number 10,000, by mid-1983, more than 1,500 had closed, with the revenues derived from these arcades declining 40 percent and profits 75 percent from the end of 1982 to mid-1983 (Kleinfield, 1983, p. D4). In 1985, Robert E. Mullane (cited in Greenhouse), who was then chair of Bally Manufacturing Corporation, aptly summarized the situation: "Even in our worst-case scenarios, we never dreamed the video game business would disappear the way it did" (p. D1). Several reasons can be posited for this decline, including the repetitive nature of some of the games, the cost of frequent play, and the rapid turnover in the available games (which makes mastering more complex games impossible).

Nonetheless, the arcades are not easily dismissed. Larger computer memories and programs, now readily available, could eliminate the repetition and rapid turnovers associated with video arcades. And it should be noted that video arcades continue to gross twice the income of all movie theaters in a given year and that a renewed interest in video arcades may occur. Indeed, in late 1986, Sontag reported that the revenues derived from the average video-arcade machine increased from $55 a week in 1984 to $70 in 1986, an increase viewed by some as a "modest rebound" and "come back" (p. F19).

A second type of video game is the video-game module, which attaches to television sets and is essentially a dedicated minicomputer. During their peak of popularity in 1983, some 15 million American households had these machines (Pollack, 1983, June 6). With over 400 different games to select from and at prices that ranged from $15 to $45 each, nearly 60 million game cartridges were purchased in 1982, twice the number sold in 1981 (Harmetz, 1983). While the number of video-game machines sold declined from 8 million in 1982 to 6.6 million in 1983, the number of video-game cartridges sold increased to 75 million in 1983 (Harmetz, 1984). During this period, the average home with a video-game module had 8 game cartridges and used the hardware 7 hours a week (Benton & Bowles, 1983). The cartridges provided by such manufacturers as Atari, Mattel, and Coleco contain such games as Donkey Kong, Pitfall, Frogger, Jumpman, and Pac-Man. In 1982, *Billboard* began to list the top-selling video games. For the week ending October 2, 1982, during the peak of home video-game sales, the cartridges listed on table 5.1 were the best-selling video games. As the weekly posting of such charts suggests, home video-games' ratings and entries changed rapidly. Each cartridge can be played 500 to 1,000 times, but boredom sets in long before the cartridge is worn out. Rather than purchase new cartridges, some players now swap cartridges with other video-game owners. In an informal survey of video-game owners in Philadelphia in 1983, we found that these swaps occurred among groups of five to six. Cartridges were swapped about once a month and kept for 1 to 2 weeks. Swaps occurred when an owner tired of a newly purchased game. Secondhand video games are also available at stores that specialize in selling and purchasing used cartridges ("Secondhand Games," 1983).

Following the plight of video arcades, the home video-game market declined in 1983. In 1983, some 6.6 million home video games were sold, down almost 2 million from 1982 sales. While cartridge sales were up 15 million, to 75 million, some 40 percent of the cartridges

Table 5.1 Top-Selling Home Video Games, September 25, 1982–October 2, 1982

1. Donkey Kong (Coleco)
2. Berzerk (Atari)
3. Defender (Atari)
4. Frogger (Parker Brothers)
5. Pac-Man (Atari)
6. Pitfall (Activision)
7. Star Master (Activision)
8. Chopper Command (Activision)
9. Yar's Revenge (Atari)
10. The Empire Strikes Back (Parker Brothers)
11. Demon Attack (Imagic)
12. Atlantis (Imagic)
13. Kaboom (Activision)
14. Star Strike (Intellivision)
15. Night Stalker (Intellivision)

sold were dramatically discounted leftovers. Some outstanding successes, such as Q-Bert and Frogger, were evident in 1983, but the number of companies making cartridges declined from about two dozen to a half dozen (Harmetz, 1984).

From a technical perspective, home video games became less attractive to consumers for several reasons. First, the quality of the graphics in home video games fell far short of that provided by arcade games. The home video games were less visually interesting. Second, the home games were not as fast or as complex as those available in arcades and were therefore less exciting. Third, home games were expensive for what they offered when compared to arcade games. The $30 paid for a home video cartridge would yield at least 120 plays in an arcade. Because the poor graphics, speed, and complexity simply did not tempt owners to play the cartridge over 100 times, the total cost of the cartridge exceeded the cost of similar entertainment in arcades.

Manufacturers therefore began taking steps to correct many of the defects of home video cartridges. Many of the manufacturers who had hoped to make a killing by releasing games of poor quality have dropped out of the market. Those remaining are upgrading both their machines and the quality of the games. Atari, for example, has released its 7800 ProSystem, which not only provides a computer keyboard but has been sufficiently enhanced to improve the quality, speed, and complexity of the games designed for its system. Beyond accepting all the games designed for Atari's 2600 and 5200 models, the new system has 1 video game built into it, and 13 new games, enhanced to equal arcade quality, can be purchased separately. Amiga has developed a new video-game machine that contains three microchips, which dramatically increase the speed and complexity as well as the graphics of games played on the system. Whether or not developments are sufficient to bring the home video-game market back to its 1982 and 1983 levels remains to be seen. By the end of 1985, only 2 million home video games (compared to 8 million in 1982) and 15 million cartridges (compared to 75 million in 1983) were sold, according to Andrew Pollack (1986, September 27). Yet on March 8, 1988, Jeffrey A. Tannenbaum proclaimed that "home video games—a spectacular but short-lived fad of the early 1980's—are making a comeback" (p. 37). He reported that the home-video revival began in 1986, when sales increased to $430 million (from $100 million in 1985), and continued in 1987, when sales doubled to $1.1 billion. By the end of 1988, Tannenbaum estimated, "the field's total U.S. sales in 1988 will reach $1.9 billion" (p. 37).

Third, video games can be played on personal computers. For users interested in programming, computer manufacturers provide basic instructions for duplicating video games and exercises in creating one's own games. In addition, a personal computer–modem connection will allow a user to tap into network games. Most providers of information services offer group games. CompuServe, for example, offers a team game, Megawar, that allows up to 10 users to play in various competitive and cooperative combinations. At peak periods of popularity, some 2,000 personal-computer users played Megawar each week at $5 per hour (Wrege, 1983, p. 84). Other popular network team games include Dogfight, Empire, and Dungeons and Dragons.

The content of video games has changed over time. Initially, the games replicated such relatively simple games as Ping-Pong, checkers, and blackjack. By 1979, however, a new set of more "masculine" games began to gain popularity: Space Invaders, for example, is a war game involving both aggression and competition within its basic rules of operation. Shortly thereafter, games such as Pac-Man, Frogger, E.T., and Return of the Jedi incorporated cartoon creatures and movie characters. More recently, best-selling novels, such as Douglas Adams' *The Hitchhiker's Guide to the Galaxy*, have been converted to video-game formats (Glatzer, 1985). The content of video games, particularly the sexism apparent in some of them, has been frequently criticized. These and other issues will be explored when we examine the effects of expressive computer programs.

Word Processing

Word processors will be central features of the office of the future. The office desk is already being replaced by the work station, the typewriter by a desktop computer terminal, keyboard, and video display screen. Office automation was recently estimated to be a $24 billion annual industry (Tydeman et al., 1982, p. 81), but the office revolution is just beginning. Only 60 of the 1,000 largest industrial firms have fully advanced office automation. In the 500 largest industrial companies, word processors have replaced less than 10 percent of their typewriters (Friedrich, 1983a, p. 18). At the same time, SRI International, a research agency, noted that 2.5 million electronic work stations exist in these automated offices. When adopted, word processors are reported to increase total productivity by 15 to 30 percent (Booz, Allen & Hamilton, cited in Friedrich, 1983, January 3, "Computer Moves In," p. 18; Rice & Bair, 1984, p. 213) and reduce by half the time required to complete a report on a typewriter (Komsky, 1984, p. 2). In this context, Vicent Giuliano (1982) predicted that "by 1990 between 40 and 50% of all American workers will be making daily use of electronic-terminal equipment" (p. 152; also see Friedrich, 1983, January 3, "Computer Moves In," p. 18); as he explained the economic incentive for this transformation, "The transition to word processing from multidraft secretarial typing can reduce secretarial costs from more than $7 per letter to less than $2" (p. 163). Indeed, word processors have made the inroads that they have—and will probably make many more—because they are time- and money-saving devices that also eliminate a great deal of annoying, stressful, and repetitive paperwork.

For the personal-computer user, many useful word-processing programs are now available, and word-processing programs exist for virtually every major model of home computer. In a random sample of all Americans, a 1983 Gallup poll indicated that 18 percent of personal-computer owners reported that they used their home computer for word processing. In a survey of its readers, *Family Computing* magazine found that word processing was ranked second to computer games in popularity; in a similar survey, *Dial* magazine found that 76 percent of home-computer users were involved in word processing (cited in Sandberg-Diment, 1984, June). We have provided a more systematic assessment of the rise of word processing from 1983 to its projected level of use in 1991 in chapter 1.

Word processors enjoy popularity in the office and in the home because of the advantages they give to their users: They are efficient and time-saving devices. Any number of users can find a periodic use for word processing, but those most likely to regularly use word process-

Table 5.2 Word-Processing Commands

Edit: The edit command allows a user to enter any message, be it a personal letter, term paper, recipe, mailing list, or book-length manuscript. The alpha and numeric characters are entered onto a kind of scroll called a "text buffer," which appears on the CRT screen. As the screen is filled, additional space appears at the bottom of the screen. Once material is entered, changes of a single character, word, or line can be made by moving a cursor to and then typing over the information to be altered.

Delete: The delete command allows a user to eliminate one or more characters, words, lines, or pages from material already entered into the text buffer.

Insert: The insert command allows a user to add one or more characters, words, lines, or pages to material already entered into the text buffer.

Move: The move command allows a user to shift entire blocks of words, lines, or pages from one place to another.

Findstring: The findstring command allows a user to locate all appearances of a word or a phrase in the text buffer and then to change this word or phrase. Such a function is particularly useful if a user has consistently misspelled a word or employed an inappropriate word or phrase and wants to correct the error throughout the text.

File: The file command is a generic name for a cluster of specific storage functions. A user can *load* a file (place stored material into a text buffer), *save* a file (place material into storage), *show* a file (display on the CRT the contents of a given storage area), and *delete* a file (eliminate unneeded material in storage).

---

ing include students and teachers, writers, and those who prepare a great deal of personal or professional correspondence at home. For these people, fast and efficient paper manipulation is highly desirable.

A description of the nature of word processing highlights some of its advantages. Word-processing programs vary greatly, but most distinguish between *editing* and *formatting* in their operations. From a technical point of view, a word-processing system is really composed of two different programs: one for editing and one for formatting. By distinguishing the editing or entering of ideas from the formatting or presentation of these ideas, a user can devote full attention to these activities one at a time. Moreover, diverse studies have shown that by separating these functions, a user can more effectively complete word-processing tasks.

The editing mode of a word processor includes commands to enter, manipulate, store, and retrieve all linguistic forms, be they letters, words, or numbers. Certain basic features are typically included in the editing mode of every word processor; some of these generic commands and their operations are indicated in table 5.2. These commands refer to only a few of the functions enabled by the editing mode of a word processor. These functions make text preparation more flexible and make changing a text less time-consuming and tedious. The user no longer has to erase letters or lines, nor does he or she have to retype entire pages. In fact, during this writing-editing process paper manipulations of every kind are eliminated.

The formatting mode of a word processor allows the user to determine how material prepared in the editing mode is to be presented or patterned. Format commands also vary from computer to computer, but formatting typically allows a user to justify the right margin of text, overstrike or underscore a word or words, set right and left margins, vary indentations, determine and vary page lengths, and alter line spacing. In addition, most word processors allow a user to have the pages of a text numbered automatically and to have a brief running head placed at the top of each page. Depending upon the program, other functions can also be carried out by the formatting mode of a word processor. In sum, once edited material is entered, the same material can be arranged in various ways without retyping the material.

Because word processors vary in the range of functions they can carry out, when selecting a word-processing program a user must consider the functions he or she is most likely to need. Word-processing programs should also be examined to determine how many characters per line and how many lines appear on the CRT screen. In some programs only 40 characters appear on the screen; this can irritate a writer who wants the material displayed on a CRT screen to duplicate exactly what will appear on a page. A user may also want to determine the size of the text buffer: For some writers, a text buffer capable of holding at least 10 to 25 pages of typed material is necessary. It may also be important to determine the speed at which a word-processing program carries out a function, the number of keystrokes necessary to initiate a command, and whether or not the program contains such special features as footnoting capability. The cost of a word-processing program varies from $100 to over $500 depending upon the number of functions the program carries out and with what speed and efficiency.

Word processing is ultimately important because of the time and energy it saves. Once the editing and formatting modes have been mastered, material can be prepared in 15 to 30 percent less time than it would take to do the same work using typewriter and paper. For some, the time and energy saved simply means that ill-conceived ideas can be more rapidly transmitted to others. For others, a word processor allows the user to devote more time and attention to conceptualizing and refining what is to be communicated to others.

Word-processing systems are being expanded to include other valuable additions. Programs are now available to help a writer correct misspellings. While some of these programs only identify misspelled words, others offer possible word substitutions from which a user

Table 5.3 Leading Information Services

Network	Owner	Subscribers
American People Link	American Home Network	40,000
Applied Videotex System	Richard Keen and Associates	40,000
CompuServe	H&R Block	380,000
Dow Jones News/Retrieval	Dow Jones	320,000
Genie	General Electric Information Services	70,000
The Source	Welsh, Carson, Anderson, and Stowe	80,000

might select replacements, providing a limited thesaurus. Thesaurus programs, also available, allow a user to consider stylistic changes suggested by the computer: These thesaurus programs provide, when requested, a list of synonyms or antonyms for any particular word in a text, and the user can elect to substitute one of these for the original word. Needless to say, the effectiveness of such a program can only be as good as the size of the dictionary built into the program. The 20,000-word dictionaries are of very limited usefulness, whereas 100,000- to 125,000-word dictionaries can be extremely useful resources. Other programs have been developed that facilitate precise proofreading. Verbal Technologies ("Technology," 1984) of New York has developed a device that reads aloud text stored in memory, pronouncing not only the words but also the punctuation and capitalization, so that proofreading requires only one person. We also envision development of similar programs that identify unusual grammatical constructions and offer conventional substitutions. In any event, the word processor increases the range of stylistic options and the efficiency with which thoughts can be expressed.

Teletext and Videotex

Teletext and videotex systems provide users with on-screen information available through computer-modem or computer-cable data interface connections. We discussed several examples of these systems when we examined electronic newspapers and encyclopedias, electronic yellow pages, and travel and entertainment reservations systems in chapter 4. These uses illustrate the generic services provided by teletext and videotex systems. Arlen Communications (1987, p. D1) has identified the nation's leading information services (see table 5.3).
   Michael Tyler (1979) has defined teletext and videotex systems as:

"Systems for the widespread dissemination of textual and graphic information by wholly electronic means, for display on low-cost terminals (often suitably equipped television receivers), under the selective control of the recipient, and using control procedures easily understood by untrained users" (p. 2). As this definition suggests, teletext and videotex systems are designed as mass communication systems that transmit requested information directly to the home of the user. Teletext and videotex systems are best perceived—at least at this time—as two different kinds of information-retrieval systems. The differences between these two systems are worth noting.

First, teletext and videotex differ in the amount and kind of information they provide. A teletext system provides only a limited quantity of information, generally some 100 "pages" of text, whereas a videotex system provides access to thousands of "pages" of information. Moreover, teletext information typically deals with the kind of current data that change daily (newspaper stories, weather reports, sports information, and so forth). The data provided are rotated throughout the day. On the other hand, a videotex system generally provides more enduring information with access to such data bases as specialized and technical journals and encyclopedias. Thus, teletext systems are geared to popular tastes and concerns, whereas videotex systems provide information relevant to those who need specialized information. In essence, then, teletext is a form of broadcasting, whereas videotex is a type of narrowcasting.

Second, teletext and videotex differ in the degree of interactive control a user can exert over the system. Because the information provided by a teletext system appeals to common and popular needs, the user's degree of control is extremely limited. Available choices are roughly equivalent to those offered by a daily newspaper. More specifically, teletext is essentially a one-way system in which a constant stream of information is broadcast to the home and in which the user stops the stream of information at a particular point to read a selected portion. The larger the teletext file, the greater will be the waiting time for requested information to appear in the home. The entire cycle of information may have to repeat itself before the needed information is in a position to be transmitted. In contrast, a videotex user can select from among a number of data bases covering many years and can receive material related to virtually any specialized interest. Because it employs what is essentially a random-access transmission system, which the user can enter at any point, a videotex system is a two-way system in which the user regulates what information is transmitted to the home. The degree of interactive control is thus greater in a videotex system than in a teletext system.

Third, the systems differ in their relative cost and availability. Teletext systems are inexpensive and can be included in the cost of a cable connection. Videotex systems require more elaborate home computer systems (interface and modem connections) and typically entail subscription and prorated hourly-use fees.

Both teletext and videotex function as expressive systems for the user because they increase the options and activities a user can carry out in the home. As we noted in concluding chapter 3, these functions can include information retrieval, transacting, messaging, computing, and telemonitoring.

In Western Europe, teletext systems are now commonplace, whereas in the United States these services are in experimental test markets or are just emerging locally. For example, KPIX, a Westinghouse Group W television station in San Francisco, offers Direct-Vision to its subscribers. DirectVision provides 18 hours a day of electronic magazines, news, weather reports, sports scores, shopping specials, and advertising. After the novelty of the system wore off, viewers reported (Kiester, 1983, p. 34) that they looked at the service about three times a week for a total of 45 minutes to 1.5 hours each week. Users found the 30 seconds required to "turn a page" an unnecessarily time-consuming inconvenience. In April 1983, CBS television network initiated the first national teletext system in the United States. Called Extravision, the system is experimental and involves only 100 decoders capable of receiving the signal. The Extravision system provides 100 pages of information ranging from news and sports reports through health, science, and communications features to food tips and ads. Extravision is advertiser supported, and users are required to pay only for the decoding equipment attached to their television sets (Arenson, 1984). Teletext is projected to become a regular feature of home reception. While several analysts (Arenson, 1984; Pace, 1982, p. D4) have predicted that 10 to 20 percent of American households will have teletext during the 1990s, others (Tydeman et al., 1982) have argued that "it is reasonable to forecast a [teletext] market approaching 40 percent of [American] households by the early 1990s" (p. 269).

Though far less popular in conception, videotex systems are widely available in the United States. They are typically used by corporations or by individuals with highly specialized research needs. DIALOG is the largest and most frequently used videotex system in the United States. Established in 1972, DIALOG currently has nearly 300 data bases and more than 152 million records. One of its data bases, SOCIAL SCISEARCH, contains over 2,288,324 records from 1972 to the present. This multidisciplinary data base indexes "every significant item from 1,500 of the most important social sciences journals throughout the world and social science articles selected from 3,000 additional journals in the natural, physical, and biomedical sciences" (DIALOG, 1988, p. 53); its records or units of information can "range from a directory-type listing of specific manufacturing plants to a citation with biblio-graphic information and an abstract referencing a journal, conference paper, or other original source" (p. 1). Beyond the data bases provided by DIALOG, the Spring 1984 *Directory of Online Databases* indexed 2,222 data bases from 1,069 producers and 327 on-line services. These data bases ranged from the biomedical data base AAMSI COMMUNICA-TION NETWORK through the marketing data base MEDIA INDEX SURVEY to the ZOOLOGICAL RECORD ONLINE system. A user of videotex should be able to locate a relevant data-base system regardless of his or her interests.

Telework

Since the late 1950s, such visionaries as Peter Drucker (1959) have believed that home computers would allow people to remain at home, receive work by computer link from a work center, complete the work at home on a home computer, and then transmit the completed tasks by computer link to the work center. People would thus communicate with rather than commute to work. By the early 1970s, such futurists as Edwin Parker, Peter Goldman, and Hazel Henderson had extended the vision of such workplace–home computer connections. Telework or telecommuting would eliminate congested urban centers, allow employees to live in whatever section of the country they preferred, free up the hours spent commuting to and from work, and end the traffic jams, gasoline shortages, pollution, overcrowding, ghettos, and even the stress associated with urban living.

Working at home is certainly not new. The 1980 census showed that more than 2 million, or 2.5 percent of the nonfarm work force, said they worked at home for money (cited in Herbers, 1986). In 1986, the United States Chamber of Commerce and AT&T estimated that more than 10 million Americans do all of their paid work at home, while an-other 12 million do some of their work there. According to Electronic Services Unlimited (cited in Goncharoff, 1985, p. 35), a New York–based research and consulting firm specializing in telecommuting, about 450 businesses across the nation, including Apple Computers, J. C. Penney, and Control Data Corporation, offered formal or informal opportunities for about 100,000 telecommuters to work with com-puters at home. In December 1985, the Office of Technology Assess-ment (cited in K. B. Noble, 1986), a research arm of Congress, estimated that only 3,000 to 5,000 people were working with com-puters at home for employers or clients. In May 1986, Yankee Group (cited in K. B. Noble, 1986), a market-research firm in Boston, reported that 30,000 full-time workers and 100,000 part-time workers were linked by home computers to their offices.

Telework is not a pervasive social experience, but it is technologically feasible for workers to work at home for several months at a time. Where employed, it has proved useful under special conditions. For disabled workers or for women during pregnancy and the first several months of a child's infancy, telework may be desirable or even necessary. Moreover, telework can provide flexibility for people experiencing personal or family crises. Nonetheless, once established as routine, telework ceases in most cases to be the preferred option. Most people enjoy the personal contacts of working together with their colleagues. John Naisbitt (1982, pp. 39–53) argued for what he called a "High Tech/High Touch" thesis, which presumes that people gain more from contacts with people than from contacts with machines. He therefore maintained that every increase in the use of technology must be compensated for with an increase in the amount of social contact available to people.

Telework may not become a national norm in the foreseeable future, but the fact remains that it can provide flexibility to virtually every information worker at one time or another. In addition, such systems expand human choices; it is no longer the case that one mode of human service must be rendered by all who engage in that service. Telework systems may in time become more popular than they are now. In any case, telework systems exist technologically. The decision to employ them seems to turn on human preferences and priorities, on, for example, whether these systems allow or can allow gratifying communicative expression.

Social Consequences

When employed as a mode of expression, personal computers directly affect the life-styles of their users. The uses described in this chapter directly increase the number of ways in which people can communicate with others. For some people, the expressive options associated with using a home computer gratifyingly reduce the time and energy devoted to formulating and conveying human expressions; for others, the gratifications of efficiency are not great. In any event, personal computers can function as a direct extension of how human beings communicate.

As was true of the study of computer transmissions, research focusing upon the expressive functions of computer use has emphasized productivity factors rather than social and subjective aspects of human responses to computers. Nonetheless, these aspects can be considered in four areas of expressive computer use.

Video Games

Playing video games does affect human relationships, but despite some clear conclusions derived from precisely executed research, the nature of its effect remains controversial. Without any real evidence to sustain their decisions, many communities have viewed video games as dangerous, if not immoral, and some communities have outlawed or restricted their use. Not all of the social effects of video games have been investigated, but several firm conclusions dispel some of these communities' misconceptions.

For most players, video games function solely as a form of entertainment and without any reported negative effects upon the individual or the family. Frederick Williams, Amy Friedman Phillips, and Patricia Lum (1984) reported that their interviews with students revealed that most associated the "playing of videogames" with "the need 'to be entertained' " (p. 12). Gerald Gibb, James Bailey, Thomas Lambirth, and William Wilson (1983), after measuring the effects on 280 players, concluded the following: that video games did not effect a sense of self-degradation or a loss in the players' self-esteem; that video games did not affect the players' achievement motivations; and that video games did not affect the players' tendencies toward social deviancy or social conformity, hostility or kindness, social withdrawal or gregariousness, obsessiveness or compulsiveness. Focusing upon the effects of video games upon family interaction, Edna Mitchell (1983) interviewed 20 families shortly after they had purchased video games and then again 4 months later. In addition, she had each family maintain a detailed daily record of all video-game and social activity within the home. Rather than detecting negative consequences, Mitchell generally concluded that the video games had enhanced family interaction during the 4 months of her study. She reported, for example, that "families (70%) reported that they watched less tv after purchasing the video games" (p. 15), that only on "rare occasions" did game playing have to be "severely regulated" (p. 18), that "in all but one family the playing of video games appeared to be kept in reasonable perspective along with responsibilities and other diverse activities of family life" (p. 18), and that 60 percent of the families saw no change in the quality of their children's homework as a result of introducing the video games into the home (p. 19). In fact, 40 percent "indicated improvement in children's school work or skills which could be a result of playing the games" (p. 19). Far more important, however, is the over-all conclusion reached in Mitchell's study:

In all families a change in family interaction was reported in a positive direction. The games brought families together in new interactive patterns, at least for a period of time. This was valued by adults and children alike.

Even in families where no effect on schoolwork was noted, the development of specific skills in eye-hand coordination, speedier reflexes, and increase in friendly competition were reported.

The most compelling outcome of the study is the extent to which families reported their enjoyment of playing video games together, and the cooperative spirit surrounding the games which had freshly emerged within the family. . . .

Technology has invaded the family in a permanent way. This study suggests that it is not inherently bad; that families may be trusted to use judgement about time and activities appropriate to their children's lives and in a context of family values. (p. 28)

In terms of the behaviors measured and the questions asked, these findings suggest that video games, as a general rule, have few known negative effects and may even have positive effects upon individual players and their families.

Other researchers have raised other questions, and they are less confident of the positive effects of video games upon video-game players. Some researchers have detected obsessive video-game playing. While Mitchell did not detect obsessions when video games were played at home, Gary W. Selnow and Hal Reynolds (1984) found that the time devoted each week to television viewing was positively related to several measures of arcade video-game playing, including frequency of arcade attendance and the amount of money spent on the games. In other words, excessive television viewing and excessive video-game playing are directly related: If children watch a great deal of television, they are also very likely to spend a great deal of time and money on video games. This correlation has several interpretations. One might speculate that the passivity of prolonged television viewing is compensated by the more active involvement of video-game playing, or one might suspect that some children are excessively dependent on multiple forms of media. It may also be that the electronic visual components of television viewing and video-game playing create a mutually reinforcing relationship. These interpretations require additional examination and investigation.

Obsessive video-game playing has also been associated with anti-social behaviors. Gary W. Selnow (1984) asked 244 children who were between the ages of 10 and 14 and who were attending a statewide summer sports camp to complete a three-part questionnaire that asked them to rate the importance of 17 value statements, to provide basic demographic information about themselves, including their television-viewing habits, and to describe their playing behaviors if they played arcade video games. Selnow found that as video-game playing increased, players increasingly viewed video games as an opportunity to escape from social interaction with others. He specifically found that "heavy" video-game players, who played 4.5 hours or more a week and spent more than $9 a week on arcade video games, preferred playing video games to being with their friends, believed they learned about people by playing video games, perceived the video-game machines as "companions," associated video-game playing with "action," and experienced positive forms of "solitude" while playing video games.

Other researchers have focused upon the male roles and the male images adopted by the teenage boys who typically play these games. After observing young males playing video games in arcades, communication specialists Paul Evangelista and Scott Tulman (1984) reported that video games facilitate and enhance male bonding and thereby influence what masculinity is to become for these teenage males. In their view, the masculinity promoted by video games is traditional: "Video games utilize and promote the theme of dominance, aggressiveness and independence" (p. 7). The consequence of this reinforcement, they assert, is " 'a coarse and unfeeling attitude toward life' " (p. 17), for "video games comprise an ironic rhetorical vision which victimizes males through the promotion of traditional sex role stereotypes" (p. 2). Although she is more supportive of video games and their impact, Sherry Turkle reported in *The Second Self* (1984) that the games reinforce a sense of "complete control" not found in social interactions (p. 72). On the other hand, the games have yet to be linked to forms of violent behavior. On November 9, 1982, Surgeon General C. Everett Koop said that "some video games may tend toward violence in their tone"; however, the following day, he noted that his "off-the-cuff comment" was not "based on any accumulated scientific evidence." "Nothing in my remarks," he concluded, "should be interpreted as implying that video games are per se violent in nature or harmful to children."

Some researchers allege that video games may have creative and intellectual consequences that are negative. In *The Brain* (1984), Richard Restak reported that video games may enhance eye-hand coordination, but their extensive use correlates with low creativity and impaired IQ. Yet a causal link is not established by merely reporting such a correlation. We have found no indication in the literature that playing video games *causes* low creativity or impaired IQ.

We are confident that the extensive playing of video games does influence the lives of the players. All studies we know of report that playing video games influences the lives of players themselves and of those in their social environment. It seems to us that video games, rather than functioning merely as a mode of entertainment, are also influencing modes of human expression, particularly among the young. Whatever these influences may be, if video games continue to decline in popularity, so may their consequences. The games themselves may be the strongest cause of their diminishing popularity. They involve, at best, only two patterns of interaction—the first requires that elements within the game be destroyed, the second that obstacles be avoided—and with time, such repetitive patterns can easily lead to boredom. Moreover, as more elementary schools and high schools provide computer courses and labs, interest in the full range of the computer's capabilities may ultimately reduce the fascination that video games held at the beginning of the 1980s. Video games may have shaped the expressive orientations of many young Americans, but perhaps their greatest impact has been to stimulate interest in a comprehensive understanding of the full capacities of a computer.

Word Processing

Word processing also exerts profound social influences on users and those in contact with users. The effects range from the obvious to the subtle.

Most obviously, word processing increases the speed with which people are able to communicate in written form. Susan Holland Komsky (1984) reported that word processors can cut "production time by one-half" (p. 2). This efficiency reduces thoughtful conceptualization for some people, while for others it provides the convenience, time, and energy necessary to refine expression. Marcel Just and Patricia Carpenter (cited in Sekuler, 1985) reported that when more time is spent refining written discourse, readers are able to more quickly and accurately comprehend intended meanings. In *Writing with a Word Processor*, William Zinsser (1983) noted that these revisions are made less conveniently and therefore are less likely to be made with a pen, pencil, or typewriter than with a word processor. More conceptual is Diane Pelkus Balestri's argument (1988, p. 17) that *hard copy*, generated on paper by hand or by the typewriter, emphasizes the final text as a fixed, immutable, and permanent record because of the physical difficulties involved in any kind of revision; in contrast, *soft copy*, "the text on a computer screen" (p. 16), is easily "expanded and contracted, split and joined, parts reserved, discarded and inserted" (p. 17). Accordingly, Balestri noted, "with softcopy, fluidity becomes a term to describe not text-as-product, but text-in-process and process itself" (p. 16). Andrew Fluegelman and Jeremy Hewes (1983), authors of *Writing in the Computer Age*, similarly argue that word processors make writing more bearable, that the blank screen is less threatening than a blank sheet of paper, that the screen encourages experimentation, and that the attractiveness of the final copy ultimately provides more positive reinforcement. In *Processing Words* Bruce L. Edwards, Jr., (1987) maintained that the dual functions executed by the word processor—text composition and transcription—free a writer "to attend to the most important issue in the writing process: the communication of ideas and experience" (p. 2). Thus, the available evidence seems to suggest that the technological structure of word processing increases productivity while encouraging revisions of written texts.

More profoundly, word processing can alter social conceptions of writing as a mode of communication. Russell Baker (1985) has aptly captured the nature of the shift, a transformation from "writing to processing words" (p. 14). The change can be cast as a basis for either a positive or a negative social transformation. When psychologists Linda Flower and John Hayes (cited in Sekuler, 1985, p. 42) concluded from their examination of students' essay writing that good writers seldom engaged in detailed mental planning before writing and often did not know precisely what they would write until they had written it, Robert Sekuler (1985) further concluded that "because it makes it easier both to produce and to modify our writing, a word processor may also make it easier to find out what we think" (p. 42). For others, however, word processing modifies the power and beauty associated with the printed word. Word processing, as a concept, possesses a functional and quantitative emphasis. Word processing is an isolating experience. The technical manipulations involved in word processing require that computer users concentrate almost exclusively upon the human-computer interaction, an intense and exclusive experience. Moreover, word processing allows a user to view words as discrete items, as capable of being manipulated independently of any social context or anticipated reader response.

Word processing reveals both the advantages and the limits of electronic modes of communication. Word processing is an efficient, productive, and open-ended method of generating human ideas. The available evidence suggests that the word-processing system itself can directly affect whether and how people express their ideas. At the same time, word processing is a self-contained process, reinforcing the link between human beings and computers. The structural features of word processing cast language creation as an isolated, functional, and pragmatic task while simultaneously shifting attention from, if not diminishing, the aesthetic characteristics and social appreciation of using words.

Teletext and Videotex

Teletext and videotex do function in the home as useful information-retrieval systems. Even after the novelty wears off, the systems are employed on a regular basis for a variety of information needs. In the view of the Institute for the Future, teletext systems will become part of 40 percent of American households by the early 1990s; the institute further predicts that videotex systems will appear in some 40 percent of American households by the end of the century (cited in Tydeman et al., 1982, p. 269). The institute projects that these systems will make the home an increasingly important feature of American life and identifies a variety of intriguing side effects: "Spouses may be drawn to each other as much for their ability to manipulate databases as for their ability to prepare gourmet meals or to play racquetball" (p. 256), and "the struggles with the outside world may increasingly become struggles in the home" (p. 257). Such consequences would tend to blur the distinction between the public and the private domains of life. If so, the sensitivity of privacy issues related to human-computer communication may slowly diminish. At the same time, as T. Andrew Finn and Concetta M. Stewart (1986) have noted, a host of problems affect the adoption of videotex systems—technical problems (protocol standards, the selection of appropriate terminal devices, and the specialization of systems), economic problems (cost, ease of use and implementation, and user friendliness) and social and political problems (needs assessments, uses, and distribution).

Telework

While not extensively used today, telework promises to exaggerate the consequences of human-computer communication. Its potential is evident. In a national, random sample of 1,019 registered American voters polled by *Time* and Yankelovich, Skelly, and White in December 1982, 73 percent of the respondents believed that the computer revolution would enable more people to work at home, but only 31 percent said they would prefer to do so themselves (cited in Friedrich, 1983, January 3, "Computer Moves In," p. 21).

People using computers to work at home have identified both positive and negative aspects of telework. Katya Goncharoff (1985) has noted that "working at home has several advantages: A person can work when he wishes, in an environment he controls. He can often set his own hours and pace" (p. 38). "Other positive aspects to telecommuting," according to Goncharoff, are "the time, stress and money saved by not having to commute, buy lunches out or buy clothing for the office. Others say they like telecommuting because their family life has become interspersed with the workday, and some say that telecommuting brings families closer together. On the negative side, telecommuters report such problems as loneliness, weight gain, family stress brought on by continued close contact, and lack of recognition for the work they do."

If such systems become increasingly popular, the distinction between work and home is likely to blur. In this scenario, a host of consequences might be anticipated. As the home functions as the work center, loyalty toward a corporation may shift to loyalty toward one's profession. The "9-to-5" timetable as a definition of a work period is likely to be displaced. As telework is combined with teletext and videotex systems, the home will increasingly function as a centralizing environment linking all dimensions of the personal life. As Joseph Deken (1982) has forecasted, the home would become an "electronic cottage," with all dimensions of human activity beginning from and terminating at this electronic center. The meaning and values of such a transformation are not immediately clear. Would the computer ultimately place an "electronic fence" around the "electronic cottage"? Consider, for example, the self-report by Gerald M. Phillips (1983, September). He has steadfastly maintained that the computer should be treated as a slave. Yet, as a result of using his own home computer, he reported that "I've become much less social. I'm very happy at home—it's like being in a cocoon. Sometimes I have to push myself to get out and be with people, and I don't engage in as much trivial socialization" (p. 18).

These careful assessments of the advantages and disadvantages of telework may ultimately prove irrelevant. Purely economic and corporate concerns may decide the issues. Goncharoff (1985) has reported that it is "less expensive" to "provide employees with equipment to use at home than it is to buy high-priced urban office space. In addition, most studies show that telecommuters are more productive, but not because people are necessarily working better; they just seem to work more hours. For example, telecommuters tend to take the commuting time they save and spend more time doing work" (p. 38). In our view, it is at least conceivable that corporate interests may reside in maximizing the financial advantages of telework. The negative interpersonal and social consequences of telework may be viewed as secondary issues and as by-products of a more fundamental decision to establish telework as the norm in the employment environment in the United States.

In chapter 9, we explore whether this scenario is an essential and necessary consequence of extensive use of personal computers. In any event, we are more likely to control our future if we can make reasonable estimations about what that future might be.

Conclusion

In this chapter, we explored uses of personal computers that facilitate human expression. Some of these uses, such as video games, appear to constitute unique modes of expression not easily duplicated by other methods of interacting. Other uses, such as word processing, provide more efficient ways for humans to express themselves. Teletext and videotex provide new sources of information that in turn influence what humans will want to express. Finally, with telework systems, the environment controlling human expression is altered: Employment itself, by being in the home rather than elsewhere, is transformed. These new circumstances are certain to alter the meanings of what is said and when, how, and to whom it is said.

6

Congruent Human-Computer Communication

In several of Isaac Asimov's science-fiction novels (see, e.g., *Robots and Empire* [1985]), robots are as intelligent as human beings; they are perhaps even more intelligent than human beings. In order to control these robots, Asimov formulated his now-famous Three Laws of Robotics: (a) A robot may not harm a human being or, through inaction, allow a human being to come to harm; (b) A robot must obey the orders given to it by human beings, except where such orders would conflict with the first law; (c) A robot must protect its own existence, as long as such protection does not conflict with the first or second law. For Asimov, these Three Laws of Robotics would ensure that human beings always dominate human-computer interactions. The laws assuage the fear that computers might someday function as the equals of human beings.

Computer programs that create an equal relationship between the computer and its user already exist. From a communication perspective, equality exists between any two entities when each can: introduce and formulate goals, tasks, and procedures; delegate or direct actions; integrate or pull together efforts; and provide transitions or interconnections among activities, thereby defining the overall meaning of an interaction. When certain computer programs are employed, both the user and the computer carry out these activities.

When these programs are employed, the human-computer interaction is typically perceived and described as useful or functional rather than as an interaction of equals. For example, when using an individualized learning program, the user must at least unconsciously admit that the program contains information new or unknown to her or him. Moreover, the user implicitly agrees to try to master the goals and tasks introduced by the computer and to do so in the order prescribed by the computer. In these ways, the computer delegates and directs the actions of the user. In addition, a comprehensive computer program determines when the user must repeat certain exercises if further progress is to be made. The computer thereby integrates or pulls together efforts, provides transitions or interconnections, and thus defines the overall meaning of the human-computer relationship at any particular point. It is true that the user, not the computer, implicitly agrees to continue through the steps outlined by a computer, and it is also true that the user may shut down the computer system at any point. In these senses, the human being controls the computer. But during the interactions themselves, when the human being follows the steps and exercises outlined by the computer, the computer functions as an equal, if not a dominant, agent in the human-computer relationship.

In this chapter, we examine several computer programs that establish such symmetrical or equal relationships between computers and users: individualized educational programs, more advanced computer-art programs, medical diagnosis and therapy programs, various games of chess, and more sophisticated data-search systems.

In all of these computer uses, the user must implicitly agree to follow the leads provided by the computer. Though the user's responses are important, the computer program controls the structure and direction of the interaction. The computer performs a *correlational* function, for it systematically integrates and links human responses to appropriate, preestablished computer-programming statements. From the user's perspective, this dependency upon a computer is acceptable or necessary because it provides the user with new skills and new information unlikely to be obtained without instruction and expert verification. Given these conditions, the user's psychological state might best be viewed as that of both manager and performer. A manager directs and supervises; a performer enacts and executes. A managing performer does not merely execute repetitive, mindless, or solely leisurely activities; rather, he or she directs and supervises while seriously engaged in a pursuit. In this regard, the term *managing performer* could as well be employed to describe the role of computers in these relationships.

Social Uses

Individualized Education Programs

Many individualized education programs are provided by computer and software manufacturers. These programs now cover virtually every traditional educational topic at all levels of the educational system (see, e.g., *Perspectives in Computing*, 1986, Fall; "Covering Computer Use," 1987). They also cover the new skills required to achieve traditional conceptions of computer literacy, such as learning a programming language or understanding the internal mechanical and electronic features of a computer. The question is generally not whether a program exists for learning a specific skill but how well a program teaches the user.

Educational programs are available from a variety of sources, including information services, computer manufacturers, software manufacturers, and users' groups. The educational programs provided by information services tend to take the form of data bases, allowing a user to select information as needed. For example, *Reader's Digest*'s The Source (1983) offers three broad categories of educational programs: foreign languages (including French, German, Greek, Italian, and Spanish); language arts (including aphorisms, English, grammar, phrase origins, poetry, quotations, and spelling); and mathematics (including addition, counting, geometry, and numbers).

In contrast, computer and software manufacturers offer more coherent educational programs that allow for progressive development from fundamental to sophisticated understandings. In addition, these programs are structured to provide appropriate exercises and reinforcement and may include game-playing formats to encourage the user. For example, Texas Instruments (1983) advertises that it is the largest producer of software and provides a wide variety of programs: a series of remedial programs that include modules designed to create interest in learning; programs dealing with beginning grammar, number "magic," and video graphs; two levels of music-recognition and -understanding modules; two levels of reading programs; four levels of spelling drills; and three levels of mathematics programs, from basic addition and subtraction to multiplication. More advanced programs include modules on physical fitness, weight control and nutrition, market simulation, bridge bidding, and statistics. In addition, Texas Instruments offers a variety of computer literacy programs, such as self-teaching programs for mastering BASIC and Extended BASIC, and of "libraries" containing information on an array of topics from electrical engineering to business. While not classified as educational, Texas Instruments' home-management and personal-finance programs provide structured formats and relationships for controlling household finances; in our view, they function more as teaching aids than as recording devices. Moreover, Texas Instruments' PLATO educational series provides in disk form some 400 hours of instruction designed to lead a user from third-grade through high-school levels in reading, writing, and arithmetic. Other computer and software manufacturers have sets of programs that come very close to offering an equally comprehensive set of educational opportunities, and some of these manufacturers are now offering highly specialized programs. For example, Harcourt Brace Jovanovich's Computer SAT is designed to help its users achieve a higher score on the Scholastic Aptitude Test (see, e.g., Belkin, 1983; Sandberg-Diment, 1983, April). In the hope that users will purchase these programs, manufacturers are typically more than eager to describe and to demonstrate them.

Users' groups are often overlooked, but they also offer impressive educational programs. These programs may lack the logical coherence and sophistication of professionally designed programs, but they frequently fill important gaps. For example, one users' group offers almost 200 tapes and disks dealing with such diverse tasks as learning how to tell time, recognizing the flags of different nations, learning Morse code, doing precious-metal conversions, learning the books of the Bible, converting dates from the Julian calendar to the Gregorian calendar, and learning about aerodynamics and spatial relationships. Users' groups also provide traditional programs in grammar, math, spelling, and foreign languages as well as an impressive set of tests and quizzes designed to measure masteries of different skills.

When assessing educational programs, one should consider not only the quantity and variety of programs but also their quality, which can vary tremendously. As early as 1982, findings reported by Vicky Cohen (cited in "Computers' Software," 1982) established norms for evaluating the quality of educational programs. Five of Cohen's conclusions are relevant to our purposes: (a) Most programs provide only drills, stressing recall of facts already learned; (b) Most programs—95 percent—deal with arithmetic; (c) Most programs do not explain why an answer provided by the user is incorrect; (d) Most programs are advertised as relevant for too wide an audience—some programs claim to be relevant to anyone from grade 3 through adulthood; and (e) Most programs do not focus upon such higher comprehension skills as criticism, analysis, and application. Indeed, Columbia University's Educational Products Information Exchange gave only 25 percent of the instructional software evaluated a high rating (cited in "Computers'

Software," 1982). The unique contributions of the computerized educational programs have also been questioned by such critics as Joseph Menosky (1984):

Though the video-gamelike graphics are new, people have been working with the idea of computer presented instruction for over 20 years. There seems to be little doubt that computers can help students learn. Various programs have reported success with arithmetic and other subjects suited to rote memorization, and the military has used computer drills to train tank gunners. But there is no evidence that students retain material better—or even learn better than if they'd been drilled conventionally. (p. 45)

Another critic is the former U.S. secretary of education T. H. Bell (cited in "Bell Is Critical," 1984), who concluded generally that "computerized educational programs" on the existing market "leave a great deal to be desired" (p. D24).

Theoretically, however, none of the deficiencies in educational programming is inherent. Indeed, in the early 1980s educators had several reasons for their high expectations for computerized instruction. First, early evaluations of computer-based instruction indicated impressive results. In a one-year assessment of kindergartners and some first graders, the Educational Testing Service (cited in Asbell, 1984) found that computer-instructed children as a group scored higher in reading skills than 89 percent of their non-computer-instructed peers, that 63 percent of computer-instructed kindergartners were composing full and original sentences and stories on paper (kindergartners typically can write only their names and a favorite word or two), and that in the first grade 92 percent of computer-instructed students were writing and reading.

As professional educators were consulted about these programs, solutions to many problems were apparently identified. For example, as early as 1983, Dan Watt had reported that on the market was a "new breed of educational software" that promised to provide " 'fun with learning at home' " (p. 65). Moreover, instruction involving computers entered all levels of the educational system, and the results provided useful feedback to computer and software manufacturers.

In addition, in several cases, particularly at the college and university levels, the link between professional educators and educational computer programmers has become more secure. This is particularly true in newly created curricula. TeleLearning Systems' educational telecommunications network, for example, is essentially an electronic university: Some 177 courses were offered via computer-modem connections during 1983–84, and about 25 colleges are making credit courses available through the system. TeleLearning plans to offer "more than 500 courses, drawing on instructors from universities, colleges, technical schools, primary schools, and trade associations" (Stahr, 1984, p. 248). Similarly, New York Institute, an independent four-year college, began in the fall of 1984 to offer 100 computer courses that lead to a baccalaureate degree (Schmidt, 1985). Roxanne Hiltz (cited in Schmidt, 1985, p. 50) coordinated a number of pilot studies of on-line learning using the New Jersey Institute of Technology's Electronic Information Exchange System and reported that 80 to 85 percent of the participants in on-line courses or seminars take an active part in discussions, whereas only 15 percent of students in traditional classroom settings do so. However, Sanger (1986, January) has reported some limitations to such systems.

In any event, it would not have been unreasonable to assume that educational programs were being consistently improved in terms of their instructional quality. Given these potentially rich and exciting educational programs, institutions at all levels of the educational system began to invest in computers. The computer craze in American public schools began during the 1981–82 academic year. Talmis Corporation (cited in Severo, 1984) has reported that there were 33,000 computers in American public schools by June 1981; 125,000 by June 1982; 300,000 by June 1983; and 630,000 by June 1984. In 1984, Menosky reported that schools had spent during that year nearly $500 million on personal computers and programs. By 1985, Market Data Retrieval (cited in Tucker, 1985, p. 14) reported that 50 percent of all high schools, 40 percent of all junior high schools, and 20 percent of all elementary schools had microcomputers. Likewise in 1985, the Department of Education's National Center for Educational Statistics reported that the percentage of all U.S. high-school students enrolled in computer-related courses has consistently increased: in 1972–73, 3.4 percent, or 407,000 high-school students; in 1981–82, 9.8 percent, or 1,244,000 students; and in 1985–86, 12.0 percent, or 1,500,000 students (cited in "Computer Education," 1985). By 1986, Henry Jay Becker, who then conducted the National Surveys of Microcomputers for the Center for Social Organizations of Schools at Johns Hopkins University, stated that 90 percent of American primary and secondary schools had educational computers and that "the average American secondary school had more than 15" (cited in Gottlieb, 1986, p. 67). By 1988, 96 percent of U.S. public schools had computers, and most of them had between 10 and 20 machines (Bulkeley, 1988). Quality Education Data (1988a) has reported:

Virtually all districts have had some micros since the 1983–1984 school year; the significant growth has been in the number of units. The critical ratio is the number of students per micro; **QED has called this micro/pupil ratio**

"Microcomputer Density." The lower the number of students per micro, the greater the opportunity for meaningful hands-on time for students and the greater the need for software.

For 1987–1988, QED found a significant increase in the number of micros per school, and therefore a lower Microcomputer Density. **There are now 1,250,000 computers in public schools enrolling 39 million students, for an average density of 32 students per micro.** This is a sharp decline from more than 50 students per micro in the 1985–1986 school year and an even more dramatic drop from 125 students per micro in the 1983–1984 school year. (p. 19)

In its "Market Target" report of May 18, 1988, Quality Education Data (1988b, pp. 1–2) detailed the particulars leading to these conclusions. These data are summarized in table 6.1.

Yet it remains unclear whether or not these computers are being employed to useful ends. Vicky Cohen stated in 1982 that most programs provide only drills, stress recall of facts already learned, are predominantly restricted to the study of arithmetic, fail to explain why an answer provided by the user is incorrect, attempt to serve too wide an audience, and do not focus upon such higher comprehension skills as criticism, analysis, and application (cited in "Computers' Software," 1982). Six years later, it remains unclear that any significant improvement has been made in the ways in which educational computer programs are used in the nation's schools. In a survey of 24,000 students, the Educational Testing Service (1988) reported the type and frequency of use of educational computing. Of the 7th and 11th graders surveyed, most used computers only rarely, and those who did used it mainly for word processing (see table 6.2).

The potential range and variety of educational computer programs as well as the increasing rate of computer penetration within American schools are certainly impressive. Yet a great deal remains to be considered in terms of actual use and types of quality controls employed in educational computing. Though we cannot confidently predict that computer education in the nation's schools will improve, we do anticipate that more students will be more actively involved with computers before they reach college age. However, the value of such exposure remains an unresolved issue.

Computer Art

In chapter 2, we hinted at the possible uses of the personal computer as an adjunct to the production of art. We noted, for example, that a light pen can be used directly on a CRT screen as an input device. It would be unfortunate if this observation left the impression

Table 6.1 Microcomputer Trends in the Schools, 1981–88

	1981–82	1982–83	1983–84	1984–85	1985–86	1986–87	1987–88
Districts:							
With micros	6,473	9,379	12,517	15,153	15,236	15,399	15,398
Without micros	10,459	7,132	4,111	1,415	1,832	1,609	1,512
% with micros	38%	57%	75%	91%	89%*	91%	91%
Schools:							
With micros	14,132	30,859	55,175	70,255	74,379	76,242	76,899
Without micros in dists. with	32,567	34,066	18,919	9,819	5,788	0	0
Without micros in dists. without	39,048	18,723	8,858	1,097	1,294	317	89
Total schools	85,747	83,646	82,592	81,971	81,333	81,408	80,999
% with micros	16.5%	36.8%	66.8%	85.7%	91.5%	93.6%	94.9%
Ratio of micros to students			1–125	1–75	1–50	1–37	1–32

*Declining percentage due to increased special units.

Table 6.2 Type and Frequency of Computer Use among 7th and 11th Graders

	Once a Week (%)	Less Than Once a Week (%)	Never (%)
7th Grade			
Write letters, reports	22.8	27.0	50.2
Draw graphs	12.2	14.8	73.0
Create data bases	7.9	7.5	84.6
Write programs	19.6	19.6	60.8
11th Grade			
Write letters, reports	19.0	27.4	53.5
Draw graphs	7.7	13.3	73.9
Create data bases	8.9	8.5	82.7
Write programs	16.5	15.6	67.8

Note: Rounding off of percentages accounts for differences above and below 100% in individual categories.

that a personal computer functions as nothing more than an electronic slate. Rather, personal computers can function as coequals in artistic design, production, and execution.

A home computer can, of course, be employed merely as an electronic blackboard, with the computer recording only what the user puts into the system. For example, Spinnaker Software Corporation's "abstract-art" program, called Delta Drawing, essentially replicates whatever the user creates. Yet even such a simple program enables a user to carry out activities not possible with a blackboard or a piece of paper. This basic program can make copies of any human creation, rearrange these duplicates, and ultimately create a new artistic conception. Other programs can transform a two-dimensional human input into a three-dimensional conception. In both cases, the computer directly contributes to the overall conception and understanding conveyed by the artistic product.

Appropriate peripherals can even more radically extend a personal computer's contribution to the design process: The computer itself can be programmed to generate original art. In February 1983, for example, the program Aaron, billed as an "intelligent" computer, was displayed at the Brooklyn Museum in New York. Using four drawing machines, Aaron produced 12 unique and original drawings every hour of the show. Aaron's drawings were described at the time as "apparently freehand and almost representational." Museum spokesperson Gerald Le Francois observed that the drawings were "not at all what one expects of a computer; even viewers who watch them being made find it difficult to believe that they had not first been made by a human artist's hand and somehow 'fed' into the computer"; Le Francois concluded that the drawings produced by Aaron were "produced autonomously" (cited in "Art Exhibition," 1983, p. TSXQ 2). As one might anticipate, some people have questioned whether or not such products should be called "art." (For a review of many of the issues involved in this question, see Robert E. Mueller's essay, "When Is Computer Art Art?" [1983].)

Beyond their aesthetic dimensions, computer-art programs have important commercial applications. Computer-aided design (CAD) constitutes nothing less than a revolution in the aerospace and electronics-engineering industries. These programs generate holistic and comprehensive designs that cannot be efficiently produced by human engineers. Moreover, computer-assisted drafting programs—such as The Producer, manufactured by Bausch and Lomb—not only eliminate repetitive and mechanical work but also encourage experimentations that, in the view of Michael J. Wozny (cited in Fowler, 1982), "lead to better designs" (p. D2). The electronic architectural design programs developed at Cornell University's Computer Graphics Laboratory, for example, enable a computer to provide a full-color, three-dimensional "walk" through any proposed architectural design. During the walk, a potential buyer can ask that the colors of walls be changed or even that walls be moved, all of which can be done immediately by the computer so that the buyer can consider each change.

At the same time, CAD programs have generated criticism. At a 1985 meeting of the American Society of Mechanical Engineers, George E. Smith argued that "junior engineers using CAD programs were simply putting in data and collecting the solutions," with "little or no thought" given "to how the program arrives at the answer or whether it is correct" (cited in Sims, 1985, p. C7). While licensed, professional engineers using CAD programs must have the minimum skill level and spend the time required to verify computer results, such is not the case with nondegreed, noncertificated junior engineers. However, as long as CAD programs remain in qualified hands, one would not expect buildings and bridges to collapse.

Despite critics' misgivings, it is clear that, as a business, computer art may become a powerful economic force. Stanley Klein (cited in Fowler, 1982), as the editor of a newsletter on computer graphics, has estimated that annual sales of graphics and drafting systems could reach $1 billion by 1990.

We have already mentioned several medical uses of personal computers: robots that serve essential medical and therapeutic functions for quadriplegics, the elderly, and arthritis victims, and the voice activators and speech synthesizers that provide similar functions for the blind and deaf. These are outstanding contributions, but computer programs have been developed in other areas to provide further improvements in medical services.

Computerized innovations have come at a time when health-care costs are soaring. Karen Davis (1983) reported that the United States in 1979 spent $215 billion on health, or 8.9 percent of the nation's gross national product; by 1982, these costs had increased $322 billion, or 10.5 percent of the nation's gross national product. This 50-percent increase in health-care costs in a 3-year period exceeded both the national inflation rate and the average increase in family income. By 1986, health care accounted for $479 billion, or 11.4 percent of the nation's gross national product (Encyclopaedia Britannica, 1988, p. 726). Expressed in terms of the Consumer Price Index (1988, p. 51), the rising costs of health care are even more dramatic: Compared to what the typical wage earner spent on medical care in 1967 (a base year), health care costs increased 20.6 percent in 1970, 68.6 percent in 1975, 167.2 percent in 1980, and 301.2 percent in 1985. There is little reason to believe that costs will decline, for just between 1985 and March 1987, the Consumer Price Index for medical care rose another 51.1 percent.

Computerization that can reduce health-care costs is especially welcome and in fact has already influenced medical practices and costs in several ways.

First, computerized medical data bases have emerged. These provide readily available, current, and comprehensive information for virtually every type of disease and tissue trauma. The *Directory of Online Databases* lists seven major medical online data bases. One of them, called MEDITEC, contains 32,000 citations to worldwide literature from 1968 to the present. Major coverage is devoted to biological sciences, biomedical measurements, medical diagnostics, medical therapeutics, artificial organs and functions, and clinical engineering.

More relevant to our immediate concerns is that computers now serve a valuable function in securing preliminary medical histories, which are frequently crucial to medical diagnosis, treatment, or therapy. Accuracy and completeness in records and the patient's honesty are vital, and the way in which the medical interview is handled can determine whether or not the patient is willing to disclose necessary information. For many patients, such self-disclosures are not easily made. Some patients are hesitant to discuss certain physical and mental problems: Sexual difficulties, alcoholism, and forms of depression are frequently embarrassing for a patient to discuss with another person. In such circumstances, patients may find a computer-human interview less threatening than a face-to-face interview. In 1980, H. C. Price (cited in Meindl, 1985) found that patients admitted to hospitals responded favorably to computer interviews. They reported that they preferred the impersonality of the computer because it spared them both embarrassment and the extra energy required in human interactions. Christopher Evans (1979) also found that patients preferred computer interviews and were in fact more truthful with the computer than with their doctor:

Computer programs have already been written which take satisfactory [medical] histories in a large variety of common complaints, make simple recommendations for follow-up studies and even offer tentative diagnoses. And they do it all with such panache that the majority of patients interviewed by the computer prefer it to the doctor. There is also clear evidence that many patients are more truthful when they talk to the computer and are more willing to reveal their secrets to it than to a human being. In some experiments in a Glasgow hospital patients suspected of being alcoholics were interviewed by a specially tailored computer program; they admitted to drinking fifty per cent more alcohol to the computer than they did to the clinic's highly trained consultants. In other experiments, patients visiting psychosexual clinics showed real eagerness to chat about sexual hangups to a computer, in striking contrast to their reluctance to talk to the most sympathetic resident psychiatrists. (p. 113)

In an attempt to determine precisely the degree to which patients respond more honestly to a computer than to a human interviewer, Terry O'Brien and Valerie Dugdale (1978) found the "mean response values to be nearer to the 'honest' end of each scale for the computer-derived data" (p. 236). The prediction that Evans reported at the end of the 1970s—"an increasing number of computer experts and doctors believe that by the 1980s, large areas of medical practice will yield up their secrets to the computer" (p. 113)—appears to have come true.

Computers can also play a central role even in psychotherapy, a treatment judiciously guarded as one in which person-to-person relationships must be sustained. The most celebrated therapeutic computer program is called Eliza. Named after Eliza Doolittle in George Bernard Shaw's *Pygmalion*, the program was originally developed by Joseph Weizenbaum for large mainframe computers but has since been adapted by Steven Gumette for personal computers. Eliza is written in BASIC and can be reworked or adapted to personalize the program's responses. Eliza is designed to deal with human feelings and emotions from a Rogerian perspective. As such, the program provides nondirective, client-centered therapeutic responses intended to let clients reveal and understand their own self-conceptions. Accordingly, the program provides a host of noncommittal and probing responses to the clients' statements.

As one might anticipate, some therapists (see, e.g., Heller & Turner, 1983; McCorduck, 1979, pp. 225, 251–56, 259, 308–9, 311, 314, 318) have criticized Eliza. They noted that the program merely repeats in question form phrases provided by the client and that the program's problems with pronoun constructions can sometimes produce gibberish. For most therapists, the therapeutic features of the program have been the central issue. Some found the program useful for at least the first therapy session, but others challenged the entire conception guiding the program. Carl Rogers (cited in Heller & Turner, 1983, p. 192), who developed Rogerian therapy, is convinced that Eliza cannot do therapy because therapy can only occur between two people. Unfortunately, Mr. Rogers has never watched Eliza perform. Still other therapists believe the inability of Eliza to contradict or offer interpretations of a client's statements is a serious limitation.

We cannot resolve the issues raised by programs like Eliza, but some distinctions are clear. Several spokespersons reject not computer therapy itself but the particular mode of psychotherapy programmed into Eliza. Others vigorously maintain that human contact is a central feature of acceptable therapeutic relationships. Still others, such as Carl Sagan (cited in Heller & Turner, 1983, p. 192), argue that Eliza is a prototype of the kinds of programs that will exist in the future.

In carefully designed attempts to determine the effectiveness of computerized psychotherapy programs, initial results have been favorable. Hartvig Dahl (1972) reports that computerized content analyses of patients' speech "can describe clinical material adequately and can discriminate between qualitatively different psychoanalytic sessions" (p. 243). These preliminary findings are impressive, but additional assessments are needed. Just how owners of personal computers could or should use psychotherapeutic programs is an especially important matter for study.

Computerized medical systems have already been employed to make diagnoses, to prescribe treatments, and to specify therapy programs. Some 19 major medical centers now employ such computers. The computer typically functions as an assistant to a doctor, but its analysis is often more complete than the physician's. The computer program MYCIN, designed to help physicians diagnose and treat certain bacterial infections, is a convenient example. MYCIN initially informs itself about the patient's symptoms, general condition, and history and about the laboratory results of tests undergone by the patient. Characterizing MYCIN as a "backward-chaining deduction system," Patrick Winston (1977) describes its diagnostic procedure:

Some 300 productions constitute MYCIN's pool of knowledge about blood bacterial infections. . . . To use such knowledge, MYCIN works backward. For each of 100 possible diagnoses, MYCIN attempts to work toward primitive facts known from laboratory results and clinical observations. Backward running is the method of choice if a production system is being used to check out one particular hypothesis. But MYCIN checks every possible hypothesis, so search economy is not the reason involved. Instead, the MYCIN system runs backward so that the questions seem focused. . . . MYCIN works in a domain where deductions are rarely certain. Thus MYCIN developers combined a primitive theory of plausible reasoning with the basic production apparatus. . . . By looking into an historical record of the productions used, MYCIN can answer questions about *why* a fact was used or about *how* a fact was established. (pp. 242–43)

Moreover, the MYCIN program allows a physician to interact with the computer and to determine how the program made its diagnostic choices.

In assessing the overall state of the art of "advanced computing for medicine" near the end of the 1980s, Glenn D. Rennels and Edward H. Shortliffe (1987) reported that with a "personal computer," doctors have access to "nationwide computer networks" that "store medical information retrieve it selectively and transmit it" and to " 'advice systems' " that "apply the information to help doctors diagnose a patient's condition" and to "help to manage a course of treatment" (p. 154). Rennels and Shortliffe also noted that several issues in medical computing remain to be resolved. Particularly needed are computing systems that can "cope with the sheer quantity of information to be represented and manipulated" (p. 159), that "ensure that the data structures representing knowledge elements will enable people to add to and correct the system's knowledge" (p. 159), and that represent "the human body" and its "functions" on a "mechanistic level," thereby allowing medical computer scientists to "develop techniques for encoding and applying such different kinds of knowledge in a coordinated way" (p. 160). Even if computing systems were to achieve such sophistication, Rennels and Shortliffe have reservations about the computer's final value in medical practice:

Computer systems do not now—nor will they soon—have a sufficiently complete understanding of medicine's technical, clinical and social considerations to approach the richness and flexibility of human expertise. The advice systems we have described do represent advances in medical computer science, but none of them is effective without the common sense and judgment of an experienced health-care worker. There are many aspects of human problem solving that we and others in the field simply do not yet know how to model within a computer. (pp. 160–61)

Nonetheless, Rennels and Shortliffe foresee that computers will be of great benefit to medical practice:

In spite of these caveats we are optimistic about the future of advanced computing for medicine. Computers are more than number crunchers. Their ability to store, retrieve selectively and transmit medical information is now well established. On the horizon are systems that will provide reasoned advice about the diagnosis and management of specific cases. Advances in materials science and chip design, in networking and parallel processing all promise greater freedom for those of us working on the software of medical information systems. We expect to see growing use of advanced systems "smart" enough to take an active, if subordinate, role in medical practice. (p. 161)

Thus, while some medical questions are currently beyond the personal computer's ability to help provide answers, the inhibiting issues appear to be predominantly technological rather than conceptual or psychological. In any event, what is important to our purposes is that the principle of coactive and coequal computer-human interaction is demonstrated by several of these procedures. Personal computers may very well come to play a role in medical diagnoses and therapy. Then they too will function in coactive and coequal interaction. We foresee many people using personal-computer programs for less complex diagnostic and therapeutic purposes than are represented by the programs discussed here.

Chess

We have postponed detailed discussion of chess because we believe that chess as a video game is inappropriately compared to Pac-Man or Donkey Kong. The computerized chess program creates a different kind of relationship between the computer and its user. Other kinds of video games are controlled by the structure of the computer program itself, but in chess both the computer and the user respond equally to preestablished rules that had been fully developed in western Europe by the 13th century. Moreover, chess programs themselves mimic prior, human, game-playing skills. Most significantly, the chess program attempts to duplicate the strategic thought of a human player. The chess game therefore establishes an excellent opportunity to explore a set of conditions in which both the computer and the human being are cast as equals.

Chess games, readily available from most computer manufacturers, typically include at least 3 levels of difficulty—beginner, intermediate, and expert. Some programs involve 6 or 7 levels of difficulty so that the human player can gradually master the full range of chess skills. In some of the dedicated home-computer versions, such as Milton Bradley's Grand-Master Chess Computer, 12 levels of difficulty are available (for a review of this program, see Pollack, 1983, January). Software Country's chess program, called Chessmaster 2000, has an opening library of 71,000 moves, 12 levels of play, a teaching mode that shows every legal move, and a library of classic chess games dating from those of the Italian master Giacchino Greco in 1620 to those played by Karpov and Kasparov in 1985. Chessmaster 2000 won the personal-computer championship at the United States Chess Federation in 1986 (Lewis, 1986, August). At the lowest of the game's levels, the computer tries to lose; at its highest levels, the computer calculates literally all possible moves in order to select the move that will allow it to win. This process of selecting a move may take days. At the highest level, the majority of chess players lose. As we will note in greater detail in chapter 8, chess programs have been developed that can beat 99.9 percent of all human chess players and that make—in the view of grand masters—unique and creative moves. What we want to stress at this point is that when a coactive and coequal but competitive relationship exists between a computer and a human being, there are clearly times when the human being must expect to lose. Computerized chess programs dramatize this fact.

Data Searches

We discussed the function of computerized data searches earlier; now we return to the subject to illustrate further the ways in which coactive and coequal principles function in computer-human interactions. We believe that a data search becomes increasingly effective as the computer assumes increasing responsibility for determining the choices made in data searches. In our view, there simply are some things that a computer can do better than human beings can.

Data searches illustrate a kind of computer-human interaction to which both the human being and the computer must bring their own forms of expertise if it is to be effective. We earlier discussed the use of electronic newspapers and encyclopedias, electronic yellow pages, electronic shopping, and electronic reservations systems. In all of these cases, a user searches for a certain kind of information, and the connection provided by the computer allows the search to be executed. In more sophisticated programs, however, the computer can do more than make a telephone connection and regulate the flow of data: A computer can decide what kinds of data will be selected, what kinds of searches to conduct, and when to shift from one type of search to another (see, e.g., Stoan, 1982). In such cases, the computer can almost be perceived as reprogramming itself in response to encountered data. In practice, then, such computer programs can sometimes generate information that the user did not know was available. A computer program might even generate a new theorem or proof and offer it as the data sought by the user. The computer program is then truly acting as an equal in the computer-human relationship, for the computer functions as the researcher and inventor while the human functions as the general theorist and user of the results obtained.

Given these possibilities, it is important to suggest the many resources that are available to users of personal computers. The Fall 1979 issue of the *Directory of Online Databases* identified and described 400 data bases. The Fall 1984 issue of this directory identified some 2,222 data bases, an increase of 450 percent in less than 5 years. Two of the data bases listed in the directory, Lexis and Nexis, provide access to many of the major newspapers, magazines, wire services, and newsletters; some 145,000 subscribers to the two data bases conduct some 35,000 searches a day (Siwolop, 1983, p. 70). One advantage of such data base researches is more conveniently and dramatically measured in terms of time: 1 hour of data-base research equals 100 hours of conventional library research.

Social Consequences

We must exercise caution in generalizing about the correlational effects of computer-human interactions because the kinds of research findings we need are not available; however, five issues are particularly relevant and warrant assessment.

Individualized Educational Programs

As indicated earlier, education seems, at least in theory, particularly susceptible to computerization. Patricia Marks Greenfield (1984) has argued that "the newest electronic media, video games and computers," have "promising applications to education" (p. 2). Milton Chen (1984) has similarly maintained that children find "a congenial match in the cognitive skills" required for using such interactive media systems as computers (pp. 283–84). He has concluded that, "on the strength of their present capabilities alone," personal computers "may be able to provide children with the literacies and modes of thought that the future requires" (p. 286).

These theoretical positions have not yet been confirmed by practical applications in local educational settings, which have proved disappointing. For example, Edward B. Fiske (1984, December 9) reported that by the end of 1984, "after investing heavily in microcomputers, public schools in the New York metropolitan area are finding that they are still far from achieving the academic revolution expected from the new technology" (p. 1). In 1985, Derek Bok, then the president of Harvard University, criticized what he called the "exaggerated claims" and "media hype" that accompanied the arrival of computers on college campuses and urged fellow educators to adopt an attitude of "cautious enthusiasm" toward the new technologies (cited in Fiske, 1985, April, p. D19). In a 1985 essay, Marc S. Tucker described the effects of theoretical promise unmet by practical experience:

Now the press is increasingly filled with stories about unused computers in school storerooms, the failure of computing to teach children to think clearly, and other similarly dreary tales. Once again, time seems to have reduced the latest enthusiasm of educators to a tale of unfulfilled and broken promises. I and others are now being asked to write articles exposing the futility of using computers in the schools—by some of the same journals that only the year before had demanded pieces extolling their promise. Conventions of school computing teachers are attracting only a fraction of the crowds they had previously attracted. (p. 12)

The availability of computers may be one of the reasons for this failure of promise. Tucker (1985) has stated that "the ratio between machines and students" will determine if the computer can function "as a tool in many, if not all, of the subjects in the school curriculum" (p. 20). In 1985 Seymour Papert has noted that a 1-to-70 ratio of computers to students has meant that schools "can't do very much" (cited in Fiske, 1985, May, p. C1). The National Surveys of Microcomputers for the Center for Social Organization of Schools at the Johns Hopkins University indicated that the average American primary school had 3 microcomputers and that the average secondary school had 16 (cited in Fiske, 1984, December 9). Available resources clearly affect the ability of schools to secure computers. John F. Hood, the chief author of Marketing Data Retrieval's 1985 survey of computer use across the country, found that the "wealthiest public school districts" had twice as many computers for their total student enrollment as the "poorest schools" (cited in Fiske, 1985, August, p. 8E). In 1987, L. R. Shannon (1987) reported that "students in the 12,000 most affluent schools were four times more likely to have access to computers than students in the 12,000 poorest" (p. C9).

The inferior quality of educational computer software may also have contributed to the reports of computers' failure to improve school curricula. In 1984, after examining more than 7,000 educational software packages, Kenneth Komoski, who was then the director of the Educational Products Information Exchange, reported that "only about one in four products met minimum technical and instructional standards, and only about three or four out of 100 were considered excellent" (cited in Hassett, 1984, September, p. 24; also see Komoski, cited in Menosky, 1984, p. 45; Komoski, cited in Fiske, 1984, December 9, p. 80).

However, even if the proper number of computers and adequate software were obtained, educational issues of critical importance remain unresolved. In other words, even if a classroom were properly equipped, it is unclear when and how computers should be used to achieve educational objectives. As Larry Cuban (1986) has broadly stated the issue, "No research evidence provides reliable guidelines and no consensus among professional educators yet exists for how machines should be used for instruction" (p. 83). There are no easy answers here, for virtually any area of education at any level of the educational process can be affected by computerized instruction (see, e.g., *Perspectives in Computing*, 1986; "Covering Computer Use," 1987). One example of the scope and kinds of issues involved in computer-aided instruction involves the effects of computerization on reading skills. As David Reinking (1987b) observed, "Professionals in reading, from educational researchers to classroom teachers, are struggling to discover the rightful place of the computer in their activities" (p. ix).

Of the multiple and complex issues involved in the area of reading alone, one unresolved question turns on the comparative effectiveness of printed versus electronically displayed text in terms of reading speed, cognitive processing, and dependency. With regard to reading speed, Paul B. Carroll (1987) has reported that "people read 20 percent more slowly from a computer screen than from paper" (p. 27), which may be due, according to Dan B. Daniel and David Reinking (1987, pp. 26–36), to the static legibility of the computer screen (e.g., illumination, color, surface, spacing, typography, and illustrations), the dynamic legibility of the computer screen, and/or the interactive nature of the computer as a medium of communication. In terms of cognitive processing, the medium of instructional choice affects what is learned and how it is learned, with printed and computerized texts conveying very different kinds of information with extremely different consequences (see, e.g., Reinking, 1987a, esp. pp. 8–11). In terms of dependency, the wide range of computer options related to reading, particularly given the development of artificially intelligent computers, can directly affect how dependent on a computer a student becomes. A comprehensive software package can contain a spelling and grammar checker, and another program, with relatively few objectives specified by a student, can generate a complete and "original" text based on Kenneth Burke's dramatistic principles (G. M. Phillips, 1986, 1987). Such programs have tremendous implications for student dependency in terms of vocabulary, comprehension, motivation, retention, and motor skills (see, e.g., Balajhy, 1987), and such a text-generated process also involves ethical issues. In all of these ways, the failure to use computer-aided instruction properly in the classroom may stem simply from the fact that all of the variables affecting the process and the consequences of such instruction are unknown.

Other reasons may also account for the computer's failure. The Early Childhood Research Center (cited in Mackay-Smith, 1985, February 13) at the University of Buffalo has charged that children have been exposed to computers at too young an age or before they exhibit an interest in computers. Joseph F. Sullivan (1986) reported that female students were not encouraged to use computers (also see Chen, 1987; L. R. Shannon, 1987), while Dan Gutman (1985) reported that educators did not employ the proper guidelines when purchasing software.

These problems deserve attention, but the fundamental educational issue may reside in the very conception of *computer literacy*. Devoting the Summer 1984 issue of *Teachers College Record* to this question, its editor Douglas Sloan noted that

This issue of the *Record* arises from a threefold conviction: that the computer offers potential for human betterment, and at the same time is fraught with great dangers to the human being; that neither the potential can be truly realized, nor the dangers avoided, without careful, far-reaching, critical questions being asked about the computer in education; and that American educators in general have been almost totally remiss in their responsibility to raise and pursue these critical questions. (p. 539)

In practice, educators have usually viewed computer literacy as computer programming or as an introduction to computer operations. In 1984, the National Surveys of Microcomputers for the Center for Social Organization of Schools at the Johns Hopkins University reported that 64 percent of the time spent in computer courses in secondary schools focused upon introductions to microcomputing, hardware or equipment, or programming, that 18 percent was devoted to repetitive drills and practice sessions, that 6 percent was spent playing "recreational games," and that 12 percent was spent on "other" activities (cited in Fiske, 1984, December 9, p. 80). David Noble (1985) argued that a programming or systems approach to computer literacy is misleading and even dangerous:

The danger is that this sense of control, or pseudocontrol, becomes a substitute for real control, deluding one into thinking that one has mastered a technology when in reality one is only playing God with a chip of silicon.

This false sense of empowerment blocks any real participation in the social control of the technology as a whole. The result is a nation of individual computer masters who can't see the forest for the trees. (p. 606)

As we noted in chapter 2, a programming or systems approach also bypasses critical computer competency issues.

When computer literacy is defined as the study of the effects of computers upon human beings, computer competency can be complementarily viewed as a methodological rather than a content skill. Tucker (1985) has aptly captured the point: "Consistent with the prevailing view in business and industry," computers "are tools for people—in this case students—to use, not electronic teachers to administer instruction" (p. 19). Tucker has specifically recommended the use of such "generic applications packages" as "word processors, data base managers, spread sheets, and laboratory instrumentation software that can be used in courses addressing very different subject matter at very different levels of difficulty" (p. 19). In this view, computer competency is not the mastery of any specific content; computer competency is the ability to use computer tools that facilitate the analysis of content.

Computer Art

As we underscored earlier in this chapter, computer art can be conceived in several ways. It can be an adjunct for artistic design, production, and execution. It can also be used to allow machines to generate their own art. Computer art can also be the foundation for computer-aided designs in a variety of industries and disciplines, including architecture, engineering, and physics. Developments in these areas are reported daily. One development came in 1985, when Graphic Communications released its Graphwriter program, which allows a user to draw 28 different kinds of charts. Similarly, computer art is the basis for modeling techniques that allow human beings to represent macro- and microscopic events normally beyond human perception. These applications may ultimately extend human productivity.

Theoretically, computer art may also constitute a base for systematic description and evaluations of visual communication, ultimately leading to reconceptions of the role of visual literacy in the study of communication. The visual is a critical component of how and what we know and may be one of the elements that make human knowledge seem relative. John Berger (1977) has observed that "seeing comes before words. The child looks and recognizes before it can speak":

> But there is another sense in which seeing comes before words. It is seeing which establishes our place in the surrounding world; we explain that world with words, but words can never undo the fact that we are surrounded by it. The relation between what we see and what we know is never settled. Each evening we *see* the sun set. We *know* that the earth is turning away from it. Yet the knowledge, the explanation, never quite fits the sight. (p. 7)

Despite the significance of visual information, few schemes exist for describing and classifying visual information. We do not have uniform vocabularies for describing shape, size, location, and perceived texture; even less agreement exists regarding how visual information might be classified in terms of such concepts.

Several computer programs, notably spreadsheets and data bases, employ visual formats as a central element of their representations of data, yet these systems remain essentially numeric and linguistic. A true visual data base would employ as its main reference framework not words or numbers but pictures. Such visual data bases would require ways of classifying information based upon shape, size, and location. Telos Software Products' Filevision is an example of a visual data base that may hold important implications for how communication researchers generate and display schemes to classify visual information.

The development of systematic visual data bases may provide new ways of conceiving, describing, and understanding reality. Kristina Hooper, when she was the director of Atari's long-range planning lab, explored the relationships between visual data bases and reality, and she coined the term *virtual realities* to describe her object of study (cited in K. C. Cole, 1984, p. 77). She defined virtual realities as sophisticated three-dimensional pictures that are real enough to work with, not unlike those used in flight simulators but free of the constraints of everyday reality. In its simplest form, the conception might lead to the development of street guides or maps using three-dimensional visual representations of landmarks, which could be particularly important when street signs are unavailable or unreadable. In more elegant forms, visual data bases might include images of unknown terrain (useful to military personnel), harmonic movements (useful to a physicist), or views of multidimensional brain activity.

Visual data bases may also benefit computer users and may ultimately redefine the concept of the user-friendly computer. Using the term *artificial realities*, rather than virtual realities, James D. Foley (1987) argued that the "reality" created by a computer should be conceived as involving "three components: imagery, behavior and interaction":

Realistic visual *imagery* helps the user to interpret the information being presented by the computer. The images may represent real objects, such as building frames, or abstractions, such as patterns of fluid flow. These images *behave* the way the objects or abstractions they represent would behave. Behavioral modeling exacts the heaviest computational toll, because it often entails solving extensive sets of equations over and over again. Finally, the user *interacts* with an artificial reality in much the same way as he interacts with the three-dimensional world: by moving, pointing and picking things up, by talking and observing from many different angles. (p. 128)

With imagery, behavior, and interaction as the defining dimensions or interfaces of the artificial realities created by computers, Foley identified the value of visual data bases for computer users:

The advent of artificial realities, foreshadowed by flight simulation, will fundamentally change the way a person works with a supercomputer. Artificial realities allow the user to interact with the computer in an intuitive and direct format and to increase the number of interactions per unit of time. The ultimate objective of artificial-reality research is to develop a simulated environment that seems as "real" as the reality it depicts. The profoundest strength of the interfaces, however, may lie in their ability to go beyond reality itself, by modeling in concrete form abstract entities such as mathematical equations and by enabling users to surmount problems of scale in manipulating atoms and galaxies alike. (p. 128)

Indeed, in advanced programs, visual data bases can generate new conceptions. For example, before using computer-generated conceptions, David A. Hoffman, William H. Meeks III, and James T. Hoffman (cited in Gleick, 1986), pure mathematicians specializing in minimal surfaces in differential geometry, reported that the class of infinite, complete minimal surfaces (i.e., the smallest possible area that can stretch over a given shape, such as a soap film stretched on a wire frame) had been conceived by humans to contain only three members—a flat plane, a spiral, and an hourglass. However, when Hoffman, Meeks, and Hoffman integrated minimal surface equations and computer representations of these surfaces, they discovered whole families of new minimal surfaces, weird shapes with holes and handles that had eluded the unaided, human, mathematical imagination. As David A. Hoffman (cited in Gleick, 1986) noted, "The computer has taken the place of soap film experiments and allowed one to bring one's visual and tactile sense to a problem that was mostly mathematical. We then used the insight from the pictures to go back and produce a formal proof" (p. E7). Beyond the implications of this finding for the design of strong, light architectural structures, the method used to generate the formal proof, computerized visual imaging, is critical. Visual data bases highlight the possibility that pictorial information might be systematically classified in ways useful to a communication specialist. The development of visual data bases can conceivably generate a grammar and a rhetoric of visual communication, ultimately providing organized data to confirm or disconfirm theories of visual communication.

Medical Diagnosis and Therapy

Computerization may introduce a variety of changes in medical and psychotherapeutic treatments. Stewart Auyash (1984) has predicted that we can expect three major changes:

1. The patient becomes the center of the care and each encounter with the computer record system allows for the development of a data base for each *unique patient situation.*
2. The caring function, usually attributed to the "art" of medicine, is becoming more a responsibility of the *allied health professional* rather than just the physician.
3. *Medical education* will be transformed over the next few decades in one of two (or both) ways. Either physicians will accept the role of computers to assist in the memorization and application of medical knowledge, or physicians will resist the change and over time be relegated to a subservient role in medical care. (p. 96)

Among the changes in psychotherapeutic treatments are those introduced by a variety of psychotherapeutic programs designed for personal computers. Michael W. Miller (1984, December 5) has referred to these programs as forms of "technotherapy" designed to "tap into the subconscious" and "reprogram the subconscious mind" (p. 1). Greentree Publishers is selling a software package—called "Subliminal Suggestion and Self Hypnosis Programs for Your Computer!"— that enables a user to rig his or her computer to blink any short message thousands of times a day while the user pursues regular computer work. Timothy Leary (cited in M. W. Miller, 1984, December 5), the 1960s psychedelic and drug guru, has recently advocated "personality construction programs" for personal computer users (p. 18). His company, Futique, sells a memory component, called Skipi, that monitors a user's personality by analyzing the way the user operates his or her computer and responds to a special series of programs. Leary claimed that Skipi will enable the user to understand and change her or his personality. In Leary's view, "The personal computer will become as much a part of your brain as oxygen" (p. 18). Such programs require thoughtful assessments of what purposes future users will want their personal computers to serve.

Data Searches

Technology has reached the point where humans must admit that computers are capable of generating information that humans simply cannot obtain with reasonable labor. A computer link can establish a comprehensive connection to an overwhelming number of diverse data bases which human beings could not manually tap in any reasonable length of time or without creating totally new priorities to govern their attention and energy.

Computers have five advantages over humans in information gathering and processing. First, computers search faster than human beings. Computer speeds are dramatically illustrated by Henry Weil's assertion (1982): "There are approximately 100,000 instructions per U.S. citizen being obeyed by computers *every second*" (p. 60). In terms of data base searches, computers operate 100 times faster than human beings. When speed counts, manual searches for information are grossly inefficient. Second, computer searches are more systematic and comprehensive. As G. Cook (1979) has observed, medical computers consider more information and diagnostic options than most doctors can remember. Similarly, while at any given moment the human chess player considers some 100 strategic options, computerized chess programs consider thousands. Third, computers are capable of a greater number of informational manipulations and are far more efficient in accomplishing them than human beings. For example, a findstring command can be used as a search technique to identify any number of new informational relationships within any text. In more complicated search techniques, a computer can pass through a data base searching for new relationships between two or more extremely different concepts in a matter of seconds. In a linguistic analysis of pronouns and values in a presidential speech, for example, a researcher can initiate a search to determine if such words as *they*, *he*, and *she* are linked to a cluster of concepts associated with a value orientation identified as materialism and if such words as *I*, *me*, and *we* are linked to a different cluster of concepts associated with idealism. Fourth, computers can generate and obtain information not available to human beings. Computerized medical programs have already demonstrated such abilities. In addition, computers have generated new understandings and theorems previously unconceived by human beings in such fields as mathematics and science. Fifth, as a result of the computer's overall efficiency, computerized searches are increasingly popular. The Online Computer Library Center ("Technology Links," 1983), a network of 3,300 libraries and information centers in the United States and abroad, reports that the number of computerized searches has increased 142 percent since 1979, from 1,666 searches per day in 1979 to 4,048 searches per day in 1983.

Several social implications are embedded in these observations. As personal computers become increasingly available to people, information itself will become democratized. Though access to on-line services can be costly, virtually all information in the public domain is now theoretically available to all. We suspect that access to information may soon be perceived as a basic right of all citizens.

Human beings must also redefine their relationship to the information-processing system. They must begin to perceive themselves not as gatherers of information but as systems analysts who create relationships among existing bodies of data in order to achieve new understandings and innovations.

Furthermore, the definition of an expert must change. Available information far exceeds any single human being's ability to read it. Moreover, computerized "stocks of information" are increasing at rates far beyond any single person's comprehension. It is no longer possible to be an expert in the popular sense of the term: No single person can be acquainted with all known facts regarding any area of specialization. Expertise must be defined by the way in which information is integrated and accounted for within a framework of understanding. The methods used for dealing with information are rapidly becoming far more important than acquisition of the facts themselves.

Finally, as information becomes available to all and functions as the content and context for all human interactions, human observations regarding physical events, the human link to the production and manufacture of physical goods, the necessity for task relationships with others in face-to-face encounters, and human contact with nature itself will all decline. The human environment is gradually becoming a solely symbolic world. The decision to preserve contacts with physical events, with other human beings, with the production of goods, and with nature itself will be a human choice rather than a necessity. We suspect that these adjustments to the Information Society will be difficult to make.

Overview

Four concerns cross or transcend the specific congruent human-computer relationships we have discussed in this chapter.

First, the home itself begins to undergo a major transformation as personal computers provide at-home educational programs, practical and occupational applications through computer-art systems, medical diagnoses and therapy, competitive entertainment through such programs as chess, and a link to virtually all data bases. Increasingly, the home becomes the new arena for explorations, displacing the role traditionally carried out by public and social institutions. In the more relaxed atmosphere of the home, these previously public activities can now be carried out in private, at one's own rate, and at whatever times one selects. Indeed, the number of people opting for at-home educational programs has been increasingly markedly. Raymond Moore (cited in Wollman, 1984) of the Hewitt Research Foundation has estimated that, with the "help of computers" designed to provide "home-study courses," "those taught at home now comes to at least 250,000 (p. C1). When the home becomes the center for a host of activities previously carried out in other social institutions, people find that a home-centered environment provides a flexibility not otherwise possible. Though forecasts in this area are risky, we may be witnessing the reemergence of the home as the center of all social activities. At the same time, however, a large number of problems once handled outside of the home will become part of the home environment, which is without the mediating forces that exist in other institutions. We are unconvinced that a solely electronic and computerized link with those outside of the home can satisfy the basic human need for contact with others, though we are convinced that many will find it difficult to admit that they have such a need. Thus, as the home becomes the focal point of human endeavors, special skills will be required to establish and to maintain face-to-face social relationships, and a renewed sense of the value of human beings may become part of the Information Society.

Second, as personal computers reduce the time and energy spent in other social institutions, we can expect these institutions to adapt to the new Information Society. Libraries, for example, are currently adapting to the computer age. Many now provide electronic delivery systems and coin-operated microprocessors. In addition, libraries are already transferring data to electronic form, subscribing to all major data bases, and acquiring new acquisitions in both hard-copy and electronic form. An increasing number of libraries provide electronic data-base searches for library members. To save time, space, and money, the Library of Congress is now placing the texts of its books and magazines on virtually indestructible 12-inch disks. Such transformations are affecting other institutions as well. For example, Ray Walters (cited in Brodkey, 1985) concluded that the computer is profoundly affecting the entire publishing industry: "The computer is affecting much more than management; it is revolutionizing the way books are written, distributed and read" (p. 44).

Third, when human beings establish a coactive and coequal relationship with a computer, this new interaction can easily foster a new form of technological dependency. As human beings shifted from agricultural to industrial and service work, they removed themselves from natural environments; as personal computers are increasingly used for educational, artistic, medical, entertainment, and research purposes, human beings may also remove themselves from other human contacts. Once the initial fear of the computer is overcome, computer activities can easily become all-consuming events. If care is not exercised, many natural contacts may be replaced by forms of computer dependency. As we noted in chapter 1, television owners engage in fewer activities outside of the home and have fewer social contacts than nonowners. Extensive computer usage can only exaggerate this antisocial condition. Although some will intentionally avoid such computer dependency and some will compensate for extensive computer usage, we can certainly expect that a significant portion of computer users will celebrate their newly discovered technology at the expense of human contact. Computer usage, like television viewing, must be carefully monitored and must be regarded as only one of several priorities within a complex social environment.

Fourth, the computer is increasingly becoming a final arbitrator and judge of disputes. Social conflicts can be too simplistically resolved by deciding to consult the information provided by computer-generated data-base searches. Information provided by a computer is seldom tested or submitted to rigorous analysis; rather, it is frequently assumed to be correct even though the sources and procedures employed to generate the information have not been carefully examined. Socially, then, the computer-generated data have the potential to intimidate, to discourage the exploration of alternative options, and ultimately to misdirect and to misinform. In this sense, computer usage may slight the critical and intellectual process.

Conclusion

In this chapter, we examined uses of the personal computer in which the user and the computer function as coactive and coequal entities generating understandings. Individualized educational programs, more sophisticated computer-art programs, medical and therapeutic programs, computerized chess, and data searches function as examples of the symmetrical relationships that can exist between human beings and computers. These programs perform particularly useful functions for users, alter our social environments by democratizing information, and reemphasize the home. They also foster a new form of technological dependency, which is altering all other social institutions and which is ultimately casting the computer as a kind of final arbitrator and judge. Clearly, the advantages of new technologies must be utilized, but constant attention must be given to recognizing and eliminating the disadvantages of these technologies.

7

Program-Dominated Computer Communication

Discussions of user-friendly computers typically turn on how closely computer responses duplicate standard English. From this perspective, the ideal computer would accept commands and would respond in everyday English. Often overlooked is the fact that such a user-friendly computer is severely limited. The ideal computer should speak the language of its user but should also automatically collect relevant data, make appropriate decisions regarding this information, and provide pragmatic applications that satisfy the needs of the user. For a computer to achieve such usefulness, the computer's programs must control the executions carried out.

In this chapter, we explore uses of personal computers that allow the computer to generate unique results with a minimum of guidance from the user. We are essentially examining a genre of computer programs that Edward Fredkin (cited in McCorduck, 1979) has identified as "semiintelligent programs" (p. 348). These programs are not yet in the mainstream of personal-computer use, but major advances in personal-computer hardware have made such programs an option in home-computer use. Noting the development of Intel's 80386 microprocessor chip for the personal computer and its rapid acceptance by the computer industry in 1986, Peter H. Lewis (1986, August 26) concluded that personal computers have the "raw power" to "facilitate advances in artificial intelligence, expert systems, robotics, speech recognition and other long-awaited promises of personal computing" (p. C7; also see "Chip May Open," 1986; Howard & Wong, 1986;

Lockwood & Honan, 1987; Rosch, 1988; Sanger, 1987, February 18). In this chapter, we specifically examine random-search or heuristic, planning, backward-chaining, and concept-learning programs. We conclude by suggesting how parallel processing and human-language systems integrate these programs.

These computer programs have common features, of which five are noteworthy. First, these computer programs exert more influence than does the user over the outcome of a computation. In fact, the author of one of these computer programs may not know the outcome. As David L. Waltz (1982) has reported, "In many cases the programmer does not know what his program can do until it is run on a computer" (p. 120). Second, the outcome of one of these computer runs is unknown. These programs are intentionally designed to generate findings that humans are unlikely to discover without the computer. Such programs have in fact generated new mathematical proofs and new, holistic conceptions of aircraft design. In computer chess applications, Arthur Bisguier (cited in Gleick, 1986, August 26), a former United States champion on the staff of the United States Chess Federation, has examined one of these more sophisticated programs and concluded that "by dint of brute force, the program has unearthed all kinds of results which eluded us. It was mindboggling for me" (p. C1). Third, external verifications of the results of these computer runs would be virtually impossible without the aid of creative and expert researchers and would likely take years to confirm. In these cases, computers are engaging in processes that for all practical purposes cannot be replicated. While the outcomes might be confirmed by expert assessment, the processes themselves would probably not be replicated by human beings. Fourth, the function carried out by these programs is essentially causal. These programs create new relationships that posit cause-to-effect patterns among data. Thus, a program might, for example, suggest new travel routes for transporting manufactured products. Fifth, the user of such a program must be psychologically dedicated to computer performance, if not to computer programming itself. In the jargon of the computer world, these users are *hackers*. Their dedication may emerge in spontaneous, frequent, inspired, and even irregular efforts, and these computer programs are often the creations of such "computer geniuses."

Given these features, our explorations in this chapter must push beyond the kinds of programs typically purchased from computer or software manufacturers. We are exploring new applications of computer principles that are producing new uses for the computer. We begin with consideration of heuristic programs.

Heuristic Programs

The word *heuristic* has a long and distinguished history. Originally derived from a Greek word meaning "to discover," the word characterizes activities designed to reveal or to discover the new. By the 1860s, heuristic acts had become formally viewed as comprising an art and logic of discovery or invention. The term has evolved to become associated with a certain frame of mind: Heuristic thought tends to be a mental process that generates questions, not answers. For a process to be heuristic, the questions must have a pragmatic function. Heuristic activities do not seek ideal solutions but rather are intended to produce useful answers, conceptions, and frequently goods and services. The essential value of a heuristic effort, then, is that, by positing answerable and useful questions, it opens up new areas for thought and investigation. In the social and engineering sciences today, heuristic endeavors are often the stimuli for new research, developments, and designs (Boguslaw, 1965, pp. 13–17, 71–98).

A heuristic computer program might be described in any number of high-level computer languages, each of which offers a different way of expressing such programs. In BASIC, for example, a direct use must be made of a "GOTO" statement, while such a statement is avoided in Pascal. Underlying all such variations, however, is a more general and universal application of the heuristic principle, as depicted in the flowchart in table 7.1. As the flowchart illustrates, this program will automatically search for a solution to a problem until a solution is found.

The introduction of heuristic principles is a formal recognition that change is needed and that change often stems from random actions. In more concrete terms, heuristic principles serve three ends. First, heuristic principles reduce the scope of a problem and therefore the time and energy devoted to it. A heuristic search of data, by limiting the range of possibilities examined, eliminates the need for a full-scale examination of all possible options or answers to a question. In commenting upon the limitations of the heuristic search in early computer efforts, artificial-intelligence specialist Pamela McCorduck (1979) observed that they did not "invariably [produce] the best strategy; sometimes they missed the unusual and the brilliant, and sometimes they didn't work at all." However, she conceded that "they were a reasonable means of pruning away the less likely possibilities of action" (p. 157). When a mass of data must be examined, then, a heuristic search can provide an efficient but not necessarily the most insightful method for dealing with a problem. Second, use of heuristic principles can yield solutions to problems. A heuristic search of data

Table 7.1 A Basic Heuristic Program

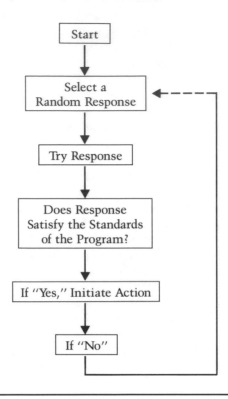

can detect patterns and relationships not previously observed by human beings. A solution, however, may be just the first available answer rather than the best answer; other relations and more effective solutions may be missed. Nonetheless, some solution can typically be provided even if the approach is solely random. Third, heuristic principles clarify human intuition. A good deal of human behavior is based upon rules of thumb or conditioning and planning. Consider, for example, the question raised in table 7.2. In the problem in table 7.2, the change involved in figure A is less radical than the change in figure B. The principle controlling this solution presumes that rotation in the same location is a less active and less severe action than a spatial change from one graphic location to another. Most respondents would intuit the answer to the question, but asking by what heuristic principle they knew the answer would require that they consciously clarify their commonsense understanding.

Uses of heuristic programming are evident in computerized chess games. A sophisticated chess program is structured to respond to hu-

Table 7.2 Which Figure Undergoes the Most Radical Change?

Compare the nature of change for figure A to the nature of change for figure B. Figure A changes *from* condition 1 *to* condition 2. Figure B changes *from* condition 3 *to* condition 4. Which of the two figures has undergone the most radical change?

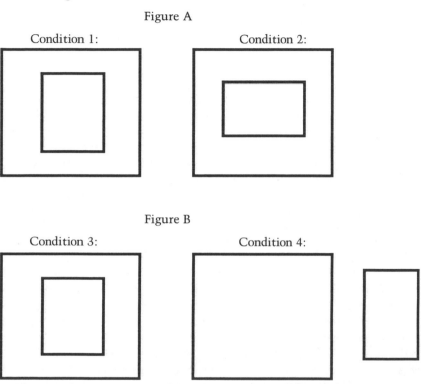

Figure A

Condition 1:   Condition 2:

Figure B

Condition 3:   Condition 4:

man actions. The solution to each human move can be thought of as governed by several standards: make no move that will result in the loss of a chess piece; if a piece must be sacrificed, lose the chess piece with the least power (as power is defined by the variety of moves the piece can make) unless the piece is the king; make a move that results in the opponent's losing his or her most powerful piece; and so forth. Given these instructions, a computer can make successive random selections until a solution is found to counteract each human move. Such programs can be fast and effective. Bell Laboratories' chess program, Belle, calculates some 160,000 chess moves per second. Moreover, Belle has a chess rating of 2,160, thus qualifying officially as an expert chess player.

Overall, heuristic programs reduce the scope of a problem, generate solutions, and frequently clarify the nature of common sense. These programs can serve invaluable ends, which are determined, of course, by the creativity and objective of the users. Whether applications include understanding the kind of human reasoning involved in playing chess or whether they serve useful ends in aircraft construction or in the control of nuclear reactors will depend upon the concerns of the user.

Planning Programs

Planning programs allow a computer to manipulate *procedures* used to deal with information. Planning programs identify and select the goals and then determine ways to achieve these goals given the available data. The user provides the general parameters of inquiry or kinds of tasks the program will execute. The user also specifies the different kinds of goals the computer may manipulate. Once the task and range of goals are established, a planning program allows a computer to determine which goal is to be pursued at any given point and to execute the steps necessary to achieve the goal.

In practical applications, planning programs are central to the development of robots that function effectively and independently in natural environments. Without planning programs, building a workable robot would be extremely difficult. Nothing would be more time-consuming than attempting to program every possible task and the exact procedure for carrying out each task. Moreover, because natural environments change, a robot would have to be reprogrammed to deal with every change that occurred. Consider, for example, the simple task of moving an object from one location to another. Without the use of a planning program, computerizing this task would be overwhelmingly difficult. Every action related to the grasping, holding, lifting, and moving of the object and the determination of exactly where to place the object would have to be specifically and precisely programmed into a robot. A planning program is intended to eliminate such specific programming and, probably more important, to provide an automatic way for a robot to adjust to changes in an environment. Accordingly, in robotic production a great deal of energy is devoted to the development of planning programs. The central task in this kind of programming is to specify all of the goals and subgoals related to a pertinent task and then to allow the robot freedom to select among those goals and to carry out the actions necessary to achieve a particular goal.

Beyond their use in robotics, planning programs can significantly improve the efficiency of heuristic programs. As we noted above, a heuristic program is essentially a random-sampling procedure; it will automatically consider whatever option is available. Accordingly, heuristic programs are structured to engage in what can be extremely time-consuming (and therefore often expensive), full-scale searches. If a heuristic program is combined with a planning program, however, the range of options to be searched can be significantly reduced. The planning program could specify which goals or subgoals to pursue first; then the heuristic program would operate within these parameters. In a game of chess, for example, some 1.3 billion moves are theoretically possible after each player has made 3 moves. If the chess computer was governed only by a heuristic program, it would take the computer 1.5 hours to make its 4th move, assuming it conducted an exhaustive search of all possible moves. The 5th move would require even more time. To avoid such delays and to introduce more realistic restrictions into the range of options to be considered, a planning program may specify the particular goal and related procedures to be examined, thereby dramatically reducing the number of possibilities investigated before each move.

Planning programs can also provide very useful services in everyday affairs. Traveling by car, for example, would be more economical and easier if planning programs were employed. A planning program could determine the shortest route to one's destination, thereby reducing gasoline consumption. To maximize driving ease, a planning program could include the goals of no more than an average of three turns per mile, periodic rest stops, and regularly encountered gasoline stations. Of course, once the general course of the trip is determined, subgoals could be introduced into the program, such as special trips to historic landmarks, visits to relatives along the way, and so forth. Comparable programs could easily be devised to function effectively for consumers.

Once the general purpose of planning programs is understood, possible applications seem almost unlimited. These programs are now used in national defense, in the operation of airplanes, in the fail-safe systems employed in nuclear plants, and in many other areas. Obviously, a planning program can only be as effective as its programming allows; therefore, if possible options are ignored or if incorrect information is placed within the system, outcomes can be less than desirable or even disastrous. However, planning programs are no longer a luxury. The complexity of modern technology requires that decisions be made, sometimes very quickly, if situations are to be handled and if large numbers of people are to be properly served. With speed and comprehensiveness, a properly programmed computer can generate a larger list of the possible actions and ways of taking those actions than humans are likely to devise, particularly during crisis conditions. Thus, the technological complexity of our social system, the speed with which we expect events to occur, and the range of goods and services we now incorporate into a minimum standard of living require that efficient planning programs become steadily increasing features of our lives.

Backward-Chaining Programs

A backward-chaining program is designed to reverse a computer's progress toward the completion of its goal. In other words, the program allows a computer to retrace the sequence already executed and to return to its original state. Rather than attempting to complete its objective, the computer works backward from the final goals sought. In chess, for example, if one move is blocked, an entire set of related moves are also blocked. A computer can terminate its efforts to carry out the original move and return to its original objective. In *Artificial Intelligence*, Patrick Henry Winston (1977) has aptly defined the backward-chaining program as "working from the goal state toward the initial state" (p. 135).

Backward chaining can serve several valuable ends. Backward chaining allows computer searches to become sensitive to the effects or influences of new information or data: New information encountered during a search will influence whether or not the search should be continued. Obviously, finding certain facts can sometimes make continued searching meaningless. In such cases, where it is more appropriate to return to the original set of goals and to select another, the user can assess which route is most likely to achieve the final objective. Routes can sometimes be measured statistically so that the user is informed of each route's precise probability of reaching the objective. Once such a comparative probability is reported, the user can direct the computer to proceed along one route rather than another. Compared to the outcomes produced by a heuristic program, backward chaining can reduce the time involved in a search and increase the likelihood that the most desired outcome is reached.

Backward chaining clearly increases the efficiency of a search. Some options or routes are so far removed from the final goal that a decision to follow them would reduce the speed of securing a goal. In some cases, it is better to return to one's beginning point. A commonsense example of the value of this maneuver sometimes occurs when driving a car. If a driver makes an incorrect turn, it can be better to turn around and return to the point of departure rather than to follow a more involved and longer route back. The same kind of efficiency is achieved with a backward-chaining program.

In sum, backward-chaining programs presume that it is frequently more desirable to retrace one's steps. New information can affect the procedures we follow. Reconsideration of one's objectives, testing the efficiency of current progress, and increasing the efficiency of a search all warrant such reversals from time to time. Especially when executing complex and extensive searches, such checks are often invaluable in terms of the time and energy expended and the final results obtained.

Concept-Learning Programs

Concept-learning programs are designed to change the programming of the computer itself. These programs are structured to generate new concepts, such as new relationships and correlations or recognition of new patterns, based upon past performance and information derived through computations. They also provide more accurate representations and uses of existing concepts. The kinds of self-change principles employed by these programs are analogous to those principles embodied in natural selection. For example, a computer can be instructed to play chess and to retain the sequences of moves that produce winning results; it can also be instructed to disregard sequences of moves that produce losing results. When the programs are actually employed, two games are typically played simultaneously, and the better of the two outcomes is retained in the computer's memory. After repeated games, the playing program of the computer gradually eliminates the weak plays and "evolves" into a stronger competitor. If an existing concept is to be perfected, a computer can be given a series of different examples of the same concept and instructed to extract the purest description of the concept. The computer would gradually develop a hypothesis and, as examples are scanned, an increasingly accurate and precise representation of the concept. Concept-learning programs can thus develop new concepts or generate more accurate representations of existing concepts.

In 1987, concept-learning programs became popularly featured subjects in the mass media. Andrew Pollack reported in the *New York Times* on September 15, 1987, that "among the recent developments" in "computers that seem to have the uncanny ability to learn by themselves" are these:

At Johns Hopkins University Terrence Scjnowsky developed a program that teaches itself to read out loud. The system is given no rules about how letters are to be pronounced; its errors are merely corrected. At first, the talk is mere gibberish. After a while it begins to utter some baby-like sounds as it learns to distinguish between consonants and vowels. After a night of computing, it reads with few mistakes.

At Avco Financial Services in Irvine, Calif. a neural network learned how to evaluate loan applications after being fed data on 10,000 past loans. One test showed that had the neural system been used in place of the company's existing computerized evaluation system, it would have increased profits 27 percent.

At Los Alamos National Laboratory, researchers used a neural network to predict whether particular DNA sequences represented genetic codes for the manufacture of proteins. The network seemed to work with greater than 80 percent accuracy, better than conventional statistical techniques. (p. C1)

In other media accounts, concept-learning programs have been described as "software that writes software." Employing this phrase, Barnaby J. Feder (1988, May) noted that "by 1985, the worldwide bill for workers who design and code software came to $139 billion annually," with the "Federal Government alone spending more than $32 billion that year to develop new software and extend the usefulness of existing programs" (p. F5). Accordingly, Feder reasoned: "The basic idea is simple enough to have attracted both computer industry giants and entrepreneurs in recent years: If computers can help design and make everything from shoes to automobiles, even other computers, why not use them to automate the painstaking, error-prone process of writing computer programs? After all, no product is more vital in the electronic age than the software that tells computers what to do and how to do it" (p. F5). From this perspective, Feder has reported that developments in computer-aided software engineering, or CASE, are emerging in two areas: "Front-end" computer applications "help a designer create the different elements of a software application like billing"; "back-end" computer applications are in fact "specifications" converted into a "code, which is written in computer languages like COBOL, Fortran, or C" and are used when companies must deal "with the taxing job of maintaining and improving existing software" (p. F5).

Concept-learning programs do at first seem to offer exciting possibilities for virtually every segment of society. Who would reject empirically derived, empirically tested, and more precisely defined concepts? However, concept-learning programs function in narrow domains. The programs are predominantly designed to generate operational definitions. We shall not repeat our analysis of operational definitions (see chapter 3). However, we note that operational definitions have little use in social situations, where contexts change the meanings of behaviors. Moreover, although concept-learning programs can recognize stable patterns unnoticed by humans and although these patterns may reveal new correlations and even new cause-to-effect relationships, knowing such relationships provides little indication of how human beings will use such information, to what ends, or in what kinds of situations. Results derived from concept-learning programs seem particularly well suited to dealing with mathematical theorems and proofs, issues in the physical sciences, and solely technical applications. Their value elsewhere is at present unknown.

The applicability of these concept-learning programs in symbolic content is by no means clear. On the one hand, symbol using deeply involves us in valuation, as we noted in chapter 3. Processes of valuation appear to fall outside the activities carried out by the concept-learning programs: Based on the performance of concept-learning programs to date, computers do not learn in the sense that they do not make the critical judgments that humans associate with understanding. On the other hand, concept-learning programs are potentially relevant to human endeavors in responding to physical events and offering accurate statements regarding how they function. Tremendous progress is being made in the development of concept-learning programs. As we noted in chapter 2, reliable computer specialists have reasoned that in the 1990s computers will be capable of symbolic inference and symbolic manipulation, and the language of fifth-generation computers may be indistinguishable from human language.

Program-dominated computer systems are frequently conceived not as functioning independently but as parts of a potentially integrated system. Parallel-processing and human-language programs provide convenient ways of discussing this integration, and we examine these programs with an eye to likely changes in the nature of program-dominated computer systems.

Parallel Programming

Parallel programming is a form of networking that is discussed in greater detail in chapters 2 and 4. It is appropriate to note here that parallel programming is a special way of linking several microprocessors or central processing units into one system. Many of the networks discussed thus far differ from parallel programming in three respects.

First, most network systems employ serial rather than parallel programming. Parallel programming involves the use of two or more central processing units wherein the activities carried out by one central processing unit depend upon the results compiled by another central processing unit. Each processing unit functions independently of the others, and thus the processing units can perform different calculations simultaneously. Once the calculations have been carried out, they are shared with the other central processing units. By contrast, the central processing units in the simpler networks using serial programming function independently and are unable to share information. Each central processing unit must perform all the calculations for any given problem. The differences between the two processing techniques are precisely defined by Hubert L. Dreyfus (1979), who has sought to identify "the limits of artificial intelligence": "Parallel processing can be simulated by a serial program, but the important logical difference remains that in a serial program each step depends on the previous ones, while in a parallel program, the operations in each series are independent of the operations in any other series" (pp. 320–21).

Second, in serial programming, several different machines are typically used. In parallel programming, the ideal is to house multiple programs within one chassis, thereby allowing for single-operator use, faster computations (because electrons have shorter distances to move), and convenience in programming and use. In an even more ideal system, several different program functions would be carried out on one machine.

Third, and probably most important, parallel programming begins to change the basic reasoning and conceptual processes of a computer. Rather than processing information bits one at a time, parallel processing approaches the method employed in human reasoning. Computers typically employ digital and binary communication systems, while humans use these and analogic and relativistic communication as well. With the development of parallel programming, a computer's reasoning process begins to shift from a digital and binary system to an analogic and relativistic system. If a computer were to exactly duplicate the analogic and relativistic communication patterns of the human being, it would still not replicate human reasoning, for the symbolic and anecdotal modes would not be employed. Nonetheless, as parallel programs are developed, the differences between human and machine communication are significantly narrowed. Michael Dertouzos (cited in Pollack, 1986, August), a computer scientist, has argued that a shift from digital back to analog computers would more closely duplicate the encoding process of the human nervous system. As Pollack's (1987) brief survey of concept-learning programs has demonstrated, early work with neural networks has also indicated great promise in such tasks as pattern recognition. Terrance J. Sejnowski (cited in Pollack, 1986, August), a biophysicist, has already developed a simulated neural network that can learn how to read out loud by trial and error.

Theoretically, parallel programming would allow heuristic, planning, backward-chaining, and concept-learning programs to operate simultaneously within one computer. When executing any kind of search or when attempting to secure a solution to a problem, the computer could operate randomly, consider multiple goal and subgoal approaches, return to original premises, and develop new concepts as a search or problem is being resolved.

Certain software packages, variously identified as "integrated," "window," or "integrated-windowing" programs, are available for personal computers and provide an illusion of parallel processing (see, e.g., S. Cook, 1984). Integrated software packages permit users to run a number of different programs on personal computers at the same time. This form of multitasking creates a new environment for personal-computer users. With an integrated software package, for example, users can access and display word-processing, spreadsheet, and data-base programs simultaneously. An integrated software package typically creates several windows, boxes, or separate display areas on the computer's screen, which make it easier for users to refer to different aspects of work being completed. Yet integrated packages provide only the appearance or image of parallel processing: Users still execute each program independently and must switch modes when moving between applications, such as between a word-processing program and a spreadsheet. The separate programs contained in an integrated package are not run simultaneously, nor do they interact when operating, as they would in a parallel-processing system.

The overall meaning of parallel programming is a contested matter. In the view of some specialists, a computer equipped with parallel programming exceeds many users' capability to employ its powers. These specialists believe that a computer can therefore be conceived of as "intelligent." Others believe that many features of human intelligence, such as symbol using and symbolic inference, are absent and would be even if parallel programming were to be further developed. We consider this dispute in the next chapter; at this point, we would simply concur with the moderate assessment of parallel programming provided by Christopher Evans (1979): "Modern computers, light barrier and inefficient software notwithstanding, still process data far quicker than brains, and when the new generation of parallel processors—many big computer companies are working on them now—come into action, their performance will be tremendously improved" (p. 204).

Human Language Programs

One of the most challenging efforts of computer specialists has been to develop a computer program that comprehends human language. To do so requires that a machine deal meaningfully with such complex issues as how humans use values in linguistic constructions, respond to context as a dimension of verbal statements, and employ such linguistic variations as contradictions, irony, and lies. The problem is not to produce a computer system that reproduces human language. A computer system with a complex voice activator and speech synthesizer system might accomplish such verbal replications. Nor is the problem to produce a computer program that merely mimics language understanding. In 1966, Joseph Weizenbaum developed a language program called Eliza that employed a rather clever set of fixed response patterns in dealing with human language. Although people were frequently convinced that the program understood and responded to their statements, Eliza only called up from its memory several all-purpose, preformulated sentences when key terms were mentioned. Such programs are not structured to understand language. The crucial problem is to develop computer programs that truly comprehend human language, and three different approaches have thus far been taken.

Developed in the 1950s, the first approach to language comprehension was essentially *linguistic-syntactical* in nature. The linguistic aspect focused on the speech units within human language: Attention was devoted to the ways in which phonemes constitute morphemes and morphemes generate meanings. The syntactical aspect attempted to codify the rules and principles that govern the ways in which the component parts of a language come together to create social meanings. When implemented, the linguistic-syntactical approach essentially employed verbatim translations of language constructions. The test of the meaningfulness of the technique typically involved translation from one language to another and then translation back to the original language. The results produced by this approach were less than encouraging. Often recalled now with amusement, one of the first of the linguistic-syntactical computers was given the following sentence to translate from English to Russian and then back to English: "The spirit is willing, but the flesh is weak." The computer produced this final translation: "The vodka is strong, but the meat is rotten."

Reactions to such translations have been mixed. David L. Waltz (1982) has observed that "good translation without understanding proved impossible, and by the middle of the 1960's the work had largely been abandoned" (p. 130). Others have viewed the approach as useful, but in limited ways. Neil Graham (1979), for example, noted that "about 80 percent of the translation could be done straightforward using a dictionary and a modest number of rules concerning grammatical functions and relationships. Unfortunately, the remaining 20 percent turned out to be very elusive" (p. 209).

We assess the linguistic-syntactical approach in quite another fashion. In our view, the issue is not whether the approach should or should not be rejected. A linguistic-syntactical thrust must be retained in any effort to create a language-comprehension computer program: Linguistics and syntax always influence language comprehension and indeed social meaning, for a language cannot be constructed without these features. At the same time, however, a solely linguistic-syntactical approach would be incomplete because language comprehension involves such nonlinguistic and nonsyntactical features as value judgments and context. We are convinced that any complete and coherent language-comprehension computer program must include linguistic and syntactical features but must not exclude other variables.

A second approach to language comprehension has been essentially *conceptual* in nature. Programs are designed to group words according to the conceptual functions they carry out in a language system. Accordingly, nouns may be grouped together because they specify existing conditions and states of being. Verbs, on the other hand, may be grouped together because they specify the ways in which conditions and states are manipulated. Moreover, these verbs or action concepts may be subdivided into more precise categories to reflect the fact that some verbs deal with the transfer of information (telling, hearing, writing, etc.), other verbs deal with possessive acts (giving, taking, selling, etc.), and still other verbs deal with sensory activities (smelling, tasting, seeing, etc.).

The conceptual approach moves toward an understanding of the place of social conventions in the construction of human language. In a computer program, this conceptual approach even allows the computer to anticipate certain human activity. For example, if a possession verb were employed, the computer would expect that something would be possessed. The sentence "John sells" makes perfectly good sense from a linguistic-syntactical perspective, but because it provides no indication of what John sells, the sentence is incomplete in terms of its conceptual meaning. The conceptual approach thus focuses on patterns that give coherence to language comprehension. Unfortunately, the linguistic-syntactical and conceptual approaches have yet to be simultaneously employed in language-comprehension computer programs.

The third approach to the development of computerized language comprehension has been *contextual* in nature. As developed by Marvin L. Minsky (1967, 1975, 1987), this approach depends on the structure of the environment or social and mental viewpoint that controls an interaction. A series of different *frames* anticipate the existence of certain controlling scripts, stereotypes, and appropriate rules in situations. Thus, the approach deals with the influence of values and value judgments as an influence in human language exchanges.

We think a profound mistake is made in attempting to select only one of these approaches to computerized language comprehension. From a theoretical perspective, no one of these approaches yields a complete view of human language. Every human language is affected by linguistic, syntactical, conceptual, and contextual variables. These influences may not be equally important in creating meaning, but all of them are present and are essential if all dimensions of human language comprehension are to be accounted for.

A complete and coherent language comprehension-computer program must incorporate at least the linguistic-syntactical, conceptual, and contextual approaches in one program. Parallel programming is essential to achieve such complexity. In fact, without parallel programming, we would predict that no one of these approaches would operate in a satisfactory fashion, at least in terms of the expectations most people have of what a sensible language exchange involves. Instead, a fully developed language-comprehension program must incorporate all three approaches. When such a program emerges, the first significant step toward the development of a truly user-friendly computer will occur.

Conclusion

We have explored the nature of computer-dominated computer systems. We examined the functions and uses of heuristic, planning, backward-chaining, and concept-learning programs. For those who wish to employ such programs on personal computers, we recommend David L. Heierman's *Projects in Machine Intelligence for Your Home Computer* (1982). Heierman's exercises and proposed uses of computer-dominated programs may fascinate many.

Each of the types of programs we discussed can be investigated and used independently, but we have stressed the ways in which these programs might be combined through parallel programming. Such integration would significantly advance the development of computers that comprehend human language.

8

Artificial Intelligence

A thinking machine or intelligent computer seems to some a frightening and unnatural application of human technology. For those convinced that only a human being can possess intelligence, the thinking machine is a utopian fantasy. For a more pragmatic group, the labels "thinking" and "intelligent" raise merely contrived issues that are largely irrelevant to the efforts to develop computers responsive to human needs. All of these views involve important issues that we explore in this chapter.

We begin by describing the discipline of artificial intelligence (AI). Once the origins of these programs are identified, we examine the questions of what constitutes intelligence and thinking and whether or not a machine can be said to produce intelligent outcomes and to carry out processes intelligently. These considerations provide a context for briefly discussing LISP, the language for representing artificial intelligence. We conclude by identifying some of the unresolved issues related to artificial intelligence.

The Discipline of Artificial Intelligence

Artificial intelligence is generally assumed to have emerged in the mid-1940s or mid-1950s. In 1945, John von Neumann developed the concept of a stored program that allowed a computer to control its own calculating sequences by modifying its own instructions (for an overview of these early efforts, see von Neumann, 1958; Chesebro, 1986). However, most see artificial intelligence as emerging in the mid-1950s. In 1956 John McCarthy coined the phrase *artificial intelligence*, and in 1958 he proposed that "all human knowledge be given a formal, homogeneous representation, the first-order predicate calculus" (cited in McCorduck, 1979, p. 42). McCarthy also conceived of and crafted LISP, the computer language still most frequently employed in artificial-intelligence research.

Artificial-intelligence researchers have remained a relatively small, isolated, and specialized group. In 1983, McCarthy estimated that only 300 people in the United States and another 200 in the rest of the world were engaged in active, full-time developmental projects classifiable under the label "artificial intelligence" (cited in Hilts, 1983, p. 28; also see Sanger, 1985, March, p. 29). With the exception of 4 or 5 outspoken advocates, these 300 researchers are programmers, mathematicians, and computer-language developers. Pamela McCorduck (1979) has observed that "the influences upon artificial intelligence" researchers can be "traced" to several "separate fields," including "computer design and construction, cybernetics, mathematical psychology and physiology, and formal logic" (p. 66). These researchers are not social critics for whom a public forum is a "natural" environment (Turkle, 1984, pp. 239–68), and their works are not available in terminologies conducive to public understanding and discussion. Rather, artificial intelligence is an esoteric topic understood by a select few. Its evolution has been strongly influenced by developments in the physical sciences, and to date there has been little agreement about the nature of artificial intelligence as a concept or as a definable area of study.

A survey of the major data bases indicates that artificial intelligence is discussed only by a small group—it is repeatedly indexed in only 2 of the 175 data systems maintained by DIALOG (1985). Within these 2 data bases—Microcomputer Index and Scisearch—some 1,027 references (by title and abstract) are found for artificial intelligence between 1975 and 1982. Of these, only 122 deal predominantly with artificial intelligence. This is a very small body of literature dealing with an eminently significant topic.

Applications of artificial-intelligence theory and research have occurred primarily in the physical sciences, in efforts to solve problems difficult, if not impossible, to simulate under laboratory conditions. Applications have occurred, for example, in efforts to synthesize organic compounds, to generate the number and identity of isomers in chemical molecules, to control nuclear reactors, and to generate developments in biocybernetics.

As we have suggested, there is little agreement among artificial-intelligence specialists concerning their collective efforts as a discipline, particularly in terms of its goals, objectives, and definitions (see, e.g., Huyghe, 1983; Schank & Childers, 1984, pp. 29–32). For some researchers, the objective of artificial-intelligence research is to understand human intelligence. For others, it is to find out what intellectual activities computers can be made to carry out. Still others measure the value of artificial intelligence by what it produces. For yet another group, the goal of artificial intelligence is the creation of programs that think. As Norman Whaland (1981) put it, "The difficulty of defining goals is a serious impediment to AI research" (p. 44).

The ambiguity of purpose facing artificial-intelligence researchers is compounded by the lack of a clearly defined conception of intelligence. For some, intelligence is only the ability to perceive, encode, and store. For others, it is the ability to employ symbols paradigmatically or abstractly. For yet another group, intelligent products do not adequately measure intelligence; intelligence only emerges from the demonstrated existence of some sort of "thinking" process involving flexibility, adaptability, and the ability to learn and understand.

The lack of a unifying purpose and of a generally shared definition of intelligence stems partly from the fact that the discipline of artificial intelligence is composed of very diverse researchers. As we have noted, artificial-intelligence researchers are predominantly specialists; they are programmers, scientists, mathematicians, and computer language developers, each involved in very narrow areas of research. They primarily see artificial intelligence not as a coherent discipline but as a means for solving their individual and different professional problems. They share only a loose conception of what artificial intelligence, as a unified discipline, can mean beyond their own specific applications.

The growing interest in social issues generated by artificial intelligence is found predominantly among those outside of the discipline of artificial intelligence. Thomas C. Hayes (1985) reported that in 1981 only 1,400 participants attended the International Joint Conference on Artificial Intelligence, a "historically sleepy, esoteric gathering," but that more than 10,000 attended the conference in 1985 (p. D2). By the end of 1985, David E. Sanger (1985, December) reported, "Artificial intelligence is beginning to break out of the lab and into factories, offices and homes" (F3). In one sense, the outsiders are best equipped to define the issues, for they are the ones who must live with the social uses and social consequences of artificial intelligence. In our discussion of these social issues, we first deal with one not systematically addressed in technical literature on artificial intelligence: What is meant by *thinking* and *intelligence*?

Thinking and/or Intelligence

Our initial concern must be with defining and tracking down the meaning of *intelligence*. Dictionaries are of little use here. *Webster's* (1981), for example, defines intelligence as "the ability to learn or understand or to deal with new or trying situations: reason; *also:* the skilled use of reason" and as "the ability to apply knowledge to manipulate one's environment or to think abstractly as measured by objective criteria (as tests)" (p. 595). Some of the descriptors in this definition are slippery, for such key words as *understand* themselves require definition. *Webster's* defines understand as "having a thorough or technical acquaintance with or expertness in the practice of" (p. 1266). This is more precise, but we must exercise caution. In limited areas, such as chess, computers appear to possess a greater "acquaintance with and expertness" than humans: As Evans (1979) reported, "by the end of 1978 computers existed which would crush 99.5% of the world's chess players" (p. 173). He further noted that some computers "have almost reached International Master level—and if this does not make you feel the computer's hot breath on your neck, then nothing will" (p. 173). If intelligence is equated with the ability to have "a thorough or technical acquaintance with or expertness in the practice of" some particular act, computers clearly have intelligence.

However, this conception of intelligence seems extremely narrow. If other features of the definition of intelligence were used—for example, the ability "to think abstractly as measured by objective criteria"—we would have to concede that some human beings would do no better than computers on certain abstraction tests, but we would question the tests' representation of the full range of skills involved in thinking abstractly. What we need is a more coherent and comprehensive *operational* definition of intelligence.

Several criteria for intelligence can be specified, six of which will guide our discussion here. (We are indebted to Christopher Evans [1979, pp. 158–66] for the initial conception of these criteria.) First, intelligence requires sensory acquisition. An intelligent organism must be capable of receiving information from its environment. Humans far exceed computers in the variety and types of stimuli they can receive. Humans employ five sensory modalities; three-dimensional information is easily processed; and both digital and analogic information is quickly acquired. In contrast, most computers can acquire only carefully prepared information, essentially in typed-in print form. Three-dimensional, analogic, and sensory information cannot easily be processed by most computers, although innovations are occurring in these areas. As noted in chapter 2, new modes of sensory acquisition are now available for computers, including a variety of physical sensors and robotic mechanisms, and, as noted in chapters 4 and 6, the data bases available for computer retrieval continue to increase. Moreover, greater attention is being devoted to eliminating the "language barriers" that exist in computer-to-computer interactions. AT&T American Bell's Net 1000, for example, theoretically allows any computer system to share the information contained in any other computer system. It is not unreasonable to foresee a fully interactive computer system that will have access to more sensory information or reports than any single human being can assimilate.

Second, intelligence requires the ability to store or to accumulate information and the ability to relate that information. In pragmatic terms, an entity changes its behavior as a consequence of accumulated experiences, and the storage or accumulation capacity of a computer is theoretically unlimited. Even as early as 1950, the notion of an "infinite capacity computer" was seriously discussed, and for very good reasons. John McHale (1972, p. 57) has detailed, for example, the steady decrease in computer storage costs and storage size and the increase in storage speed since 1955. In 1972, he projected that storage costs would decrease by a factor of 300 in the next 10 years, that the size of fully integrated circuits would reduce storage size by a factor of 1,000, and that storage speed would increase by a factor of 200. These expectations have already been reached and exceeded (Meindl, 1987). But we must remember that stored information in a computer is only as useful as the programs' ability to retrieve it in forms that can be employed by a user. Over 300 software companies now create programs for a wide range of uses, and a number of other enterprises contribute to selective, organized retrieval of stored information. In 1981, W. Sullivan argued that "a quiet revolution" was occurring "in the coordination, storage and delivery of data" in "the scientific world, with far-reaching effects on operating procedures of libraries, professional journals and their readers" (p. E9). He particularly detailed the development of field stations that translate journal articles onto optical disks—each disk capable of holding 50,000 pages—which are transmitted by satellite to the system's organizers (also see Broad, 1988; Fabun, 1968, p. 15; Kranzberg, 1988, p. 36; Machlup & Leeson, 1978–80; Naisbitt, 1982, p. 24). Subscribers can thus receive any particular article electronically on their home computers at roughly one tenth the cost of photocopying. Sullivan observed that some 200 of these electronic warehouses now exist. Information in a computer can thus be related and used in many ways.

Third, intelligence requires the ability to process conclusions quickly. While basic time cycles vary from computer to computer, a commonly used time measure is the number of instructions in 500 billionths of a second. Univac's 1100/90 series, for example, is able to perform 25 million instructions per second. IBM's 3084 translates at a speed of about 26 million instructions per second. Raj Reddy (cited in Wilford, 1987), a specialist in robotics, has specified an execution rate of 1 billion instructions per second as the next interim goal for computer processing. In practice, computers regularly process calculations at amazing rates. The daily weather forecast, for example, requires trillions of calculations for one computer prediction. Compared to humans, then, computers are virtually unbeatable number crunchers.

Fourth, intelligence requires the ability to create new linkages among existing patterns of information. Humans are virtually unbeatable in this category. As Evans (1979) has noted, "In really complex brains there may be millions, perhaps billions, of interlocking programs, and they are constantly restructuring in order to take account of the changes in the average organism's environment" (p. 162). He concludes, "No one is pretending that the learning programs which control the human brain—or those that control the rat, the fish, or even the earwig—are anywhere near as simple in execution [as those in computers]" (p. 162). William Shoemaker (cited in Begley, Carey, & Sawhill, 1983) has stated that the human brain contains between 10 billion and 100 billion neurons, each forming bridges to so many others that the brain is "abuzz" with as many as 1 quadrillion connections; the average neuron "is as complex as an entire small computer" (p. 41). Comparing the human brain and the computer, John David Sinclair (1983) has noted: "To simulate the 100 trillion or so synapses in the human brain would require a computer with several times this many transistors. If 100 transistors are required to simulate each synapse, a 32-bit processor doing a million operations per second would require several hundred years to address each location once" (p. 11). "Several thousand years," concluded Sinclair, "would be needed to make the calculations for simulating a single event, an event that for humans occupies only a fraction of a second" (p. 11).

There is no denying the power of the human being to create new information links, but there is progress in computers that needs to be recognized. As we pointed out in chapter 6, computers are proving almost as good as expert clinicians at diagnosing certain illnesses and in securing medical information. Moreover, the "expert computer system" is on the market (B. Davis, 1985; Deane, 1985; Ham, 1984; Hertz, 1988; Linden, 1988; Mace, 1986; Marcus, 1983, August 29; M. W. Miller, 1984, December 14; Sanger, 1987, October; Waldrop, 1987). Expert systems are programmed to duplicate the reasoning and inference systems of particular human experts. Human experts are asked to describe, in detail, the ways in which they make decisions.

These processes are operationalized, and they become the foundation for the expert system's program. Although the system functions only in narrow areas of application, the principle of the expert system nonetheless suggests that the human being's ability to create new linkages among existing information is potentially within the reach of a computer. Linkages are already made by such systems as the federal government's Computer Matching Project, which creates new informational linkages whenever it cross-lists welfare expenditures and tax records in order to track down cheaters. Evans (1979) captured the point: "The goal of creating an Ultra-Intelligent Machine will prove too tempting to be ignored" (p. 203).

But the ultraintelligent machine does not yet exist. Even given the remarkable information links computers can now create, parallel programming is only emerging. Furthermore, parallel programming is unlikely to duplicate human thought processes, though it will generate a new form of synthesis or analogic reasoning. Even the so-called expert computer systems do not learn from experience; they will make the same diagnosis twice, even if the first one has been proven wrong. On balance, then, humans are far more capable than computers in creating new links among different information systems.

Fifth, intelligence requires efficiency. Living organisms develop efficient systems through evolution, adaption, and experience. Humans can intuit answers, can make leaps of faith with successful results. Computers lack this kind of efficiency. Computers move through a program step by step; leaps are impossible. No matter how many times a computer has moved through the same program, it cannot make a leap of faith to solution at the end of the program. As Evans (1979) put it, "Computers are wildly inefficient and will remain so for some time to come" (pp. 163–64). Even in the more recently developed computer systems, as we noted in chapter 2, computers continue to rely on linear and discrete data conceptions and on sequential and independent programs (Fox & Messina, 1987; Gelernter, 1987, esp. p. 92) and therefore remain, in Evans's words, wildly inefficient. A computer may compensate for this inefficiency by increased computation speeds, but to devote computer time to "intuitive" or generalized activity prevents it from carrying out other functions at which it is superior. It is the human being who naturally performs as an efficient information processor.

Sixth, and finally, intelligence requires the ability to exercise a wide range of capabilities. The range of tasks required for human survival is obviously much greater than that required for the survival of a bee. For a computer, the range of programs handled by a central processor constitutes an equivalent measure of intelligence. By this standard, humans are far more intelligent than computers. Computer manufacturers compensate for this limitation by linking increasing numbers of computers together. Univac's and IBM's computers are in fact combinations of four different computers. Some of the new 64K computer chips are actually composed of four 16K chips; this is equivalent to having four different computers process information at the same time. The factors limiting the range of a computer's capabilities seem to be affected by costs, size, and human creativity. Though we expect some limitations to be overcome, computers seem nonetheless unlikely to best humans at exercising a wide range of abilities.

Three conclusions regarding the comparative intelligence of humans and computers seem warranted. First, if we agree with the sixfold comparison just completed, humans are far more intelligent than computers. In two of the six skills associated with intelligence—sensory acquisition and the linking of different information systems—humans are overwhelmingly more efficient than computers. In two other areas—information storage and processing speed—computers outperform humans. In the last two areas—efficiency and the ability to execute a wide range of activities—comparison is virtually impossible because the two systems operate in such different ways. Without a doubt, the human being is at present the more intelligent agency. However, as Evans (1979) noted, in less than 10 years the computer has moved from the IQ of a tapeworm to that of "substantially above a tapeworm" (p. 170).

Second, innovations in computer programming have allowed computers to generate creative or novel outcomes, by which we mean outcomes or manipulations produced by computers and unexpected by the persons writing the computer programs. These outcomes sometimes lead to formulations of theorems, procedures, proofs, and manipulations never before known to have been produced by human beings. We have detailed the nature of several of these programs: the heuristic, planning, backward-chaining, and concept-learning programs. The ability to produce creative or novel outcomes is for many people a measure of intelligence regardless of whether or not another kind of entity, such as a human being, can also produce useful information.

Third, and probably most importantly, we do not think that human and computer understandings will ever be equivalent. A distinction needs to be made between intelligence (a product or outcome) and thinking (a process or mode of procedure). The outcomes of humans and computers may become increasingly similar, but the processing systems governing humans and computers are more likely to become even more dissimilar. Computers are increasingly capable of generating analogic and relativistic outcomes, and the fifth-generation computers may be capable of manipulating symbols and producing symbolic inferences. In these ways, the outcomes of humans and computers are likely to become increasingly similar, yet the processes by which these outcomes are derived continue to become increasingly dissimilar. The mechanical innovations controlling the development of computers in no way resemble the operations of the human brain. Humans and machines simply do not operate in the same mode. Humans think; machines process. In our view, human beings and computers will continue to be two different kinds of information-handling entities. Different processes can yield the same outcome, but thinking as a process yielding outcomes remains within the province of the human being alone.

To some, our distinction between thinking and intelligence seems to avoid the central question. Many continue to wonder if computers will ever become as intelligent as human beings. These critics require a precise operational definition of intelligence and an impartial test of intelligence as defined. Such a test, one viewed as a classic measure for determining if human and computer intelligence will ever be equivalent, has been devised by Allen M. Turing (1937a, 1937b, 1950; also see Chesebro, 1982, 1983, 1986, 1988).

The Turing Test

In the October 1950 issue of *Mind: A Quarterly Review of Psychology and Philosophy*, Turing proposed "to consider the question, 'Can machines think?' " and to answer the question through an "information game" (p. 433). His game, now called the Turing Test, presumes that a computer and a human being are equally intelligent if other human beings are unable to distinguish between the responses of a computer and those of a human being.

To determine whether such a distinction could be made, Turing proposed an "imitation test" (p. 433). Teleprinters would connect two rooms: In one room would be a human interrogator, and in the other room a human being at one teletype machine and a computer at another teletype machine would answer questions. Assuming that both the computer and the interviewed human could lie, Turing posited that the computer is thinking—for all practical purposes—if the interrogator, using solely the teletyped answers, could not distinguish the responses of the human from the responses of the computer.

The testing condition generates all sorts of intriguing possibilities. A clever interrogator might ask each to provide a poem, reasoning that a computer is not artistic. But what if the computer had a poem within its memory and the human being interviewed is simply not poetic? Perhaps a question on love would reveal which was which. Yet the computer might have within its memory personal and psychological descriptions of love, while the human might be unable to articulate his or her feelings on the topic. Questions that would distinguish the human being from the computer might be more difficult to frame than it at first appears.

We do not know what we would ask if conducting the Turing Test, but we suggest that questions requiring the use and manipulation of highly figurative analogies and the synthesis of anecdotal reasoning would constitute a telling test. We offer this possibility because diverse data banks may not be tied into one computer and because parallel-processing techniques are currently limited. Questions requiring symbolic inferences and relativistic communication techniques might also reveal interesting limitations of the computer.

What is something like the Turing Test likely to produce? Turing speculated that by the end of the 1990s "an average interrogator will not have more than a 70 percent chance of making the right identification after five minutes of questioning" (p. 442). Considering that the interrogator has a 50 percent chance of identifying the computer without asking any questions, Turing seemed to imply that the typical interrogator would have only a slightly better than average chance of distinguishing the computer from the human being. McCorduck (1979, pp. 225, 243) has noted that the Turing Test measures only one type of intelligence, but she has observed that, at least under one set of conditions, a computer appears to have passed the Turing Test. Michael A. Guillen (1983) has been far less optimistic about the computer's performance:

Today, some 30 years later, we are nowhere near fulfilling Turing's prophecy. In fact, our basic understanding of human and artificial intelligence is so incomplete, says Marvin Minsky, MIT computer scientist, that "nobody is even trying any such thing" as programming computers to play the imitation game. The problem, he says, is that nobody imitates human conversation or intelligence in any but the crudest way. Given this, Minsky predicts, it will probably be at least another 300 years before we are able to program a computer to make a decent showing on Turing's test. (pp. 80–81)

Erik Sandberg-Diment (1986, March) has been equally direct: "Going by the normal definition of the word 'intelligent,' there is no such thing as intelligent software, nor is there likely to be in this millennium" (p. F14). Others, however, remain positive. The Turing Test and Turing's analysis of it continue to intrigue some computer specialists. Some 30 years after Turing published his analysis, Christopher Evans (1979) viewed Turing's analysis as "of lasting interest," "logically unassailable," of "classic status," and the product of a "genius" (p. 177). Accordingly, in dealing with the broader question of whether or not a computer can think, we might return to Turing's 1937 paper, "On Computable Numbers," where Turing concluded that a computer, no matter how well it is programmed, will never be able to solve *every* problem. Without intending to complicate matters, we must observe that a single human being will probably also never be able to solve *every* problem.

LISP: A Language for Representing Artificial Intelligence

Artificial intelligence finds its fullest expression in its programming language, called LISP. The theories of artificial intelligence can be operationally defined, represented, tested, and verified in LISP. In fact, LISP is the major source of the concepts and theories defining artificial intelligence. There are other artificial-intelligence languages, such as IPL, POP-2, and SAIL, but LISP is the most dominant and productive of these languages (see, e.g., Friedman, 1974; Siklossy, 1976; Winston & Horn, 1981).

LISP is specifically designed for coding only intelligence-exhibiting human-language processes. Moreover, it is a predominantly descriptive language, designed to represent symbolic mathematical expressions both conceptually and in pragmatic formulations. LISP employs some 61 functions or commands for representing symbolic expressions. The same syntax is employed to characterize both data and commands. In one sense, it is impossible to distinguish the content from the rules of procedure in LISP. Accordingly, the most common features of LISP are its *lists* or groups of elements in a particular order. Some of the 61 functions add an element to a list, whereas others eliminate an element from the list; some functions add one group to another group, whereas others distinguish one group from another.

An example of the use of LISP reveals the general kinds of configurations in the language. Obviously, the example will not specify all of the rules governing LISP, but it will provide a general indication of LISP's forms. The example we use here employs terminology used only in the early stages of LISP's development.

In the initial uses of LISP, if one wishes to return an element to a list of symbolic expressions, the CAR function would be used. Winston (1977) has provided the following example of the CAR function:

```
(CAR '(FAST COMPUTERS ARE NICE))
    FAST

(CAR '(A B C))
    A
```

(CAR '((A B) C))
(A B)

Note in the last example that the argument given to CAR was the two-element list ((A B)C). The first element is itself a list, (A B), and being the first element of the argument, (A B), is returned by CAR. (p. 266)

We find LISP particularly intriguing because its logic and structure appear capable of dealing simultaneously with linguistic-syntactical, conceptual, and contextual approaches to development of a human-language program. The parentheses used in LISP allow particular linguistic and syntactical units to be isolated and grouped, if meaningful, with certain equivalent words but not with nonequivalent words (a process not unlike the creation of various dictionaries of synonyms and antonyms). At the same time, concepts can also be isolated as units, and these concepts can govern, by virtue of where the parentheses are placed, the understanding of any particular group of linguistic-syntactical units. Even contexts can be likewise isolated and can function as larger frames of reference for sets of concepts that share a common viewpoint. In this sense, linguistic-syntactical units, concepts, and contexts are ordered formally from a common perspective in LISP. As a logical and structural system, then, LISP would apparently satisfy McCarthy's concern (cited in McCorduck, 1979) that artificial intelligence initially provides a "formal, homogeneous representation" of "all human knowledge" (p. 42). We are not experts in manipulating LISP in all of its various orders or levels of abstraction, but we find its logic and structure immediately compelling, at least as a foundation for developing one mode of artificial intelligence. LISP certainly appears worthy of further exploration.

LISP is available for personal-computer users. At least two companies, Microsoft in Washington State and the Soft Warehouse in Honolulu, provide a sequential file access version of LISP, called MuLISP-80, and a more powerful random access file version, called MuLISP-83.

Unresolved Issues

As our discussion has shown, we are unable to resolve all of the issues that emerge when computers are called intelligent. We are confident that computers will not duplicate the processes of human thinking, but we are unable to determine whether computers are or will become as intelligent as human beings. Many questions are unanswered; many of the questions may, in fact, be unanswerable. Nonetheless, some issues need to be thought about by all of us—computer experts and novices alike.

First, we do not know what human intelligence is, let alone what machine intelligence is or might be. In some people's views, intelligence can never be satisfactorily defined in operational terms. One thing seems clear. If we refuse any kind of operational definition of intelligence, we will never be able to say whether or not a machine can be intelligent.

Second, the value of the entire question regarding machine intelligence is unclear. Is the controversy surrounding artificial intelligence motivated by a fear of computers and technological control or by a fear that computers might outperform humans? Is the most unique feature of the human being the ability to reason? Many believed so during the Age of Reason, but since that era human beings have recognized that they are multifaceted creatures. In the 20th century, most follow Freud in believing that motivations and psychic determination are equally powerful human characteristics. Human beings also judge, evaluate, and posit critical assessments that determine the ends to which reason is applied. Clearly, intelligence is only one of the dimensions defining humanness, and we remain unconvinced, then, that the significance given to the issues embedded in artificial intelligence has been justified.

Third, will intelligent computers help us or hurt us? This implies a policy problem, for both the advantages and the disadvantages of this technology must be weighed. On balance, we suspect that at present the gains far exceed the losses.

Fourth, can computers function as our companions, as intellectual and emotional companions? Beyond the therapeutic computer programs that can be written, both Norbert Wiener (1950, pp. 163–86) and Leonard Pinsky (1951) have argued that machines are capable of "breakdowns under pressure which cannot be distinguished from the nervous breakdowns of human beings" (Pinsky, p. 398). Do humans create technologies only in their own image? More immediately, will computers destroy the social bonds that unify people? Will anyone care? Television has reduced social cohesion, yet the medium continues to dominate the American life-style. Neil Frude (1983) is one observer who foresees that computers will be America's next technological companion:

Many people have a deeply held belief that no object or animal should be able to replace a human being in a person's life. It may be felt that there is a sanctity about human relationships that renders them beyond artificial simulation, but arguments of this kind cannot rule out the psychological possibility that a person may, in fact, come to regard a nonhuman object as an adequate substitute for a human friend. It is clear, for example, that some people set the value of their relationship with an animal above that of any human alliance, and the possibility that a computer might achieve such favor cannot be rejected merely on the grounds that it is not human. . . . If we use the available evidence as a basis for predicting the likely reactions to "softer" and more sophisticated devices, then it will be seen that the concept of the companion machine is in fact highly plausible. . . . It can be anticipated that computer systems will be future friends and intimates as well as colleagues. (pp. 23–24)

As computers invade our lives, we must compensate for the energy we devote to computers and must work at being social. As Naisbitt (1982, pp. 39–53) has compellingly argued, every increase in high technology should be countered with an equally important increase in human touch.

Fifth, will we encounter the "limits of technology"? Can we make computers evolve as far as we hope? Will we suffer a more profound technological shock if we are unable to develop artificial intelligence? Will the visions of computer science slowly give way to a form of science fiction? In the early part of 1988, "setbacks for artificial intelligence" (Pollack, 1988) and fears that "the artificial intelligence industry is retrenching" (Markoff, 1988, May) were reported, predominantly because practical and dedicated artificial-intelligence systems and viable market outlets had not been developed. Though suggestive of a larger trend in the computer industry, such reports also have a way of reinvigorating and challenging computer specialists to respond more directly to emerging needs. However, these questions are as much philosophical as practical, for we are also concerned about those who metaphorically view their computer manuals as their bibles. The faith being placed in computers might rapidly transform computer science into a religion in which beliefs in future progress are substituted for present inability to generate technological advancement.

Sixth, are we maintaining a proper balance among nature, production, and information? During the Industrial Age, we lost contact with nature, and we retain this contact only with great difficulty. Now we seem to be losing our appreciation of the skills necessary to make objects, whether beautiful or useful. The production of physical objects is becoming a lost art. Do we not need to reinstate a commitment to a truly ecological balance in which nature, production, and information operate equally?

Conclusion

In this chapter, we have examined computer programs designed to independently produce knowledge never before produced by any hu-

Table 8.1 Types of Computer-Human Relationships

Content Variable	Chapters				
	4	5	6	7	8
Name of Relationship	Communicating by computer transmission	Human communication in a computer context	Congruent human-computer communication	Program-dominated computer communication	Artificial intelligence
Typical Computer Service	Electronic mail	Video games	Individualized education programs	Heuristic programs	Artificial intelligence
Function	Transmissive	Expressive	Correlational	Causal	Creative
Input- or Program-Oriented	User's input controls	User and program equally control	Program controls but responses depend upon the user's input	Program controls	Program controls
Anticipated Outcome	Known with a high degree of confidence	Known but new information is expected	New skills and new information	Unknown	Unknown
Possible Media Alternatives	Multiple mass and personal alternatives	Fewer in number and more difficult to access	Specialized institutions of learning	Creative and expert researchers	Creative and expert researchers
Verification System	Multiple mass and personal confirmation systems	Fewer mass communication systems	Expert verification	Expert verification requiring years to confirm	Pragmatically unverifiable
User's Psychological State	Dispassionate user	Enthusiast	Managing performer	Hacker	Computer scientist

man being. The essential function of these programs is therefore *creative* in nature. The computer program alone controls the outcome of its computations, and the outcome is unknown. Moreover, the most creative and expert human researchers might not be able to replicate the efforts of these programs. Given the researchers' training, energy, and lifetime commitment and the complexity of the undertakings involved in creating such programs, nothing less than a scientific (specifically, a computer-scientific) psychological state is required to carry out the efforts needed to develop these programs. The efforts of these small and specialized groups of researchers may profoundly affect us all.

In our view, computer-dominated relationships create more issues than they resolve. It is helpful to define the discipline of artificial intelligence as well as to define and distinguish human and computer intelligence. It is equally useful to understand at least the basic configuration of LISP, the language that has generated so many of the concepts and theorems of artificial intelligence. We have explored all of these issues, yet we are nonetheless left with unanswered questions of the most basic and profound kind. While we are confident that major advances will be made in the development of computer intelligence and that they will serve social ends, we remain unsure of their social consequences. We suspect that each of us will shape the future we each experience either unconsciously or, hopefully, consciously, by selecting those ends we require to develop as human beings.

This chapter concludes an extended discussion, which began in chapter 4, of the actual and potential relationships that define computer-human communication. In chapter 4, we considered the relationships in which humans dominated computer-human interactions. From chapter 4 through chapters 5, 6, and 7, the computer is increasingly cast as dominating its relationship with the human user. Accordingly, in this chapter we examined the relationship in which the computer ultimately determines the outcomes of what begins as a joint computer-human relationship. Table 8.1 summarizes the relationships among these types of computer-human relationships.

III.
Societal Issues

9

Computing as Rhetoric

Fantasy, Vision, and Ideology

Personal computing is increasingly perceived as a national issue. Not only is the personal-computer industry a major economic force in the United States, but personal computers dramatically affect their users. As we repeatedly demonstrated in part 2, personal computers have identifiable and extensive social consequences. For users, the impact is difficult to deny. The first preassembled personal computer was introduced in 1977. Ten years later, 17 million families, or some 20 percent of all American households, had personal computers. For this group, personal computers have typically functioned as transmission and expressive devices. For a growing number of users, personal computers are also used as correlational, causal, and creative media systems.

Far more intriguing is how personal computers have captured the public's attention. As early as 1983, a Gallup poll indicated that 28 million families, or 36 percent of American households, were "very" or "fairly" interested in buying a personal computer. Paradoxically, at approximately the same time Evans (1979) reported that "most people" have "very little understanding" of what computers "can and might do" (p. 96). In any event, the American language has been decisively altered by the appearance of personal computers (Rice & Boan, 1985). Individuals have been classified as *computerphobic* or *computer obsessive*. *Computer literacy*, whatever it might mean, has become a national educational objective. Such terms as *computerized banking, electronic work stations, teletext,* and *artificial intelligence* are rapidly becoming part of our vocabulary. A new rhetoric is pervading the terminologies Americans use to express themselves.

In this chapter, we ask why this new vocabulary has gained popularity and then suggest how this vocabulary is affecting our national identity. In other words, we examine the ways in which the terminologies of the computer specialist and the computer industry have spread throughout the United States and ultimately function as part of an emerging philosophy, if not ideology, in American culture. We are thus shifting from the descriptive and interpretative frameworks governing earlier chapters to an evaluative mode in this chapter. We believe our analysis would be incomplete were we not to evaluate some of the issues created by personal computers as societal technologies.

Two methods guide our evaluation. In the first part of this chapter, we employ portions of the fantasy-theme analysis developed by Ernest G. Bormann (1972, 1985). Bormann's method seems particularly useful as a way of accounting for the actions of personal-computer users, for Bormann (1972) has posited that any group may engage in "group fantasy events" in which verbal exchanges become "dramatized" (p. 397). The characters and events created in these dramas are "removed in time and space from the here-and-now transactions of the group" and gradually are "chained out" into increasingly larger social settings (p. 397). As Bormann has detailed the chaining-out process,

> When group members respond emotionally to the dramatic situation they publicly proclaim some commitment to an attitude. . . . Values and attitudes of many kinds are tested and legitimatized as common to the group by the process of fantasy chains. . . . The dramatizations which catch on and chain out in small groups are worked into public speeches and into the mass media and, in turn, spread out across larger publics, serve to sustain the members' sense of community, to impel them strongly to action (which raises the question of motivation), and to provide them with a social reality filled with heroes, villains, emotions, and attitudes. (pp. 397–98)

As these dramas "catch up larger groups of people in a symbolic reality," a "rhetorical vision" is created (Bormann, 1972, p. 398). In this chapter, we trace the evolution of the personal-computer vision from intimate and personal levels to increasingly larger societal systems. Bormann (1972) has provided a basic structure for such an analysis: "A rhetorical vision is constructed from fantasy themes that chain out in face-to-face interacting groups, in speaker-audience transactions, in viewers of television broadcasts, in listeners to radio programs, and in all the diverse settings for public and intimate communication in a given society" (p. 398). We thus examine these personal-computing fantasies successively from the highly personal to the international level. At each of these levels, we seek to isolate the rhetorical techniques that give credence to personal-computer use and to identify particular issues involved in these rhetorical transactions. We believe that the time to deal with these issues is now, at the inception of the microprocessor revolution.

In the second half of this chapter, we isolate the unifying features of the personal-computer rhetoric that constitutes an emerging public philosophy, perhaps even a proclaimed ideology, in American culture. We are guided at this juncture by a line of reasoning developed by Michael Calvin McGee (1980a, 1980b; McGee & Martin, 1983). McGee (1980a) has posited that "human beings in collectivity behave and think differently than human beings in isolation. The collectivity is said to 'have a mind of its own' distinct from the individual qua individual" (p. 2); he then specifically noted that, "if a mass consciousness exists at all, it must be empirically 'present,' itself a thing obvious to those who participate in it, or, at least, empirically manifested in the language which communicates it" (p. 4). In this sense, we treat the "chained-out" fantasies or visions associated with personal computers as an ideology. As McGee (1980a) has also noted, an "ideology in practice is a political language, preserved in rhetorical documents, with the capacity to dictate decision and control public belief and behavior" (p. 5). The fantasies and visions associated with personal computers are rapidly becoming part of a public philosophy or ideology that promotes certain values as normative. In the last half of this chapter, we isolate the particular cluster of values associated with personal computers and identify the controlling ideology that governs these values. We begin by identifying the fantasies and visions associated with personal computers and note the ways in which the terminologies and concepts of these fantasies and visions have increasingly moved from private to public domains.

Personal Computer Fantasies and Visions Chain Out

Psychological Attitudes: Computer Obsessions and Computerphobia

Personal computers could be viewed solely as tools, much as we view a hammer or a saw, but they are seldom approached in a dispassionate or neutral fashion. The personal computer has been elevated from mere tool to, in the words of Sherry Turkle (1984), "a projective device" that "resembles" the "Rorschach, perhaps the best known and most powerful of psychology's projective measures" (p. 14). Personal computers are cast as extensions of the individual's psychological needs and frequently as representative of the individual's repressed subconscious urges. When so conceived, the personal computer becomes a symbol of the individual's basic drives. Nothing in a personal computer or in the functions it executes warrants such a conception, but the psychological association persists, and it alters perceptions of the personal computer. In this fantasy, the basic urges of each individual are apparently revealed through this machine. The personal computer therefore appears to have mysterious powers, and the reports of these psychological reactions always appear to reveal the unknown.

COMPUTER OBSESSIONS.   For some users, we are told, a "natural" affinity with the computer emerges as soon as contact is made. We could speculate about why certain individuals are thus immediately attracted. Motives undoubtedly vary among individuals. Certainly some use a personal computer because it extends their range of skills for accomplishing tasks. Some are attracted to the computer simply because it is a machine. For others, a power motive may exist, for the mastery of a machine can be perceived as representative of an individual's social status (a motive some might interpret as a form of repressed social hostility). For still others, the computer is the archetype of a new era to which one may belong simply by owning and operating a computer, or the computer may function as a symbol of their intellectual curiosity. For the economically and materially motivated, it is a passport to a better position within a corporation or a potential source of income. Any one of these motives possesses the kind of attraction necessary to create an obsession—a computer obsession. Regardless of the reason for this obsession, use of a machine is being employed to define the psychological essence of a human being. Machine using becomes the controlling metaphor for explaining human motives; a machine is specifically employed to account for excessive and self-destructive human behavior. Yet, in public statements, computer obsessions are treated positively. The personal computer becomes a symbol of, if not a justification for, excessive self-indulgence.

Computer obsessions are now gaining public attention. In some cases, these obsessions are treated in a humorous fashion. In 1982, for example, one of the lead articles in *TV Guide* was entitled "Help! I'm the captive of my home computer! (And I love it!)." The author, James Fallows, cast his obsession as a relatively harmless activity carried out in "the small hours, long after midnight, when the rest of my family lies unsuspecting in bed" (p. 26). He noted that the home computer might be used to "sort out your family finances and learn calculus or a foreign language," but he conceded that is like saying "people spend Sundays watching pro football because they are concerned with physical fitness" (p. 2). Ilis conclusion: "The dirty little secret of home computers is that they are addictive," an addiction, Fallows admitted, he shares with a host of others (p. 2).

However, not all obsessions are harmless, personal habits. Sooner or later, others can be affected. Yet computer obsessions, associated with self-indulgence and entertainment, are treated as equivalent to extensive watching of football games. The extreme possibility is noted, but computer obsession ultimately becomes testimony of an abiding satisfaction with the machine. In this context, consider Georgia Dullea's (1983) "report": "The so-called 'computer widow' and, to a lesser extent, the 'computer widower' are becoming familiar figures in psychotherapists' offices. Their complaint: Their mates cling like barnacles to the machine, staring for hours at illuminated characters on the screen. They are withdrawn, unresponsive, uncommunicative. In extreme cases, the computerized spouse begins giving commands to family members as one does to the machine" (p. A17). Even less tongue-in-cheek reports on computer obsessions contain embedded assumptions that personal computers create satisfaction and enjoyment. Thomas McDonald (cited in Dullea, 1983), a psychotherapist and one of several computer-obsession counselors, not only leads group therapy sessions for computer widows and their mates but has designed psychological tests to measure computer obsessions. He reported that these obsessions initially emerge as absorbing and enjoyable, albeit isolating, experiences. These experiences become obsessions, McDonald noted, if people begin to feel a pleasing sense of power over the computer or to perceive computer-human communication as a mode of self-expression not experienced with others and if the computer provides forms of positive reinforcement not present when the user deals with other people. In psychologist Philip Zimbardo's (cited in Dullea, 1983) view, these computer obsessions constitute a "social disease," an excessive involvement with computers fostered by the positive feedback and confidence they inspire, even though they produce diverse forms of social isolation.

Computer obsessions are not, as far as we know, a common problem with users. Rather than discouraging their use, the descriptions we have cited appear to encourage involvement with personal computers. None of the descriptions appears to outline the classic elements of an obsession: a persistent and disturbing preoccupation with an unreasonable idea, feeling, or commitment to an activity. We suspect that few users find their use of a personal computer all consuming; it is difficult to engage in persistent, unreasoned, and disturbing preoccupations when using a home computer. The possibility for such behaviors exists, but we expect that compulsions are no more likely to occur with personal-computer use than with television viewing.

What intrigues us, however, is the fact that a psychological perspective is used to describe personal-computer use. The association suggests, from a rhetorical perspective, that personal computers are critical to the individual's psyche, an assumption that we have yet to see empirically demonstrated.

COMPUTERPHOBIA. While computers immediately intrigue some, they create an initial, unreasoned fear in others. To cast personal computers as the source of a phobia reinforces the use of a psychological model, and it also implies that personal computers function within the realm of the powerful, are agents capable of dominating others. From a rhetorical perspective, personal computers thereby become part of the family of "power terms," objects requiring attention and perhaps a set of mastery skills designed to deal with them. In this view, computerphobia "reports" might also be examined for more subtle indications that personal computers are cast as power agents.

In his survey of several hundred managers and college students who use computers, Sanford Weinberg (cited in Dullea, 1983) found that nearly one third, as measured by galvanic skin responses, experienced a fear of the computer. About 5 percent actually showed such classic symptoms of phobia as nausea, dizziness, cold sweat, and high blood pressure.

Among corporate executives and managers, computerphobia has been similarly used to explain "resistance to computers" (Carroll, 1988, p. 17). This resistance is cast in decidedly psychological terms, with computerphobia employed as the governing and integrating concept to describe the "difficult attitudes" and "troublesome types" that computer-training firms have encountered in corporate environments; in terms of causation, "computerphobic" executives are also viewed as "technophobic" personalities who are also "technologically illiterate" (p. 17).

The sources of fear can vary for each individual. For some, the fear of any new machine, particularly those powered by electricity, explains their behavior. For others, the computer symbolizes an ever more dehumanized society in which technology promotes social isolation. For another group, the use of a computer represents a kind of ultimate loss of control over one's personal life, a fear that the computer will control them. The computer critic Erik Sandberg-Diment (1982, August 17) has given voice to similar fears:

Computers are by their very nature intimidating to the uninitiated. Sure, they have a television-like video monitor, and a typewriter-like keyboard, both familiar devices. But there is also an aura of mystery, even fear, surrounding the computer as an entity.

I've seen people, driven by curiosity, approach a small computer and then stop dead in their tracks to stare. They ask questions. They are obviously intrigued. But their hands remain behind their backs, or if they are induced to peck at the keyboard, they do so with the reluctance of touching a hot stove.

I myself am well acquainted with Computer Fear Syndrome. The first few times, I too looked, but dared not touch. I can't, however, say the same for my children—and here may be the widest current gulf of all in the so-called generation gap. (p. C2)

While a certain amount of hesitation is to be expected when dealing with a new piece of machinery, all of these "computerphobia reports" reinforce the image of the personal computer as an agency of power. If a fear of personal computers exists, a more gradual introduction to the personal computer by way of video games or the assistance of a knowledgeable but sensitive friend may eliminate some of these fears. Computer manufacturers themselves have tried to deal with the problem by designing programs particularly designed for those new to computers. The programs begin at "ground zero"—first introducing the user to the keyboard, then to the most basic functions of the computer—and typically include references to the users as well as interesting games for users. These introductory programs do much to eliminate the fears a user might have of a home computer. Given these training options, the psychological and power-oriented descriptions of personal computers appear to serve rhetorical rather than functional ends.

Other fears of computers may initially appear more justified. As we noted in chapter 1, the transformation from a manufacturing to an information-based economy will create major economic and employment transformations, if not dislocations, during the coming decades. Similar observations are now beginning to appear in the media, fostering a concern about or even a fear of the impact of computers on the lives of many Americans. The media terminologies are probably designed to underscore a neglected issue, but they also reinforce an association between computers and power. For example, in one of the first reports calling for a link between the economy and computers as a matter of national policy, Pat Choate (1982) argued that microtechnologies "are making millions of existing jobs obsolete" (p. 3). His report was written only for congressional representatives from states then experiencing technological transformations, but its findings were widely circulated in daily newspapers. Other newspaper headlines have noted that "worry grows over upheaval as technology reshapes jobs," with the observations that "computer-based technologies" will "mean wrenching change for many workers," that a computer " 'revolution' " is occurring " 'that will leave virtually no form of work unchanged,' " and that "the new technology will radically change what will be required of workers and will contribute to economic disarray" (Serrin, 1982, p. 1). When confronted with such news reports, fear would seem to be one of several reasoned responses, particularly when such reports conclude that "there are no definitive answers," "little research has been done," and "there are some fears that the nation lacks the knowledge to make informed policy decisions or even the ability fully to explore the matter" (cited in Serrin, 1982, p. 1). Policies may certainly have to be reconsidered if these fears are substantiated, and we will explore the dimensions that such reconsiderations may involve. In any event, for some, the fear of computers cannot really be perceived as a phobia or unreasoned fear. For one likely to be displaced by a computer or automated robot in the workplace, the personal computer may not seem a welcome addition in one's home. At the same time, such descriptions reinforce a computer-power association, making it difficult to ignore computers wherever they exist.

Interpersonal Relationships: Computer Friendships

We have already discussed several aspects of computers' actual and potential impact on friendships. We pointed out that users report that computer friendships are being formed on local bulletin boards throughout the United States. There is reason to believe that 30 percent of the messages left on these systems are interpersonal (Chesebro, 1985, p. 218). Similarly, on task-oriented or professional networks, as we noted in chapter 4, researchers have observed that network links are frequently used to make new friends. Others have reported that the heavy users are most likely to employ the computer networks for social purposes.

In the media, computer networks have increasingly been cast as potential sources and opportunities for interpersonal relationships. Computer networks offering dating or match-making services have received most of the attention. However, other media reports have noted the more diverse interpersonal functions that these computer networks serve. Indeed, one reporter described the networks as "a social system," "an entire society on-line . . . a town, a club, a clique, a fantasy work, a dating service . . . or anything one wants it to be" (Carpenter, 1983, pp. 9, 11).

In terms of the fantasy-theme, chaining-out process, the descriptions we have of computer networks cast them as positive environments serving important social functions or associated them with the achievement of social needs and objectives. Even if users do not actually use computer networking, computers are described as creating an option for social contacts. For those contemplating the purchase of a computer and for those with an emerging interest in computer use, the social functions linked to networking may constitute an additional motive or rationale for conceiving of computers as useful technologies. The issue here is not whether computer networking actually creates a social network or computer contacts function as interpersonal communication or computer networking is a desirable and healthy form of interpersonal communication. The issue turns on a question of perceived association or image. Regardless of what the "facts" may be, mass-media systems have increasingly cast computers as devices that create new social options for computer users.

The Social Structure: The "Electronic-Cottage" Thesis

In chapter 6, we underscored the educational, artistic, medical, recreational, and informational advantages of possessing a home computer center. Yet, in chapters 1 and 5, we also noted that such systems may isolate people, diminish the emotional gratification of human relationships, and require that conscious attention be paid to other ways of dealing with people. These social features of using computers constitute a sort of balance sheet of what increasing computerization is going to mean to us. The balance sheet says in effect that the use of computers, including personal computers, will promote efficiency at the expense of social contact.

The home communication system has been of concern to many. Joseph Deken has been one of the foremost advocates of such systems. His best-selling book, *The Electronic Cottage: Everyday Living with Your Personal Computers in the 1980s* (1982), provided one of the first popular descriptions of the home computer center and a reasoned analysis, bolstered by the author's commitment and enthusiasm, justifying the home computer center. Deken specified his reasons for advocating the development of a comprehensive and coherent home communication system, but he also recognized the social limitations of a comprehensive personal-computer system. He argued, for example, that "the more powerful computers become, the more disastrous will be the human consequences of letting them get out of control" (p. 14). The greatest of these dangers, in Deken's view, would be when computers "are consciously directed by one human against another, or when computer systems are recklessly given a great deal of power" without adequate " 'fail-safe' controls for human monitoring and takeover when necessary" (p. 15). He also suggested that computer users must critically examine the results of computer analyses as well as avoid excessive dependency upon and addiction to computers.

Yet, comprehensive home computer systems have been most consistently and persistently described as the "wave of the future." Early visionaries usually viewed the home computer as a foundation for a communication system that, by allowing people to remain at home and "communicate" to work, would also allow them to live wherever they wished and would ultimately eliminate traffic jams, urban congestion, overcrowding, and air pollution. Employing a more rational style, Deken (1982, p. 307) has also extended these visions.

In practice, however, telework has failed to produce these results. On balance, we know that people prefer to work with other people; human contact has remained a primary objective even when telework options have been created. However, the research findings outlining these cautions have not attracted the public attention that Deken's book has. The computer is predominantly perceived as a technology capable of restructuring the social system. In this vision, the home computer can reestablish the home as the primary unit of the American culture, reinforce family links, resolve urban issues and conflicts, and function as an efficient and useful means for satisfying employment obligations.

The Legal System: Privacy and Deciphering

Beyond the attractive role computers are said to play in personal life, computer terminologies and issues have also begun to enter the legal system, which has provided sanctions for certain computer activities and issued prohibitions against others. These legal actions are reported in the press almost daily. In one of the first of these legal actions, the *New York Times* reported, for example, that Hitachi pleaded guilty to the theft of IBM computer designs and agreed to pay $540,000 for the information it had received ("Hitachi Guilty," 1983; also see Pollack, 1983, November; Pollack, 1984, July). Particularly before computer trespassing laws had been formulated (Gargan, 1984; Greenhouse, 1986), the media repeatedly publicized cases in which computer hackers had been indicted for the destruction of property, fraud, and the invasion of privacy when entering and altering computer files maintained by various corporations and institutions (see, e.g., Baris, 1988; Burnham, 1984; "Laws in U.S.," 1983; Lewis, 1987).

Regardless of their merits, these cases have established that computer behaviors can be assessed within a legal context. Computer terminologies have, in Bormann's terms, "chained out" and affected the legal system, producing new definitions of legal and illegal behaviors.

The legal actions have linked computers with a new family of power terms, a set of power terms associated with control, regulation, and restraint. While not positive for most people, these legal associations reinforce the significance of computer activities.

Some of the legal decisions have potentially profound societal implications, particularly in terms of the right to privacy. Court decisions have sanctioned computers as legitimate detection and investigation devices. Computers have become powerful detection and investigation technologies within our society in part because they have been "endorsed" by the legal system. As legal investigative tools employed by the government, computers are further associated with the emergence of an "all-knowing" government. In these cases, computers may not be positively perceived, but they gain significance as legitimate instruments of the powerful. Privacy cases before the courts illustrate many of the issues that have contributed to this image of the computer within our society.

As a point of departure, we initially observe that computerized interceptions have been legally sanctioned as an investigative tool of certain government agencies. Computer interceptions gain significance because corporations and government agencies have persistently abused the right to privacy. The abuses may not be illegal, but they nonetheless have diminished the right and scope of privacy available to every American. The issue became especially clear when the United States Court of Appeals for the Sixth Circuit ruled that the National Security Agency could lawfully intercept through electronic and computerized means *all* overseas calls made by Americans, regardless of whether or not the agency suspected illegal activities. The court specifically noted that these "taps" did not constitute "unreasonable searches and seizures" and that the National Security Agency could transmit to and store within the Federal Bureau of Investigation's computers the information derived from these interceptions (see, e.g., Burnham, 1983; Burnham, 1983, March).

Because this information is gathered by a national security agency, access to it is exceedingly difficult. Moreover, the quality of the information derived from these interceptions is suspect. The Office of Technology Assessment (cited in Slade & Biddle, 1982), a research branch of Congress, estimated at the end of 1982 that "almost half" of the records kept by the FBI were "incomplete or inaccurate" (p. E7). When one considers that the number of central processing units within the federal bureaucracy has increased from 11,305 in 1980 to 26,682 in 1985, not including the hundreds of thousands of word processors that store more personal information ("More Mainframe Computers," 1988), it becomes clear that verification of the information derived from or maintained in computers becomes almost impossible. As Benjamin H. Alexander (1983) has so eloquently observed in a speech delivered on December 7, 1982, and later printed in *Vital Speeches of the Day*, "Most of this information is cold, hard, unexpurgated, one-dimensional data that may or may not be accurate. Much of it is inaccessible to the individual, and there is no certain way to verify or challenge its accuracy, in most cases" (p. 187). The point is thus particularly clear. Computer abuses are a consistent feature of computer use; it is not unreasonable to assume that abuses are common rather than exceptional.

While some groups' use of computers as investigative tools has been sanctioned, others have not been granted equivalent legal protection. Personal-computer users are particularly susceptible to invasions of privacy. Existing and emerging technologies are far outstripping our ability to protect computer information (Broad, 1983, April; Broad, 1983, September; Fialka, 1985; Markoff, 1988, June 5). As personal computers become popular within the American home, these problems will be aggravated. As the personal computer becomes the vehicle for carrying out an increasing number of activities, users subject themselves to an increasing number of monitoring systems in at least three different ways.

First, records of transactions can be sold by those providing information services and products. We suggested the ways in which a personal computer might be employed to shop and to bank electronically, to function as a method for receiving newspapers, magazines, and other forms of information, and for making travel and entertainment reservations. In all of these cases, once the services are electronically requested and received, the information agencies or cable-television systems providing the services possess records of the transactions. In his tenure as attorney general of Connecticut, Joseph I. Lieberman (1983) pointedly noted, "If you are overdrawn on your checking account, the cable company will know it. If you like to watch soft-core pornography, it will know that, too" (p. A21). The records of computerized transactions can be sold or exchanged much as mailing lists are today. Even though some states prohibit sale of such information (very few do), the information can still be privately exchanged. In sum, the current management of electronic records of all personal-computer transactions creates possibilities for abuse of the privacy rights of computer users.

Second, technological devices exist for eavesdropping on computer manipulations, even on those carried out within the privacy of one's home. A host of these devices can be used, but a spectrum analyzer is an excellent example of surveillance mechanisms. A spectrum analyzer decodes the radio-frequency signals of certain electronic equipment. Every computer constantly and inadvertently emits radio waves when it operates, and the radio-wave signals change as each function is executed. For example, striking the letter *a* will produce a signal quite different from that of *s*. The spectrum analyzer decodes these radio-frequency signals. The signals can be picked up from the screen, chassis, wiring, or power lines. In smaller computers, the signals are cleaner, and only a room lined with copper will prevent leakage. Thus, even if a personal-computer user employs the computer only for data storage within the home, that stored information is technologically susceptible to access by others.

Third, virtually any code used to prevent access to a computer file can be broken. If one person can gain access to a computer file, anyone can. The power of decipherers has been vividly and repeatedly illustrated. They receive the most attention when a code breaker enters a banking system and electronically transfers funds to a personal account. When one considers that banks electronically "move" some $300 billion every day (Samuelson, 1985, p. 73), one begins to appreciate the energy that has to be devoted to prevent deciphering. Yet even the code devised by Stanford University, one involving a branch of mathematics known as complexity theory and estimated to take 1 million years to decipher, was cracked within 5 years. In covering this deciphering event in an October 1982 issue of *Time*, Philip Faflick, Russell Leavitt, and Marlin Levin noted that the case raised "questions about whether computers can ever be made to keep their secrets" (p. 88). Edward H. Currie (cited in "Battling the Computer Pirates," 1983), who was then president of a software firm, bluntly said that they could not: "As fast as you can think up a new code, someone else can break it" (p. D1). Deciphering is now a science; virtually any computer is susceptible to access.

From a larger perspective, a political issue may be involved. Certain groups have been granted the legal right to employ computers for detection and investigation purposes, which violates the right to privacy. Other computer users face potential invasions of privacy without clear forms of legal protection. Given this apparent imbalance, some may argue that it is appropriate to consider comprehensive policies to correct it. Our main point here, however, is that computer activities now function within a legal context. More precisely stated in Bormann's words, computer terminologies and issues have clearly "chained out" and now affect a major societal institution, the legal system.

The Economic System: "Computer Economics"

Computers have been linked to the American economic system predominantly through a series of fantasies that creates a vision of a future in which computers are a potentially decisive economic force affecting all dimensions of the country's economy. In one scenario, computer firms are an emblem of the American economy. Cast as a coherent industry, the "high-tech industry," computer firms are said to represent the ingenuity, creativity, and competitive spirit that has defined traditional American economic initiatives. The enemy in this scenario is Japan, and the victory sought is control of the international computer market. The struggle is aptly illustrated in the effort to control the market for computer memory chips, a $2-billion-a-year industry. Published in the *New York Times*, Montgomery Securities' analysis of the international computer-chip market (cited in Markoff, 1988, September, pp. D1, D10) reinforces this fantasy:

Computer Memory Chips

Size of Chips in RAMS	United States' Share of the Market (%)	Japan's Share of the Market (%)
1K	95	5
4K	84	15
16K	57	40
64K	29	70

The futuristic nature of the fantasy is reflected in Edward A. Fiegenbaum and Pamela McCorduck's *The Fifth Generation* (1983). They have argued that the emerging fifth generation of computers will be dominated by Japan. The subtitle of their book, *Artificial Intelligence and Japan's Computer Challenge to the World*, reveals the kind of impact they expect. In Feigenbaum and McCorduck's vision, this "struggle" can be "won" only if the United States developed a comprehensive national policy in which computer research and development become its primary economic priorities. Continued into 1987, the scenario repeats itself, with some modifications: "In the trade dispute with Japan over computer chips, the real issue," which "has rarely been what it seemed," is "the role that Japan will play in the American economy in the 1990's" (Sanger, 1987, March; also see Pollack, 1986, September 30; Prokesch, 1987).

A related economic fantasy emerges in assessments of the competitive nature of computer firms within the United States. In this scenario, antitrust efforts have been evaluated as a mechanism to prevent the development of *de facto* monopolies in the manufacture and distribution of both mainframe and personal computers. At the same time, these monopolistic tendencies are weighed against how effectively the United States can compete in international computer markets. In this scenario, IBM is a constant presence, frequently functioning as a symbol of the ideal American corporation (Mc-Dowell, 1983; Sanger, 1984, June). IBM's share of the mainframe-computer market had increased from 70 percent in 1967 to more than 80 percent by the end of the 1970s (Pollack, 1983, March). During the first half of the 1980s, IBM continued to control 80 percent of the mainframe market, a share characterized as an indication of "unmistakable aggressiveness" but also of a "lessening of competition" in the computer industry (Pollack, 1985, January).

Similarly, IBM has occupied an increasingly important role in the manufacturing and distribution of personal computers. In 1981, IBM controlled only 1.9 percent of the personal-computer market. By 1983, IBM accounted for 21 percent of personal-computer sales. Moreover, during 1983, three computer manufacturers for the first time accounted for 50 percent of all personal-computer sales; in 1981, these firms had accounted for only 39 percent of the personal-computer market (Pollack, 1983, March; also see Pollack, 1985, January). In 1987, IBM was again cast as an aggressive but monopolistic force in the personal-computer market when its share of this market increased to 25 percent (Sanger, 1987, February 24). Concern centers around the fact that once a major firm, such as IBM, gains a controlling interest in a market, its economic base allows it to temporarily reduce prices, which forces less financially secure firms out of the market.

Yet what would appear to be an undeniable monopoly has been "assessed" in ways that ultimately justify it in terms of other economic considerations. The analysis offered by Franklin M. Fisher, John J. McGowan, and Joan E. Greenwood in *Folded, Spindled, and Mutilated: Economic Analysis and U.S. v. IBM* (1983) identified some of the ways in which the IBM monopoly has been assessed. They noted that the Justice Department has engaged IBM in legal actions, but they also noted that the prosecutions, which involved years of litigation and millions of dollars, ultimately concluded without even a clear definition of competition or a monopoly. In the case of IBM, the Justice Department finally assumed the rather unusual, if not contradictory, position that IBM's monopoly had produced better products at lower prices. The government failed to focus on the innovative advantages that emerge in a competitive market. Whether intended or not, the outcome has left one firm, IBM, as the dominant corporate entity in the United States computer industry, a result that provided a corporate force and mechanism for securing the larger future vision governing the economic conception of the computer industry in the United States and in the world.

We have already considered a related fantasy regarding employment in a "computer economy" when we considered computerphobia. We do not wish to duplicate that analysis here, but it is appropriate to suggest how these two fantasies are related. Computerphobia frequently stems from the fears and anticipated dislocations that may occur as the economy shifts from an industrial to an information-based system. A dominant theme of the analyses of both computerphobia and corporate monopoly has been that a price must be paid for progress, although interim adjustment programs are also advocated to ease the hardships of the transformation.

In this context, the computer industry begins to affect the educational system. Computer-related economic dislocations have thus been cast as affecting all levels of the educational system and retraining programs. As we outlined in some detail in chapter 6, educational training and retraining programs have been cast as a solution, often a permanent solution, to the dislocations created by economic consequences of computerization.

Beyond creating a computer-education link, this fantasy also seems to imply, if not require, a redefinition of the nature of work itself. In an information-based economy, an entirely new cluster of employment issues is created. As the anticipated number of workstations reaches 17.5 million by 1990, the nature of many data-entry jobs has been negatively assessed. As experienced keypunchers have frequently noted, data-entry work is often extremely dull and menial. It may be necessary to introduce appropriate work breaks and physical comforts into employment environments to counter the notion that computerized work experience can be demoralizing (Bonsall, 1984).

Moreover, as new technologies are introduced, downward pressure is exerted on the wage scales of those working in jobs susceptible to immediate automation. In these cases, those already experiencing employment discrimination, such as women, are more likely to face these pressures. Some critics of the technological age have already coined the term *electronic sweatshop* to dramatize these working conditions (Pollack, 1982, October; Reinhold, 1984, January; Serrin, 1984). We anticipate a series of fantasies that deals more directly with these issues.

In all of these ways, the computer-economy fantasy has spun out, manifesting itself in a host of international and national arenas, and, as several of these linkages indicate, some of these associations have been pointedly negative, as with such references as the electronic sweatshop. Moreover, computer-related industries have not always been associated with increasing levels of productivity. In 1987 the *New York Times* published an article headlined "Services Hurt by Technology: Productivity Is Declining" (Schneider, 1987), and in 1988 the *Wall Street Journal* published a similar article entitled "Service Industries Find Computers Don't Always Raise Productivity" (Wessel, 1988). These associations, although negative, continue to reinforce the link between the U.S. economy and computers, a link made stronger by those who seek to reverse the negative image associated with the economic effects of computers. James Brian Quinn, Jordan J. Baruch, and Penny Cushman Paquette (1987), for example, have predicted great things for the computer economy:

> The technologies that are now transforming the service industries have profound implications for U.S. manufacturing, economic stability and growth, for national and regional job markets and for the position of the U.S. in world politics and international competition. Perhaps more important for the future is the fact that technology, properly applied, can enhance productivity, quality and economic output in the services sector just as it has in manufacturing. This means that a U.S. economy dominated by services can continue to support real increases in income and wealth for a very prolonged period. (p. 50)

It appears clear that computers have now been linked to the economic system of the United States. As Bormann might put it, computer terminologies have "spun out" and been employed to create symbolic links with the American economic system. The rhetoric establishing this association is, admittedly, often a futuristic conception, but the link has at least cast computer activities as a currently powerful economic force. Moreover, rather than diminishing the power of the computer-economy fantasy, the futuristic component may in fact enhance it by providing a new direction, a novel set of goals to be achieved, or a new future for what many people feel is a sluggish American economic system.

The Political System: "Computer Politics"

Computer specialists, particularly corporate executives in computer industries, have also explicitly sought to forge an association between computers and politics. The effort has been to establish national priorities and developmental goals that are linked to computer activities. The ideal within this fantasy is the establishment of a national information act whose objectives would be similar to those of the 1946 Full Employment Act, which established full employment as an economic objective in the United States. Although a national information act might only be a formal statement of objectives, the act, like its earlier counterpart, would establish formal recognition and a set of standards for evaluating the information economy as well as a formal set of issues that could be assessed and fully debated. Without such a formal statement of goals, we are told, a set of haphazard economic policies is likely to replace a more coherent understanding of where we are going as a nation and why. Once computerization is recognized as a political issue or a foundation for realizing the goals that regulate the Information Society, actions must also, in this fantasy, be taken to realize these objectives.

This computer-political fantasy has emerged in a number of different situations. One occurred in October 1982, when a report written by 15 of the most prominent members in the disciplines of mathematics, physics, and computer science was jointly released by the National Science Foundation and the Department of Defense (cited in Pollack, 1982, October 28). The report warned that the United States is "seriously undermined" in the development of "supercomputers" (p. D9). The report further warned that there was "little likelihood" that the United States would lead in the development of these computers "under current conditions" (p. D9). The panel concluded by calling for a "national program" that would provide financial and commercial incentives for the development of these computers, increase access to supercomputers, improve training of personnel, and increase research on new machines and the software related to supercomputers (p. D9).

Computer manufacturers have similarly called for a "national high-tech policy." Led by such firms as Intel Corporation, Hewlett-Packard, and Systems Industries, to name but a few, these proposals are for a high-tech policy that would include a national commitment (not unlike that made during the *Sputnik* era) to provide adequate scientific and mathematical training in elementary and secondary schools, to institute tax incentives for research and development and new capital formations (essential to the development of the supercomputer), to allow development of a "free-trade" international market, to carefully regulate high-tech exports, to permit temporary suspension of anti-trust policies in research and development to allow for a coherent computer policy similar to Japan's, and to provide increased federal funding of university research related to computer development (Pollack, 1983, February).

Computers have also been cast as a "political right" whose denial constitutes a form of "information discrimination." In this view, the United States has become a society in which the majority of work is related to information processing and in which the substance of work itself becomes information. To withhold access to the tools that promote information constitutes a form of discrimination. In his much-publicized "maiden address" to the Senate, Frank R. Lautenberg (cited in Perlez, 1983) argued that the electronic media are creating the "potential for new and distressing divisions in our society" (p. B1). Senator Lautenberg reported that 70 percent of wealthy school districts had microprocessors, while 60 percent of poor schools did not. Senator Lautenberg's conclusion: "In an age that demands computer literacy, a school without a computer is like a school without a library" (p. B22). To avoid such a social division, Lautenberg argued, a national policy is required to equalize these differences.

We can also envision extensions of this "information-discrimination" fantasy, for information discrimination might also be said to operate in a host of less overt ways. Insofar as only middle- and upper-class homes are able to purchase personal computers, those in low-income families will lack an initial exposure to the computer. These economic differences could also be said to reinforce racial differences, thereby casting information discrimination as an implicit form of racism (see, e.g., Bonsall, 1984). Information discrimination against women might also be alleged. Insofar as video games are designed to appeal to teenage boys, girls are discouraged from exposure to computers, and insofar as most word-processor operators are women, they are more susceptible than men to electronic-sweatshop conditions, a form of "technosexism" in Leveen's (1983) view.

A computer-political connection has also been used in assessing international politics. In this view, the United States is cast as part of an international context, as influenced by and responding to the actions of other nations. Other nations are viewed as important sources of the raw resources, imports, personnel, and information required to sustain the American economy and way of life. These complex ties among nations have fostered the development of multinational corporations based in the United States but tied through complex interrelationships to industrialists in other nations.

In this fantasy, the global web of interconnected corporate relationships requires a constant flow of communication. This information includes essential exchanges regarding inventories, personnel records, and financial data. Data banks must be monitored on a daily, if not constant, basis. Such surveillance is essential to the multinational corporate structure, and telecommunication computers, connected by telephone lines or satellites, serve as the vehicles creating this "global village." Multinational corporations are thus already computer-dependent. Their complex economic systems presuppose that a rapid transfer of computerized information can occur across national borders, now commonly identified as "transborder data flows" (Wigand, Shipley & Shipley, 1984).

In this scenario, the United States is especially dependent on this international computer communication system. To sever the computer links of multinational corporations would eliminate much of the economic base of the United States. American-based multinationals account for 80 percent of all data processing performed worldwide (Sanger, 1983, p. F26), and the National Telecommunications and Information Administration of the Department of Commerce (cited in

Sanger, 1983) has warned that any restrictions on the flow of this information could produce "catastrophic" effects on the long-term development of the American economy (p. F26).

Increasingly, the information transferred through such computer links, we are told, is being perceived by other nations as a "commodity," "product," or "entity" whose intrinsic value can be measured, taxed, and restrained to protect national self-interests. In some cases, the restrictions are cast as reasonable. For example, the Organization for Economic Cooperation and Development's guidelines for the 1980s (cited in Sanger, 1983) prevent the transmission of personal information to any jurisdiction that fails to guard against its unauthorized use (p. F26). In other cases, restrictions on transborder data flows are cast as destructive to the interests of the United States. For example, recent actions taken by Brazil have been cast as political. In order to ensure that local equipment and labor are employed, Brazil has required that computer bases be established within its borders (rather than allowing use of existing data bases in other nations) and that compatible Brazilian software be employed whenever possible (Riding, 1985). Other restrictions on transborder data flow, such as those initiated by West Germany, Canada, and France, have also been cast as political acts. France has proposed that the intrinsic value of the informational context of computer links, and not just the computer medium, be taxed. The retail value of a computer program, rather than just the quantity of plastic involved in the production of a computer disk, would be estimated and taxed (Sanger, 1983, p. F1). A host of problems are associated with this proposal (what, for example, is the value of a government memo?); nonetheless, such proposals illustrate the kind of actions that can be viewed as computer-related political actions in an international environment. These are the kinds of actions that led the National Telecommunications and Information Administration to forecast "catastrophic" consequences for the United States.

The official policy of the United States has been to endorse a free flow and exchange of information, yet even such a seemingly reasonable policy can be viewed as a profoundly political conception. A free flow of information can be cast as working against the self-interests and potential gains of other nations. In dealing with transborder data flows, a clear majority of the world's governments have, in fact, perceived information as a commodity to be regulated much as any other import or export is controlled. The breadth as well as the complexity of prospects arising from this attitude are suggested in a resolution adopted by the United Nations General Assembly on December 10, 1982 ("Text of U.N. Document," 1982). The resolution held that "activities in the field of international direct television broadcasting by satellite should be carried out in a manner compatible with the sovereign rights of states" (p. 6; for an overview and context for these issues, see Martelanc, 1982). The principle implies that each nation may regulate the flow of electronic information from space.

In all of these ways, efforts have been made to establish a computer-political connection. Fantasies that promote this connection are easily identified, yet, at this time, it is unclear if the fantasies have "chained out" and become part of the national rhetoric of the United States. Certainly, direct efforts are underway to achieve this end, and the agents involved in this campaign appear to possess both the means and the conviction necessary to succeed in their rhetorical effort. As we assess these forces, we would not be surprised to see the computer-political association become a dominant mode of communication in the United States.

There are many reasons why computers have become an important component of the personal life of Americans. We remain convinced that one of the factors that have contributed to Americans' current attitudes about computers stems from the way in which these machines have been discussed. Computers have not been described as mere tools. The terminologies employed to describe computers have consistently cast computers as agencies of power. These discussions have simultaneously related computer activities to an increasing number of different spheres of human action. They have been cast as agencies capable of altering individual psychological orientations, interpersonal relationships, family structures, and the American legal, economic, and political systems. As a result, computers now command respect. Any decision to ignore computers would now seem to challenge an entire way of understanding the transformation of the American system. It seems to us that only a few would be willing to undertake such a challenge.

Computing and Ideology

In our view, the fantasies linking computers to the American way of life are not randomly related. In a general fashion, the links can be viewed as suggesting that the computerization of America is a struggle against agents who would deny progress and the requirements of life in the 21st century. The rhetorics creating these links are unified, at the least, by their common use of power terminologies and references. Moreover, the power terms used to associate the computer with the groups and social systems identified earlier bear certain characteristic relationships with each group or system. A formal statement of these relationships would generate the following "equations":

Psychological Orientation = Hedonistic Power
Interpersonal Relationships = Social Power
The Social Structure = Organizational Power
The Legal System = Regulatory Power
The Economic System = Material Power
The Political System = Institutional Power

Beyond the use of power terms, the fantasies we have discussed also possess a unifying substantive coherence or logic. The coherence begins to emerge if we recall that it is the computer, a technology, that has been associated with these power terms. In this sense, the rhetorical scheme we have been discussing is designed to infuse technology with power. It is a discourse that would create technological power. In a phrase, we have a "rhetoric of technological power."

Philosophically, an emphasis upon technology as a dominating force promotes a form of pragmatism. Kenneth Burke (1962, pp. 127–31) has explored this relationship, and he has argued that pragmatism, as a "philosophy of means" (p. 128), ultimately "prescribes the means necessary to the attainment of happiness" (p. 275). Burke detailed earlier pragmatic philosophies that have captured the human imagination, but he stated that the pragmatism of "modern science is *par excellence* an accumulation of new agencies (means, instruments, methods). And this locus of new power, in striking men's fancy, has called forth 'philosophies of science' that would raise agency to first place" over other competing philosophical orientations (p. 275).

In the context we have established, Burke's analysis suggests that, in a world of high technology, science is given a dominant place. As the extension of science, technology becomes the way in which individual psychic experiences are understood, social relationships are created, social structures are organized, and legal, economic, and political systems are governed. In other words, the computerization of America implies, philosophically, that human beings are to delegate their responsibility for action to science and technology. Science and technology are to become the new "religion" of 20th-century America.

The power of science in America has been repeatedly underscored, but personal computers have dramatically altered the power of science and technology. With the emergence of home computers, science and technology have now entered the personal lives of Americans. Computer terminologies have become a way of describing psychic, interpersonal, and social structures as well as legal, economic, and political institutions. The home computer is now, indeed, the personal computer.

This philosophical perspective provides the foundation for answering the 10 questions we raised at the end of chapter 1. As we close this last chapter, we return to these questions and offer our best responses as stimuli for the assessments of the reader, whom we encourage to mentally argue with us as we posit answers to these issues.

1. *Are we substituting a "paper and electronic reality" for the world of physical phenomena?* Yes. As the structure of the American economy shifts from a world of manufactured and crafted goods to a world of information processing and as the home increasingly merges an ever-increasing number of electronic media, our understandings of "what is" depend increasingly on what others pass on to us as information. In our view, we need to compensate for this tendency by pressing ourselves to explore a truly ecological balance among nature, the world of human goods, and relayed information about the world.

2. *Does the Information Society promote the use of isolated facts without a consideration of the political-cultural context in which these facts occur?* Yes. Search techniques encourage users to select independent facts and to create new patterns for the organization of these facts. The contexts of generated information are frequently ignored, for people are expected to generate knowledge by creating new patterns of existing information. In our view, overall patterns of social meaning are lost when isolated facts are readily and narrowly employed. In an even larger context, computers fundamentally change the meaning of knowledge itself. Massive quantities of data are slowly being defined as information and ultimately as knowledge, and the consumption of mass quantities of information is being equated with understanding. Knowledge is becoming a corporate product rather than an aspect of personal comprehension, utility, and growth.

3. *Are the Information Society and the use of the computer promoting a world of number?* Only temporarily. Computers are likely to become increasingly user friendly. As the fifth generation of computers emerges in the 1990s, we expect that these computers will function as sophisticated symbol manipulators. We believe that it is a mistake to expect that the values promoted by science and technology will always be associated with numeric analyses and anticipate that science and technology will become very sophisticated rhetorical agents invoking the most humane of concepts in support of the efficiency they promote.

4. *Are information and computer friendships replacing human interactions?* Yes. As personal computers become increasingly popular, we anticipate that personal-computer owners will engage in fewer human interactions than non-personal-computer owners.

5. *As people increasingly use computers, will they develop computer friendships, in which the electronic messages transmitted among people become the only basis for the friendships?* Yes. They

lack the physical intimacy of face-to-face friendships, but computer friendships, in our view, will function as powerful psychological relationships at least equal in the importance to many face-to-face contacts. We anticipate that relationships developed through computers will eventually be recognized as a significant form of interpersonal communication and also that an increasing number of people will view their computers as intimate social and emotional companions, a "social" development that will probably remain unadmitted until such relationships can no longer be avoided or ignored.

6. *As home computers are increasingly linked into all sectors of the economy, will there be sufficient privacy safeguards?* No. But we are not convinced that privacy will continue to be as strong a motivating force as it has been.

7. *Will computers displace other communication media?* No. As computer usage increases, computer technology should facilitate development of other media while reducing the real costs of their production and encouraging the use of other media, particularly those enabling human communication. We believe that these technologies will continue to multiply in number and forms and that they will continue to be employed to compensate for isolation and loneliness. In the long term, we anticipate that these technologies will not function as an adequate substitute for face-to-face communication. When this recognition occurs, we fully anticipate that it will constitute a profound cultural shock, which will in turn constitute a foundation for reassessment of the most basic notions regarding human communication.

8. *Will we rigorously test the information we receive from computers?* No. The mystery and aura surrounding the computer distract users from rigorous examination of the information and analyses it provides. Moreover, as the computer begins to manipulate symbolic information, thereby becoming more user friendly, the quality of computer information will become virtually impossible to verify.

9. *Does a computer create new social responsibilities?* Yes. The emergence of an Information Society is creating important problems whose resolution requires nothing less than the adoption of a national agenda. In our view, the most important social goal will initially be the elimination of information discrimination. Until all groups of people are guaranteed the right to information, we believe the primary social obligation of an Information Society will not be met. In the long run, the most difficult task before an Information Society will be to demonstrate that information can be used to attain humane objectives.

10. *Can we control our futures in a world of computers?* Human beings create technologies, but these technologies in turn control

their creators. Once technologies become our tools, we begin to operate in ways that allow us to maximize their use. Conscious attention to the nature and functions of these technologies can enable us to determine what the technologies will become and how they will be used, but such conscious attention is difficult to maintain. As personal and other computers become part of our life-styles, we may begin to accept as "natural" the ways in which they control human-computer interactions. In our view, only the most constant surveillance of the social uses and the social consequences of computers can ensure that we control our own destinies. We doubt that the burdens of analyzing and sometimes resisting computers' controls over behavior will be assumed by most of the population, although we hope that a dedicated band of advocates and dissenters will keep social and humanistic issues in the public eye. For most people the advantages of using computers will outstrip the conscious attention given to the consequences of these uses. Precisely because of this we expect information discrimination—in all of its possible forms—to become a new human-rights issue in legal arenas and also in interpersonal, social, and political activities.

Will all readers agree with our answers? We hope not. We would prefer that readers see our questions as open-ended problems that will continue to be with all of us. As new information emerges, all of us will probably change our minds about how the questions just posed should be answered.

Conclusion

We have come a long way in this book. In chapter 1, we argued for the existence of an Information Society in which computers function as a central element. In chapter 9, we asked the reader to remain constantly skeptical about the value of these computers and alert to the ways in which these technologies might enhance or diminish our development of humane attitudes, beliefs, and actions. We can offer no definitive solutions guaranteeing that we will retain and develop our humane activities. We are at the inception of a revolution, and each of us will individually decide—through conscious and deliberate efforts or through passive and conditioned responses—how this revolution will alter and shape our lives.

Bibliography

The bibliography contains references for all citations in the introduction and nine chapters. Because many readers will be new to the world of computers, the majority of the references are to readily available, popular, and nontechnical sources, and because we examine human responses to computer experiences, the references represent a wide range of reactions and perspectives—polemical, popular, specialized, political, educational, scientific, philosophical, moral, personal, technical, economic, and social.

Abelson, P. H. (1986). Instrumentation and computers. *American Scientist, 74,* 182.

Aborn, M. (1988). Machine cognition and the downloading of scientific intellect. *The Annals of the American Academy of Political and Social Science, 495,* 135–43.

Abraham, E., Seaton, C. T., & Smith, S. D. (1983, February). The optical computer. *Scientific American,* pp. 85–93.

Administration says burden of paperwork is now eased. (1984, February 12). *New York Times,* p. 35.

Adoni, H., Cohen, A. A., & Mane, S. (1985). Social reality and television news: Perceptual dimensions of social conflicts in selected life areas. In M. Gurevitch & M. R. Levy (Eds.), *Mass communication review yearbook* (Vol. 5, pp. 189–204). Beverly Hills, CA: Sage Publications.

Agostino, E., Terry, H., & Johnson, R. (1980). Home video recorders: Rights and ratings. *Journal of Communication, 30,* 28–35.

Aitken, J. E. (1985, November). *Microcomputer associations with interpersonal communication.* Paper presented at meeting of the Speech Communication Association, Denver, CO.

Alexander, B. H. (January 1, 1983). Impact of computers on human behavior: The future is not now. *Vital Speeches of the Day*, pp. 185–88.

Allen, T. J., & Hauptman, O. (1987). The influence of communication technologies on organizational structure: A conceptual model for future research. *Communication Research, 14*, 575–87.

All-time film rental champs [of U.S.-Canada market]. (1986, January 8). *Variety*, p. 26.

And still champion: Cray's chess computer. (1986, June 17). *New York Times*, p. C3.

Angeles, P. A. (1981). *Dictionary of philosophy*. New York: Barnes & Noble.

Angell, J. B., Terry, S. C., & Barth, P. W. (1983, April). Silicon micromechanical devices. *Scientific American*, pp. 44–55.

Appelbaum, J. (1983, January 16). Good news amid the gloom. *New York Times Book Review*, p. BR31.

Appelbaum, J. (1983, June 5). Cashing in on computers. *New York Times Book Review*, pp. BR39–40.

Appelbaum, J. (1983, September 4). Eyes on the mid-80s. *New York Times Book Review*, p. BR19.

Arenson, K. W. (1984, February 15). CBS, IBM, Sears join in videotex venture. *New York Times*, p. D4.

Arlen Communications, Inc. (1987, September 15). Personal computer information networks. *New York Times*, p. D1.

Art exhibition is the work of computer. (1983, February 6). [New York] *Daily News*, p. TSXQ2.

Asbell, B. (1984, February 26). Writer's workshop at age 5. *New York Times*, p. 64.

Ascione, F., & Chambers, J. (1985). *Video game behavior*. Paper presented at meeting of the Society for Research in Child Development, Toronto, Canada.

Asimov, I. (1985). *Robots and empire*. New York: Del Rey/Ballantine Books.

Atwan, R., Orton, B., & Vesterman, W. (Eds.). (1986). *American mass media: Industries and issues*. New York: Random House.

Auyash, S. (1984). Exploring the impact of technology on communication in medicine and health. *Communication Quarterly, 32*, 91–97.

Badre, A., & Shneiderman, B. (Eds.). (1982). *Directions in human computer interaction*. Norwood, NJ: Ablex.

Baker, R. (1985, February 10). The processing process. *New York Times Magazine*, p. 14.

Balajhy, E. (1987). Implications of artificial intelligence research for human-computer interaction in reading instruction. In D. Reinking (Ed.), *Reading and computers: Issues for theory and practice* (pp. 40–54). New York: Teachers College Press.

Baldwin, C. S. (1959). *Ancient rhetoric and poetic: Interpreted from representative works*. Gloucester, MA: Peter Smith.

Balestri, D. P. (1988, February). Softcopy and hard: Wordprocessing and writing process. *Academic Computing*, pp. 14–17.

Baris, J. G. (1988, February 21). Electronic watchdogs for computers. *New York Times*, p. F15.

Barnes, P. W. (1984, August 24). A risk for Federal Express. *New York Times*, pp. D1, D3.

Battling the computer pirates. (1983, January 5). *New York Times*, pp. D1, D7.

Beckson, K., & Ganz, A. (1975). *Literary terms: A dictionary* (rev. ed.). New York: Farrar, Straus & Giroux.

Beckwith, B. P. (1967). *The next 500 years: Scientific predictions of major social trends*. New York: Exposition Press

Begley, S., Carey, J., & Sawhill, R. (1983, February 7). How the brain works. *Newsweek*, pp. 40–47.

Belkin, L. (1983, November 13). Cramming by computer: New approach to SATS. *New York Times*, sec. 12, p. EDUC3.

Belkin, L. (1984, July 21). Computers cross-checking use of medicines. *New York Times*, pp. 1, 52.

Belkin, L. (1986, April 1). The crafting of a catalogue. *New York Times*, pp. D1, D5.

Bell, D. (1976). *The coming of the postindustrial society*. New York: Basic Books.

Bell is critical of computer fad. (1984, January 19). *New York Times*, p. D24.

Beniger, J. R. (1986). *The control revolution: Technological and economic origins of the information society*. Cambridge, MA: Harvard University Press.

Beniger, J. R. (1988). Information society and global science. *The Annals of the American Academy of Political and Social Science, 495*, 14–28.

Benjamin, R. L. (1970). *Semantics and language analysis*. Indianapolis, IN: Bobbs-Merrill.

Bennett, C. H., & Landauer, R. (1985, July). The fundamental physical limits of computation. *Scientific American*, pp. 48–56.

Bennett, R. A. (1983, December 7). Banking goes into the home. *New York Times*, p. D1.

Bennett, R. A. (1986, November 30). Pick a card, any card, every card. *New York Times*, sec. 3, pp. 1, 8.

Benton & Bowles. (1983, June 4). Pay-TV interest increasing. *TV Guide*, p. A–4.

Berg, E. N. (1984, December 16). One industry is cheered by rising postal costs. *New York Times*, p. E22.

Berg, E. N. (1987, September 9). Humanizing bank machines. *New York Times*, p. D8.

Berger, J. (1977). *Ways of seeing*. New York: Penguin.

Berger, P. L., & Luckmann, T. (1966). *The social construction of reality: A treatise on the sociology of knowledge*. Garden City, NY: Doubleday.

Bergmann, G., & Spence, K. (1951). Operationalism and theory construction. In M. H. Marx (Ed.), *Psychological theory* (pp. 56–57). New York: Macmillan.

Berleau, J., (1978). Computer science, computers, and education. *Impact of Science on Society, 28*, 269–74.

Berlo, D. (1960) *The process of communication*. New York: Holt, Rinehart & Winston.

Bertelsen, D. (1983). *Video games: The unknown cultural phenomenon*. Unpublished manuscript.

Biddle, W., & Slade, M. (1982, September 12). Tomorrow's unemployed. *New York Times*, sec. 4, p. E7.

Billboard. (1982, October 2). "Top-selling videogames," p. 14.

Bills offer protection for chips. (1984, June 11). *New York Times*, pp. D1, D5.

Blankenship, J. (1966). *Public speaking: A rhetorical perspective.* Englewood Cliffs, NJ: Prentice-Hall.

Blodgett, A. J., Jr. (1983, July). Microelectronic packaging. *Scientific American* pp. 86–96.

Blumenfeld, Y. (1982, July). Francis Crick. *Geo*, pp. 13–16.

Boffey, P. M. (1983, January 9). Panel warns of computer lag. *New York Times*, p. D6.

Bogan, C. (1984, November). Future u. *American Way*, pp. 71–74.

Boguslaw, R. (1965). *The new utopians: A study of system design and social change.* Englewood Cliffs, NJ: Prentice-Hall

Bonsall, D. G. (1984, March). *Employment transformations in a high-tech economy.* Paper presented at meeting of the Eastern Communication Association, Philadelphia, PA.

Boorstin, D. J. (1961). *The image: A guide to pseudoevents in America.* New York: Atheneum.

Bormann, E. G. (1972). Fantasy and rhetorical vision: The rhetorical criticism of social reality. *Quarterly Journal of Speech, 58*, 396–407.

Bormann, E. G. (1980). *Communication theory.* New York: Holt, Rinehart & Winston.

Bormann, E. G. (1985). *The force of fantasy: Restoring the American dream.* Carbondale: Southern Illinois University Press.

Bouchez, C. (1986, December 14). Prime-time spending. [New York] *Daily News*, New York Life, pp. 1, 6.

Bowden, B. V., Strachey, C., & Turing, A. M. (1953). Digital computers applied to games. In B. V. Bowden (Ed.), *Faster than light: A symposium on digital computing machines* (pp. 286–310). London: Sir Isaac Pitman & Sons.

Boyd, D. A. (1987). Home-video diffusion and utilization in Arabian gulf states. *American Behavioral Scientist, 30*, 554–55.

Broad, W. J. (1983, April 5). Every computer "whispers" its secrets. *New York Times*, pp. C1, C8.

Broad, W. J. (1983, September 25). Computer security worries military experts. *New York Times*, pp. 1, 40.

Broad, W. J. (1984, March 8). Digital revolution breeds smart new appliances. *New York Times*, pp. C1, C8.

Broad, W. J. (1984, August 7). Does genius or technology rule science? *New York Times*, pp. C1, C10.

Broad, W. J. (1985, May 22). Light may be key to new generation of fast computers. *New York Times*, pp. C1, C12.

Broad, W. J. (1988, February 16). Science can't keep up with flood of new journals. *New York Times*, pp. C1, C11.

Broadcasting. (1984). VCRs: Impacts on the film, television, and cable industries. In R. Atwan, B. Orton, & W. Vesterman (Eds.), *American mass media: Industries and issues* (3rd ed.), (pp. 406–13). New York: Random House.

Brockman, J. (1983, June 5). 26 million desktop home computers by 1986. *New York Times Book Review*, p. BR39.

Brodkey, H. (1985, November 24). Reading, the most dangerous game. *New York Times Book Review*, pp. 1, 44, 45.

Bronstein, S. (1985, October 6). A check-writing nation. *New York Times*, pp. F12, F13.

Brooke, J. (1984, September 23). The pros and cons of "computer commuting." *New York Times*, p. F15.

Brooks, G. (1984, October 3). "Magnetic resonance" advances a revolution in science of diagnosis. *Wall Street Journal*, pp. 1, 22.

Brown, E. (1984, January). Fear and lurking on CB simulator. *PC World*, pp. 182–91.

Brown, H. (1976). *Brain and behavior*. New York: Oxford University Press.

Browne, M. W. (1985, October 15). Robot with laser eyes takes lumbering first step. *New York Times*, pp. C1, C14.

Bulkeley, W. M. (1988, June 6). Computers failing as teaching aids: Heralded revolution falls short due to lack of machines, training. *Wall Street Journal*, p. 23.

Bunch, B. (Ed.). (1984). *The science almanac* (1985–86 ed.). Garden City, NY: Doubleday.

Burke, K. (1962). *A grammar of motives and a rhetoric of motives*. Cleveland, OH: World. (Originally published in 1945 and 1950)

Burke, K. (1965). *Permanence and change: An anatomy of purpose*. Indianapolis: Bobbs-Merrill. (Originally published in 1935)

Burke, K. (1973). *The philosophy of literary form: Studies in symbolic action* (3rd ed.). Berkeley: University of California Press. (Originally published in 1941)

Burnham, D. (1983). *The rise of the corporate state*. New York: Random House.

Burnham, D. (1983, March 27). The silent power of the NSA. *New York Times Magazine*, pp. 60–67.

Burnham, D. (1984, June 11). Survey outlines computer crimes. *New York Times*, p. A16.

Cable gets the word: Getting ready for videotex, teletext, and the interactive worlds beyond. (1981, June 1). *Cablevision*, pp. 233ff.

Capron, H. L., & Williams, B. K. (1982). *Computers and data processing*. Menlo Park, CA: Benjamin/Cummings.

Cardwell, D. S. L. (1972). *Turning points in western technology*. New York: Neale Watson.

Carpenter, T. (1983, September 6). Reach out and access. *The Village Voice*, pp. 8–11, 23.

Carroll, P. B. (1987, December 14). Computer firms step up efforts to make machines easier to use. *Wall Street Journal*, sec. 2, p. 27.

Carroll, P. B. (1988, June 20). The tough job of training computerphobic managers. *Wall Street Journal*, p. 17.

Case, D., & Daley, H. (1983). *Personal computers: The new academic medium*. Paper presented at meeting of the International Communication Association, Dallas, TX.

Cassette use beats sales of movie tickets. (1987, January 3). *TV Guide*, pp. A-1, A-32.

Cathcart, R., & Gumpert, G. (1985). The person-computer interaction: A unique source. *Information and behavior*, (Vol. 1, pp. 113–24). New Brunswick, NJ: Transaction Books.

Center for the Social Organization of Schools, Johns Hopkins University. (1985). *1985 survey*. Baltimore, MD: Author.

Chapanis, A. (1975, May). Interactive human communication. *Scientific American*, pp. 36–42.

Chapanis, A. (1976). *Human factors in teleconferencing systems: Final report.* Baltimore, MD: Johns Hopkins University. (ERIC Document Reproduction Service No. ED 163902).

Chemical Bank. (Undated). Introducing Pronto: The home information system from Chemical Bank (advertising brochure).

Chen, M. (1984). Computers in the lives of our children: Looking back on a generation of television research. In R. E. Rice (Ed.), *The new media: Communication, research, and technology* (pp. 269–86). Beverly Hills, CA: Sage Publications.

Chen, M. (1987). Gender differences in adolescents' uses of and attitudes toward computers. In M. L. McLaughlin (Ed.), *Communication yearbook 10* (pp. 200–216). Newbury Park, CA: Sage Publications.

Chesebro, J. W. (1982, October 9). *Media and cerebral technologies as communication futures.* Paper presented at meeting of the New York State Speech Communication Association, Syracuse, NY.

Chesebro, J. W. (1983, April). *Rhetorical implications of artificial intelligence.* Paper presented at the meeting of the Eastern Communication Association, Ocean City, MD.

Chesebro, J. W. (1984a). The media reality: Epistemological functions of media in cultural systems. *Critical Studies in Mass Communication, 1*, 111–30.

Chesebro, J. W. (1984b). The symbolic construction of social realities: A case study in the rhetorical criticism of paradox. *Communication Quarterly, 32*, 164–71.

Chesebro, J. W. (1985). Computer-mediated interpersonal communication. In B. D. Ruben (Ed.), *Information and behavior* (Vol. 1, pp. 202–22). New Brunswick, NJ: Transaction Books.

Chesebro, J. W. (1986). *Communication and computability: The case of Alan Mathison Turing.* Unpublished manuscript.

Chesebro, J. W. (1988). Computer science as a rhetoric. In B. D. Ruben (Ed.), *Information and behavior* (Vol. 2, pp. 74–91). New Brunswick, NJ: Transaction Books.

Chesebro, J. W., Foulger, D. A., Nachman, J. E., & Yannelli, A. (1985). Popular music as a mode of communication, 1955–82. *Critical Studies in Mass Communication, 2*, 115–35.

A chip that may open the way to the future. (1986, November 12). *New York Times*, p. D10.

Choate, P. (1982). *Retooling the American work force: Toward a national training strategy.* Washington, DC: Northeast-Midwest Institute.

Christensen, K. (1985, August 13). Home PC: People don't need it, but they fear life without it. *Wall Street Journal*, p. 35.

Cohen, A. A. (1987). Decision making in VCR rental libraries: Information use and behavior patterns. *American Behavioral Scientist, 30*, 495–508.

Cole, B. (1983, September). Computer languages. *Popular Computing*, pp. 80–151.

Cole, K. C. (1984, June). Kristina Hooper building bridges for the brain. *Discover*, pp. 74–80.

Computer clubs growing as hobbyists share data. (1986, July 24). *New York Times*, pp. C1, C10.

Computer education. (1985, September 23). *Wall Street Journal*, p. 33.

A computer in every home? (1987, May 31). *New York Times*, Guide to the personal computer, pp. 48–49.

Computerized system helps a paralyzed woman to walk. (1982, November 12). *New York Times*, p. A23.

The computer moves in. (1983, January 3). *Time*, pp. 12–40.

Computer rights stir legal snarl. (1983, July 5). *New York Times*, pp. A1, D5.

Computers as Poison [Special Issue]. (1984, December/1985, January). *Whole Earth Review*.

Computers: Digitising the Oxford Dictionary. (1986). *Inter Media, 14*, 2.

Computers: Focus on schools. (1982, November 23). *New York Times*, p. D1.

Computers' software found weak. (1982, April 20). *New York Times*, p. C4.

Comstock, G. (1980a). Television and its viewers: What social science sees. In G. C. Wilhoit & H. deBock (Eds.), *Mass communication review yearbook* (Vol. 1, pp. 491–507). Beverly Hills, CA: Sage Publications.

Comstock, G. (1980b). *Television in America*. Beverly Hills, CA: Sage Publications.

Condon, J. C., Jr. (1966). *Semantics and communication*. New York: Macmillan.

Connor, J. (1981, February). I compute—therefore I am. *Creative Computing*, pp. 56–60.

Consumer Price Index. (1988). *The 1988 information please almanac*. Boston, MA: Houghton Mifflin.

Cook, G. (1979). Rx for the maladies of health care: A medical revolution in the making. *The Futurist, 13*, 179–89.

Cook, P. (1984, May). Look homeward, (electronic) angel. *Science 84*, pp. 75, 78.

Cook, R. (1984, August). Operating systems. *Popular Computing*, pp. 111–14, 135–48.

Cook, S. (1984, January). Microsoft does windows. *PC World*, pp. 58–61.

Covering computer use in higher education [Special issue]. (1987, September). *Academic Computing*.

Cowell, A. (1982, September 13). Selling artificial intelligence. *New York Times*, pp. D1, D2.

Crawford, C. (1983, September). Why you should learn to program. *Popular Computing*, pp. 153–56.

Crichton, M. (1983). *Electronic life: How to think about computers*. New York: Alfred A. Knopf.

Crick, F. H. C. (1979). Thinking about the brain. In *The brain* (pp. 130–37). San Francisco, CA: W. H. Freeman.

Cuban, L. (1986). *Teachers and machines: The classroom use of technology since 1920*. New York: Teachers College Press.

Cuddon, J. A. (1984). *A dictionary of literary terms* (rev. ed.). New York: Penguin.

Cushman, D. P., & Cahn, D. D., Jr. (1985). *Communication in interpersonal relationships*. Albany: State University of New York Press.

Cytowic, R. E., & Wood, F. B. (1982). Synesthesia: 1. A review of major theories and their brain basis. *Brain and Cognition, 1*, 23–35.

Dahl, H. (1972). A quantitative study of a psychoanalysis. *Psychoanalysis and Contemporary Science, 1*, 237–57.

Dance, F. E. X., & Larson, C. E. (1976). *The functions of human communication: A theoretical approach*. New York: Holt, Rinehart & Winston.

Daniel, D. B., & Reinking, D. (1987). The construct of legibility in electronic reading environments. In D. Reinking (Ed.), *Reading and computers: Issues for theory and practice* (pp. 24–39). New York: Teachers College Press.

Daniels, T. D., & Frandsen, K. D. (1984). Conventional social-science inquiry in human communication: Theory and practice. *Quarterly Journal of Speech, 70*, 223–40.

Danko, W. D., & MacLachlan, J. M. (1983). Research to accelerate the diffusion of a new invention. *Journal of Advertising Research, 23*, 39–43.

Danowski, J. A. (1982). Computer-mediated communication: A network-based content analysis using CBBS conference. In M. Burgoon (Ed.), *Communication yearbook 6* (pp. 905–24). Beverly Hills, CA: Sage Publications.

Davis, B. (1985, June 10). Mechanical minds: Some firms try to put skills of key staffers in computer programs. *Wall Street Journal*, pp. 1, 15.

Davis, D., & Malone, M. (1984, May 14). Offices of the future. *Newsweek*, pp. 72–75.

Davis, K. (1983, August 26). Health care's soaring costs. *New York Times*, p. D2.

Deane, B. (1985, November 26). Electronic experts. *American Way*, pp. 73–76.

De Fleur, M. L., & Ball-Rokeach, S. (1983). *Theory of mass communication* (4th ed.). New York: David McKay.

Deken, J. (1982). *The electronic cottage: Everyday living with your personal computers in the 1980s*. New York: William Morrow.

DeVito, J. A. (1983). *The interpersonal communication book* (3rd ed.). New York: Harper & Row.

DIALOG Information Services. (1988, January). *DIALOG database catalog*. Palo Alto, CA: Author.

Dickerson, M. D., & Gentry, J. W. (1983). Characteristics of adopters and non-adopters of home computers. *Journal of Consumer Research, 10*, 225–35.

Directory of online databases. Santa Monica, CA: Cuadra Associates.

Dizard, W. P., Jr. (1985). *The coming information age: An overview of technology, economics, and politics* (2nd ed.). New York: Longman.

Dolnick, E. (1987, August 23). Inventing the future. *New York Times Magazine*, sec. 6, pp. 30–33, 41, 49, 59.

Douglas, J. D. (1969). The rhetoric of science and the origins of statistical social thought: The case of Durkheim's *Suicide*. In E. A. Tiryakian (Ed.), *The phenomenon of sociology* (pp. 44–57). New York: Appleton-Century-Crofts.

Dozier, D. M., Hellweg, S. A., & Ledingham, J. A. (1983). Implications of interactive cable systems: Reduced consumer contact. In R. N. Bostrom & B. H. Westley (Eds.), *Communication yearbook 7* (pp. 828–36). Beverly Hills, CA: Sage Publications.

Dozier, D. M., & Rice, R. E. (1984). Rival theories of electronic newsreading. In R. E. Rice (Ed.), *The new media: Communication, research, and technology* (pp. 103–27). Beverly Hills, CA: Sage Publications.

Dreyfus, H. L. (1979). *What computers can't do: The limits of artificial intelligence* (rev. ed.). New York: Harper & Row.

Drucker, P. F. (1959). *Landmarks of tomorrow*. New York: Harper & Row.

Dullea, G. (1983, January 10). New marital stress: The computer complex. *New York Times*, p. A17.

Dullea, G. (1985, March 4). Computers promote candor. *New York Times*, p. C12.

Dutton, W. H., Rogers, E. M., & Jun, S. (1987). Diffusion and social impacts of personal computers. *Communication Research*, *14*, 219–50.

Eckholm, E. (1984, October 2). Emotional outbursts punctuate conversations by computer. *New York Times*, pp. C1, C5.

Edersheim, P. (1985, July 23). Electronic mail hasn't delivered, but backers say it is on the way. *Wall Street Journal*, p. 35.

Educational Testing Service. (1988). *The nation's report card*. Princeton, NJ: Author.

Edwards, B. L., Jr. (1987). *Processing words: Writing and revising on a microcomputer*. Englewood Cliffs, NJ: Prentice-Hall.

Ehrenhalt, S. M. (1986, August 15). Work-force shifts in 80s. *New York Times*, p. D2.

Electronic Industries Association. (1988a). *Consumer electronics annual review*. Washington, DC: Author.

Electronic Industries Association. (1988b). *Consumer electronics: U.S. sales*. Washington, DC: Author.

Ellis, D. C., Weerber, W. S., & Fisher, B. A. (1978). Towards a systemic organization of groups. *Small Group Behavior*, *9*, 452–69.

Elton, Carey, J. (1983). Computerizing information: Consumer reactions to teletext. *Journal of Communication*, *33*, 162–73.

Encyclopaedia Britannica. (1988). *1988 Britannica world data/1988 Britannica book of the year*. Chicago, IL: Author.

Erisman, A. M., & Neves, K. W. (1987, October). Advanced computing for manufacturing. *Scientific American*, pp. 163–69.

Ernst, M. L. (1982, September). The mechanization of commerce. *Scientific American*, pp. 133–45.

Ernst, M. L. (1985). Electronics in commerce. In T. Forester (Ed.), *The information technology revolution* (pp. 336–49). Cambridge, MA: MIT Press.

Evangelista, P., & Tulman, S. (1984, March). *Macho machine: The rhetoric of pinball and video games*. Paper presented at meeting of the Eastern Communication Association, Philadelphia, PA.

Evans, C. (1979). *The micro millennium*. New York: Viking.

Fabun, D. (1968). *The dynamics of change*. Englewood Cliffs, NJ: Prentice-Hall.

Faflick, P., Leavitt, R., & Levin, M. (1982, October 25). Opening the "trapdoor knapsack." *Time*, p. 88.

Fallows, J. (1982, December 18). Help! I'm the captive of my home computer! (And I love it!). *TV Guide*, pp. 26–29.

Feder, B. J. (1985, January 31). Computer chip juggles tasks. *New York Times*, p. D2.

Feder, B. J. (1988, May 8). Computer helper: Software that writes software. *New York Times*, p. F5.

Feder, B. J. (1988, June 15). The drive to speed automation. *New York Times*, pp. D1, D8.

Feigenbaum, E. A., & McCorduck, P. (1983). *The fifth generation: Artificial intelligence and Japan's computer challenge to the world*. Reading, MA: Addison-Wesley.

Fialka, J. J. (1985, October 18). Study sheds light on vulnerability of computers to electronic spying. *Wall Street Journal*, p. 31.

Fildes, R., & Toffler, A. (1988, February 21). High tech's next twist. *New York Times*, sec. 3, p. F1.

Finn, T. A., & Stewart, C. M. (1986). From consumer to organizational videotex applications: Will videotex find a home at the office? In M. L. McLaughlin (Ed.), *Communication yearbook 9* (pp. 805–25). Beverly Hills, CA: Sage Publications.

First complete on-line encyclopedia. (1983, July). *Popular Computing*, pp. 26–27.

Fisher, F. M., McGowan, J. J., & Greenwood, J. E. (1983). *Folded, spindled, and mutilated: Economic analysis and U.S. v. IBM*. Cambridge, MA: MIT Press.

Fiske, E. B. (1982, April 4). Computers alter lives of pupils and teachers. *New York Times*, pp. 1, 42.

Fiske, E. B. (1983, September 8). Americans in electronic era are reading as much as ever. *New York Times*, pp. A1, B12.

Fiske, E. B. (1984, December 9). Schools' use of computers disappointing. *New York Times*, pp. 1, 80.

Fiske, E. B. (1984, December 11). School computers: Vision and reality. *New York Times*, p. B2.

Fiske, E. B. (1985, April 19). Educator assails computer "hype." *New York Times*, p. D19.

Fiske, E. B. (1985, May 12). Interview: Seymour Papert on computers. *New York Times*, pp. C1, C7.

Fiske, E. B. (1985, August 4). There's a computer gap and it's growing wider. *New York Times*, p. E8.

Fitter, M. J., & Cruickshank, P. J. (1983). Doctors using computers: A case study. In M. E. Sime & M. J. Coombs (Eds.), *Designing for human-computer communication* (pp. 239-60). New York: Academic Press.

Fitzgerald, J. (Speaker). (1984, May 31). "Local area networks," *Computer chronicles* [Television series]. Channel 21, WLIW (PBS), Garden City, NY, 6:00–6:30 PM EDT.

Fluegelman, A., & Hewes, J. (1983). *Writing in the computer age: Word-processing skills and style for every writer.* New York: Doubleday.

Foley, J. D. (1987, October). Interfaces for advanced computing. *Scientific American*, pp. 127–35.

Fowler, E. M. (1982, June 3). Drafting on a computer. *New York Times*, p. D2.

Fowler, E. M. (1983, September 7). Global public relations. *New York Times*, p. D20.

Fox, G. C., & Messina, P. C. (1987, October). Advanced computer architectures. *Scientific American*, pp. 67–74.

Freedman, A. M. (1982, May 9). When machines talk, business listens. *New York Times*, p. E9.

Friedman, D. (1974). *The little LISPer.* Palo Alto, CA: Science Research Associates.

Friedrich, O. (1983, January 3). Glork! a glossary for gweeps. *Time*, p. 39.

Friedrich, O. (1983, January 3). The computer moves in. *Time*, pp. 14–24.

Friendly, J. (1982, October 2). Study finds no mass market for newspapers on home TV. *New York Times*, p. 14.

From behind the silence, a mind edges forward. (1982, October 5). *New York Times*, p. C4.

Frude, N. (1983, December). The affectionate machine. *Psychology Today*, pp. 23–24.

Fuchs, I. R. (1983, March). BITNET—because it's time. *Perspectives in Computing*, pp. 16–27.

Gallup Organization. (1977, April). Leisure-time activities. *The Gallup Opinion Index*, pp. 14–15.

Gallup Organization. (1982, May). Relationship between television violence and crime. *The Gallup Report* (Report No. 200), p. 36. Princeton, NJ: Author.

Gallup Organization. (1983, April). *A Gallup study of consumer attitudes toward an interest in owning computers for the home.* Unpublished manuscript.

Gardner, H. (1983). *Frames of mind: The theory of multiple intelligence.* New York: Basic Books.

Gardner, H. (1985). *The mind's new science: A history of the cognitive revolution.* New York: Basic Books.

Gargan, E. A. (1984, June 10). Computer-tampering bill passes in Albany. *New York Times*, p. 50.

Gelernter, D. (1987, October). Programming for advanced computing. *Scientific American*, pp. 91–98.

George, F. H. (1977). *The foundations of cybernetics.* London: Gordon & Breach.

Gibb, G., Bailey, J., Lambirth, T., & Wilson, W. (1983). Personality differences between high and low electronic video-game users. *Journal of Psychology*, 114, 159–65.

Ginsberg, E. (1982, September). The mechanization of work. *Scientific American*, pp. 67–75.

Ginsberg, E., & Vojta, G. J. (1981, March). The service sector of the U.S. economy. *Scientific American*, pp. 48–55.

Giuliano, V. E. (1982, September). The mechanization of office work. *Scientific American*, pp. 149–64.

Glatzer, H. (1985, January 31). "Hitchhiker's" trip: From best seller to computer game. *Wall Street Journal*, p. 26.

Gleick, J. (1983, August 21). Exploring the labyrinth of the mind. *New York Times Magazine*, pp. 23–27, 83, 86–87, 100. See also Cowell (1982).

Gleick, J. (1986, August 24). Mathematicians finally log on. *New York Times*, p. E7.

Gleick, J. (1986, August 26). Machine beats man on ancient front. *New York Times*, pp. C1, C8.

Glossbrenner, A. (1983). *The complete handbook of personal-computer communications: Everything you need to go on-line with the world.* New York: St. Martin's.

Goleman, D. (1983, February). The electronic Rorschach. *Psychology Today*, pp. 36–43.

Goleman, D. (1986, April 22). Investigations of the brain finding clues to the mind. *New York Times*, pp. C1, C7.

Goncharoff, K. (1984, November 18). Bulletin boards go electronic. *New York Times*, pp. LI1, LI33.

Goncharoff, K. (1985, March 24). Telecommuters say there's no workplace like home. *New York Times*, pp. 35, 38.

Gottlieb, A. M. (1986, January 5). Computer-literacy race: A global printout. *New York Times*, Winter Education Survey, sec. 12, pp. 67–68.

Graham, N. (1979). *Artificial intelligence: Making machines "think."* Blue Ridge Summit, PA: Tab Books.

Gratz, R. D., & Salem, P. J. (1984). Technology and the crisis of self. *Communication Quarterly, 32*, 98–103.

Greenberg, B. S., & Heeter, C. (1987). vcrs and young people: The picture at 39 percent penetration. *American Behavioral Scientist, 30*, 509–21.

Greene, B., (1983, October 26). A plaintive wail for mail. [New York] *Daily News*, p. 29.

Greenfield, P. M. (1984). *Mind and media: The effects of television, video games, and computers.* Cambridge, MA: Harvard University Press.

Greenhouse, S. (1985, March 15). Bally diversification pays off. *New York Times*, pp. D1, D17.

Greenhouse, S. (1986, June 1). The wiretapping law needs some renovation. *New York Times*, p. E4.

Greer, W. R. (1986, August 7). Remote controller, *New York Times*, p. C2.

Gregg, R. B. (1984). *Symbolic inducement and knowing: A Study in the foundations of rhetoric.* Columbia: University of South Carolina Press.

Guillen, M. A. (1983, December). The test of Turing. *Psychology Today*, pp. 80–81.

Gulino, S. J. (1982, May 9). How the computer fails the course. *New York*

Times, sec. 11, p. 22.

Gumpert, G., & Cathcart, R. (Eds.). (1986). *Inter/media: Interpersonal communication in a media world* (3rd ed.). New York: Oxford University Press.

Gunter, B., & Levy, M. R. (1987). Social contexts of video use. *American Behavioral Scientist, 30*, 486–94.

Gutman, D. (1985, September 1). Hints on choosing instructive software for your children. *Philadelphia Inquirer*, p. 7.

Haight, T. R., & Rubinyi, R. M. (1983). How community groups use computers. *Journal of Communication, 33*, 109–17.

Ham, M. (1984, January). Playing by the rules. *PC World*, pp. 34–41.

Hammonds, K. H. (1984, March 25). "Human" computer is coming of age. *New York Times*, pp. 52–53.

Hardie, A. E. (1986, August 17). Catalogers move up from mail. *New York Times*, p. F12.

Hardy, A. P. (1984). *Diffusion of new communication/information technology for the home.* Paper presented at the Annual Meeting of the International Communication Association, San Francisco, CA.

Harmetz, A. (1983, January 13). Makers vie for millions in home video games. *New York Times*, p. C17.

Harmetz, A. (1984, January 10). Sigh of relief on video games. *New York Times*, pp. D1, D5.

Harris, Z., & Mattick, P., Jr. (1988). Science sublanguages and the prospects for a global language of science. *The Annals of the American Academy of Political and Social Science, 495*, 73–83.

Hartmann, T. (1984, March). Molecular computers. *Popular Computing*, pp. 65–70.

Hassett, J. (1984, January). Hacking in plain English. *Psychology Today*, pp. 38–39, 42–45.

Hassett, J. (1984, September). Computers in the classroom. *Psychology Today*, pp. 22–28.

Hawken, P. (1983). *The next economy.* New York: Holt, Rinehart & Winston.

Hawkes, T. (1977). *Structuralism and semiotics.* Berkeley: University of California Press.

Hawkins, J. (1983). *Learning LOGO together: The social context.* Paper presented at meeting of the American Educational Research Association, Montreal, Canada.

Hawkins, R. P., Gustafson, D. H., Chewning, B., Bosworth, K., & Day, P. M. (1987). Reaching hard-to-reach populations: Interactive computer programs as public-information campaigns for adolescents. *Journal of Communication, 37*, 8–28.

Hayes, T. C. (1985, August 22). Computers that reason. *New York Times*, p. D2.

Heierman, D. L. (1982). *Projects in machine intelligence for your home computer.* Blue Ridge Summit, PA: Tab Books.

Heise, D. R. (Ed.). (1981). *Microcomputers in social research.* Beverly Hills, CA: Sage Publications. A special publication of vol. 9, no. 4, of *Sociological Methods and Research.*

Heller, S., & Turner, J. A. (1983, July). Eliza: Turn your computer into a therapist. *Popular Computing*, pp. 187–92.

Hellerstein, L. (1986, May). *Electronic messaging and conferencing with an emphasis on social use: An exploratory study.* Paper presented at meeting of the International Communication Association, Chicago, IL.

Hellweg, S. A., Freiberg, K. L., & Smith, A. F. (1984, November). *The pervasiveness and impact of electronic communication technologies in organizations: A survey of major American corporations.* Paper presented at meeting of the Speech Communication Association, Chicago, IL.

Herbers, J. (1986, May 13). Rising cottage industry stirring concern in U.S. *New York Times*, p. A18.

Hertz, D. B. (1988). *The expert executive.* New York: John Wiley & Sons.

Hiemstra, G. (1982). Teleconferencing, concern for face, and organizational culture. In M. Burgoon (Ed.), *Communication yearbook 6* (pp. 874–904). Beverly Hills, CA: Sage Publications.

Hiemstra, G. (1983). You say you want a revolution?: "Information technology" in organizations. In R. N. Bostrom & B. H. Westley (Eds.), *Communication yearbook 7* (pp. 802–27). Beverly Hills, CA: Sage Publications.

Hill, I. D. (1983). Natural language versus computer language. In M. E. Sime & M. J. Coombs (Eds.), *Designing for human-computer communication* (pp. 55–72). New York: Academic Press.

Hillman, J., & Shyles, L. (1984, November). *Improving the legibility of digital type: A comparison of some current videotex fonts against a new design.* Paper presented at meeting of the Speech Communication Association, Chicago, IL.

Hilts, P. J. (1983, January). The dean of artificial intelligence. *Psychology Today*, pp. 28–33.

Hiltz, S. R. (1984). *On-line communities: A case study of the office of the future.* Norwood, NJ: Ablex.

Hiltz, S. R., & Turoff, M. (1978). *The network nation: Human communication via computer.* Reading, MA: Addison-Wesley.

Hitachi guilty in IBM case. (1983, February 9). *New York Times*, p. D1.

Holden, C. (1986, October). The rational optimist. *Psychology Today*, pp. 54–60.

Hollie, P. G. (1982, August 11). Apple fighting counterfeits in Orient. *New York Times*, pp. D1, D4.

Hollie, P. G. (1983, November 25). Risky growth in catalogues. *New York Times*, p. D1.

Hollie, P. G. (1984, May 15). Western Union's Easylink. *New York Times*, p. D29.

Holusha, J. (1984, September 13). Standardizing computer talk. *New York Times*, p. D2.

Home banking by computer. (1983, March 29). *New York Times*, pp. D1, D18.

Horn, B. K. P., & Ikeuchi, K. (1984, August). The mechanical manipulation of randomly oriented parts. *Scientific American*, pp. 100–111.

Howard, B., & Wong, W. G. (1986, November 25). Compaq leads the way to speed and compatibility. *PC Magazine*, pp. 134–60.

Huyghe, P. (1983, December). Of two minds. *Psychology Today*, pp. 26–35.

IBM announces a 4-megabit chip. (1987, February 26). *New York Times*, p. D4.

IBM Data Processing Glossary. (1977). White Plains, NY: IBM Corporation.

Inman, V. (1984, March 16). MCI mail, falling short of expectations, begins campaign to increase service's use. *Wall Street Journal*, p. 29.

Integrated software. (1984, November 28). *New York Times*, Guide to the personal computer, Vol. 2, pp. 54, 74. Also see S. Cook (1984).

Jacobson, H. (1950). The information capacity of the human ear. *Science, 112,* 143–44.

Jacobson, H. (1951a). Information and the human ear. *Journal of Acoustical Society of America, 23,* 463–71.

Jacobson, H. (1951b). The information capacity of the human eye. *Science, 13,* 292–93.

James, W. (1950 [1890]). *The principles of psychology* (Vol. 2). New York: Dover/ Henry Holt.

Jennings, L. (1984). Computers in the world of 1985. *American Educator, 8,* 42–46.

Jernick, R. (1984, July 1). Frisky, how could you? *New York Times*, p. LI20.

Johansen, R., Vallee, J., & Spangler, K. (1979). *Electronic meetings: Technical alternatives and social choices.* Reading, MA: Addison-Wesley.

Johnson, B. M., & Rice, R. E. (1984). Reinvention in the innovation process: The case of word processing. In R. E. Rice (Ed.), *The new media: Communication, research, and technology* (pp. 157–83). Beverly Hills, CA: Sage Publications.

Jones, A. S. (1984, April 18). Carter Hawley's coveted unit. *New York Times*, pp. D1, D6.

Joselow, F. (1983, October 9). Advice to high-tech millionaires. *New York Times*, p. F10.

Jung, C. G. (1968). *Man and his symbols.* New York: Dell.

Kalman, R. E. (1978). An introduction to informatics. *Impact of Science on Society, 28,* 227–32.

Kaufman, L. (1979). *Perception: The world transformed.* New York: Oxford University Press.

Keen, P. G. W. (1987). Telecommunications and organizational choice. *Communication Research, 14,* 588–606.

Kendig, F. (1983, April). A conversation with Roger Schank. *Psychology Today*, pp. 28–36.

Kerr, E. B., & Hiltz, S. R. (Eds.). (1982). *Computer-mediated communication systems: Status and evaluation.* New York: Academic Press.

Kerr, P. (1982, June 3). Should video games be restricted by law? *New York Times*, pp. C1, C8.

Kerr, P. (1982, September 16). Now, computerized bulletin boards. *New York Times*, pp. C1, C7.

Kiesler, S., Siegel, J., & McGuire, T. W. (1984). Social psychological aspects of computer-mediated communication. Unpublished manuscript.

Kiesler, S., Sproull, L., & Eccles, J. S. (1983, March). Second-class citizens? *Psychology Today*, pp. 41–48.

Kiesler, S., Zubrow, D., Moses, A. M., & Geller, V. (1984). Affect in computer-mediated communication. Unpublished manuscript.

Kiester, E., Jr. (1983, January 15). Information, please. *TV Guide*, pp. 32–34.

Kleinfield, N. R. (1983, October 17). Video-games industry comes down to earth. *New York Times*, pp. A1, D4.

Kleinfield, N. R. (1986, February 2). Turning McGraw-Hill upside down. *New York Times*, pp. F1, F27.

Kleinfield, N. R. (1988, May 1). A tight squeeze at video stores. *New York Times*, p. F4.

Klieger, D. M. (1984). *Computer usage for social scientists*. Boston: Allyn & Bacon.

Kneale, D. (1985, September 5). Computer price cuts seem likely despite industry's lackluster year. *Wall Street Journal*, p. 35.

Kneale, D. (1988, April 25). "Zapping" of TV ads appears pervasive. *Wall Street Journal*, p. 29.

Kohl, K., Newman, T. G., Jr., & Tomey, J. F. (1975). Facilitating organizational decentralization through teleconferencing. *IEEE Transactions in Communications*, COM-23 (10), 1098–1103.

Komatsuzaki, S. (1981). The impact on communication theory of the evolution of media. *International Social Science Journal*, 33, 91–98.

Komsky, S. H. (1984, November). *The role of communication in the implementation of word-processing systems*. Paper presented at meeting of the Speech Communication Association, Chicago, IL.

Koop, C. E. (1982, November 10). *Statement*. (Available from Office of the Surgeon General, Washington, DC).

Kranzberg, M. (1988). Interdependence of scientific and technological information and its relation to public decision making. *The Annals of the American Academy of Political and Social Science*, 495, 29–39.

LaPlante, A. (1986, July 14). Software testers to establish quality guidelines. *InfoWorld*, p. 8.

La Rosa, P. (1984, May 30). Computer becomes a chatterbox. [New York] *Daily News*, p. XQ4.

Larson, E. (1985, February 13). Working at home: Is it freedom or a life of flabby loneliness? *Wall Street Journal*, p. 33.

Lasden, M. (1985, August 4). Of bytes and bulletin boards. *New York Times Magazine*, pp. 34–35, 37, 40, 42.

Lawler, R. W. (1985). *Computer experience and cognitive development: A child's learning in a computer culture*. New York: Halsted Press/John Wiley & Sons.

Laws in U.S. called inadequate to block abuse of computers. (1983, September 18). *New York Times*, sec. 1, pp. 1, 42.

Lederman, L. C. (1984, March). *Communication, information, and alienation: The impact of information systems and high technology on human interaction*. Paper presented at meeting of the Eastern Communication Association, Philadelphia, PA.

Ledgard, H., McQuaid, E. P., & Singer, A. (1983). *From Baker Street to binary: An introduction to computer programming with Sherlock Holmes*. New York: McGraw-Hill.

Lemley, B. (1984, June). Synesthesia: Seeing is feeling. *Psychology Today*, p. 65.

Leonard, G., (1986, May). Secrets of the body. *Esquire*, pp. 105–6.

Leveen, S. (1983, November 12). Technosexism. *New York Times*, p. 23.

Levin, D. P. (1984, May 14). Westinghouse move into robotics shows pitfalls of high-tech field. *The Wall Street Journal*, p. 29.

Levin, H. M., & Rumberger, R. W. (1983, February). *The educational implications of high technology* (Project Report No. 83–A4). Stanford, CA: Stanford University School of Education, Institute for Research on Educational Finance and Governance.

Levy, M. R. (1980a). Home video recorders: A user survey. *Journal of Communication, 30*, 23–27.

Levy, M. R. (1980b). Program playback preferences in VCR households. *Journal of Broadcasting, 24*, 327–36.

Levy, M. R. (1981). Home video recorders and time-shifting. *Journalism Quarterly, 58*, 401–5.

Levy, M. R., & Fink, E. L. (1985). Home video recorders and the transience of television broadcasts. In M. Gurevitch & M. R. Levy (Eds.), *Mass communication review yearbook* (Vol. 5, pp. 569–84). Beverly Hills, CA: Sage Publications.

Levy, S. (1984, February). Touring the bulletin boards. *Popular Computing*, pp. 54, 59–62.

Lewis, P. (1984, April 30). Computer linkups spurred by France. *New York Times*, p. D8.

Lewis, P. H. (1986, April 29). Software gets its day in sun. *New York Times*, p. C5. Also see S. Cook (1984).

Lewis, P. H. (1986, May 20). As computers get smarter, so do the users. *New York Times*, p. C7.

Lewis, P. H. (1986, July 1). The answer? Sold separately. *New York Times*, p. C7. Also see Mace & LaPlante (1986).

Lewis, P. H. (1986, July 8). The summer break. *New York Times*, p. C5.

Lewis, P. H. (1986, August 12). Chess program beckons. *New York Times*, p. C5.

Lewis, P. H. (1986, August 26). New chip: Vast power on horizon. *New York Times*, p. C7.

Lewis, P. H. (1987, October 4). Hackers, thieves, and carelessness. *New York Times*, p. F16.

Lieberman, J. I. (1983, May 31). TV's watching you. *New York Times*, p. A21.

Linden, E. (1988, March 28). Putting knowledge to work: Suddenly, artificial intelligence produces some results. *Time*, pp. 60–63.

Lindsey, R. (1983, December 2). Computer as letterbox, singles bar, and seminar. *New York Times*, p. A18.

Lindsey, R. (1985, March 3). VCRs bring big changes in use of leisure. *New York Times*, pp. 1, 24.

Link Resources Corporation. (1988, February 8). Software sales. *Wall Street Journal*, p. 27.

Lockwood, R., & Honan, P. (1987, November). 386 computers head to head: IBM model 80 vs. Compaq 386. *Personal Computing*, pp. 106–21.

Look and listen. (1985, February 15). *Wall Street Journal*, p. 25.

Lubar, D. (1981, February). The problem of defining intelligence. *Creative*

Computing, pp. 52, 54.

Lueck, T. J. (1983, January 13). Retailing by computer. *New York Times*, p. D2.

Luria, A. R. (1968). *The mind of a mnemonist*. New York: Basic Books.

Mace, S. (1986, August 18). Lower-priced expert systems debut at AI show. *InfoWorld*, p. 11.

Mace, S., & LaPlante, A. (1986, May 12). CEOS say products poorly tested. *InfoWorld*, p. 1, 8.

Machlup, F., & Leeson, K. (1978–80). *Information through the printed word: The dissemination of scholarly, scientific, and intellectual knowledge* (Vols. 1–4). New York: Praeger.

Mackay-Smith, A. (1985, February 12). Epic program: Computer is used in new search for divine insight. *Wall Street Journal*, p. 33.

Mackay-Smith, A. (1985, February 13). A computer can hone a child's writing and creativity, but don't expect all As. *Wall Street Journal*, p. 33.

Mander, M. S. (1983). Communication technologies, rhetoric, and social change. *Communication Research, 10*, 138–52.

Marcom, J., Jr. (1985, July 26). Consumers are taking a back seat as computer stores court business. *Wall Street Journal*, p. 23.

Marcom, J., Jr. (1985, September 19). Computer firms confused on how to advertise to changing market. *Wall Street Journal*, p. 35.

Marcus, S. J. (1983, June 2). As computers eliminate jobs. *New York Times*, p. D2.

Marcus, S. J. (1983, June 16). A small robot with "feeling." *New York Times*, p. D2.

Marcus, S. J. (1983, August 29). Computer systems applying expertise. *New York Times*, pp. D1, D3.

Margulis, L., & Sagan, D. (1986). Strange fruit on the tree of life. *Science, 26*, 38–45. Also see Margulis & Sagan (1987).

Margulis, L., & Sagan, D. (1987). *Microcosmos: Four billion years of evolution*. New York: Summit Books.

Markoff, J. (1988, April 25). Top-secret, and vulnerable. *New York Times*, pp. D1, D5.

Markoff, J. (1988, May 15). The artificial-intelligence industry is retrenching. *New York Times*, p. E7.

Markoff, J. (1988, June 1). Wider threat to privacy seen as computer memories grow. *New York Times*, pp. A1, C10.

Markoff, J. (1988, June 5). A new breed of snoopier computers. *New York Times*, p. E32.

Markoff, J. (1988, June 6). New computer network is faster. *New York Times*, p. D3.

Markoff, J. (1988, June 16). Faster computers: Race is on. *New York Times*, pp. D1, D5.

Markoff, J. (1988, September 14). The chip at 30: Potential still vast. *New York Times*, pp. D1, D10.

Marks, L. E. (1974). On associations of light and sound: The mediation of brightness, pitch, and loudness. *American Journal of Psychology, 87*, 173–88.

Marks, L. E. (1975). On colored hearing synesthesia: Cross-modal translations of sensory dimensions. *Psychological Bulletin, 82,* 303–31.

Markus, M. L. (1987). Toward a "critical-mass" theory of interactive media: Universal access, interdependence, and diffusion. *Communication Research, 14,* 491–511.

Martelanc, T. (1982, November). *The right to communicate.* Paper presented at meeting of the Council for Media Research, Queens College of CUNY, Flushing, NY.

Martin, R. C., & Caramazza, A. (1982). Short-term memory performance in the absence of phonological coding. *Brain and Cognition, 1,* 50–70.

Marvin, C., & Winther, M. (1983). Computer-ease: A 20th-century literacy emergent. *Journal of Communication, 33,* 92–108.

McCarthy, J. (1983, December). The little thoughts of thinking machines. *Psychology Today,* pp. 46–49.

McClellan, S. T. (1985). The automated office. In T. Forester (Ed.), *The information technology revolution,* (pp. 298–335). Cambridge, MA: MIT Press.

McCorduck, P. (1979). *Machines who think: A personal inquiry into the history and prospects of artificial intelligence.* San Francisco, CA: W. H. Freeman.

McCroskey, J. C., & McCain, T. A. (1974). The measurement of interpersonal attraction. *Speech Monographs, 41,* 261–66.

McDowell, E. (1983, April 17). How the U.S. flubbed the IBM case. *New York Times,* sec. 3, p. F15.

McDowell, E. (1983, June 5). Sales up of hardcover best-sellers, study shows. *New York Times,* sec. 1, p. 52.

McDowell, E. (1984, April 12). Fewer youth read books, study finds. *New York Times,* p. C19.

McDowell, E. (1985, April 22). Trade paperbacks reshaping book publishing. *New York Times,* p. C13.

McEliece, R. J. (1985, January). The reliability of computer memories. *Scientific American,* pp. 88–95.

McGee, M. C. (1980a). The "ideograph": A link between rhetoric and ideology. *Quarterly Journal of Speech, 66,* 1–16.

McGee, M. C. (1980b). The origins of "liberty": A feminization of power. *Communication Monographs, 47,* 23–45.

McGee, M. C., & Martin, M. A. (1983). Public knowledge and ideological argument. *Communication Monographs, 50,* 47–65.

McHale, J. (1972). *World facts and trends: Where man is headed—a multidimensional view.* New York: Macmillan.

McLuhan, M. (1964). *Understanding media: The extensions of man.* New York: New American Library.

McWilliams, P. (1983, June 19). Learning BASIC's basics is no longer a necessity. *Philadelphia Inquirer,* sec. P, p. 10.

Medical diagnoses made by computer. (1982, August 19). *New York Times,* p. C11.

Mehrabian, A. (1968, April). A communication without words. *Psychology Today,* pp. 52–55.

Mehrabian, A. (1981). *Silent messages: Implicit communication of emotions and attitudes* (2nd ed.). Belmont, CA: Wadsworth.

Mehrabian, A., & Wiener, M. (1966). Nonimmediacy between communication and object of communication in a verbal message: Application to the inference of attitudes. *Journal of Consulting Psychology, 30,* 420–25.

Meindl, J. D. (1985). Micros in medicine. In T. Forester (Ed.), *The information technology revolution* (pp. 359–73). Cambridge, MA: MIT Press.

Meindl, J. D. (1987, October). Chips for advanced computing. *Scientific American,* pp. 78–88.

Menosky, J. A. (1984, May). Computer worship. *Science 84,* pp. 40–46.

Meyrowitz, J. (1985). *No sense of place: The impact of electronic media on social behavior.* New York: Oxford University Press.

Mikita, R. (1986). Computer communications—coming of age. In R. Atwan, B. Orton, & W. Vesterman (Eds.), *American mass media: Industries and issues* (pp. 427–31). New York: Random House.

Miller, C. R. (1978). Technology as a form of consciousness: A study of contemporary ethos. *Central States Speech Journal, 29,* 228–36.

Miller, M. J., & McMillan, T. (1984, May). Windows while you work. *Popular Computing,* pp. 96–102. Also see S. Cook (1984).

Miller, M. W. (1984, December 5). The latest frontier of the programmers is all in the mind. *Wall Street Journal,* pp. 1, 18.

Miller, M. W. (1984, December 14). Expert-system software finds place in daily office routines. *Wall Street Journal,* p. 29.

Miller, M. W. (1985, January 15). Whether playing the market or horses, computerized data banks might help. *Wall Street Journal,* p. 37.

Miller, M. W. (1985, June 3). Productivity spies: Computers keep eye on workers and see if they perform well. *Wall Street Journal,* pp. 1, 15.

Miller, R. J. (Ed.). (1983). Robotics: Future factories, future workers [Special issue]. *The Annals of the American Academy of Political and Social Science, 470.*

Minnick, W. C. (1957). *The art of persuasion.* Boston: Houghton Mifflin.

Minsky, M. L. (1967). *Computation: Finite and infinite machines.* Englewood Cliffs, NJ: Prentice-Hall.

Minsky, M. L. (1975). A framework for representing knowledge. In P. H. Winston (Ed.), *The psychology of computer vision* (pp. 139–53). New York: McGraw-Hill.

Minsky, M. L. (1987). *The society of mind.* New York: Simon & Schuster.

Mitchell, E. (1983, May). *The effects of home video games on children and families.* Unpublished manuscript.

Monforte, J. (1984, December). The digital reproduction of sound. *Scientific American,* pp. 78–84.

Monk, A. (Ed.). (1984). *Fundamentals of human-computer interaction.* Orlando, FL: Academic Press.

More mainframe computers in federal agencies. (1988, April 25). *New York Times,* p. D1.

Morowitz, H. (1983, January 29). Paperwork's two sides: Reality/noisulll. *New York Times,* p. 23.

Mosco, V. (1982). *Pushbutton fantasies: Critical perspectives on videotex and information technology.* Norwood, NJ: Ablex.

Mueller, R. E. (1983, January). When is computer art art? *Creative Computing,* pp. 14–18.

Muson, H. (1982, April). Getting the phone's number. *Psychology Today*, pp. 42–49.

Nadler, G., & Robinson, G. H. (1983). Design of the automated factory: More than robots. *The Annals of the American Academy of Political and Social Science, 470*, 68–80.

Naisbitt, J. (1982). *Megatrends: Ten new directions transforming our lives.* New York: Warner Communications.

New data explain lag in productivity. (1983, April 7). *New York Times*, p. D6.

A new medical network is announced. (1982, September 14). *New York Times*, p. C2.

New York Stock Exchange Office of Economic Research. (1982, November). *People and productivity: A challenge to corporate America.* New York: Author.

Nielsen Media Research. (1987a). *1987 Nielsen report on television.* Northbrook, IL: Author.

Nielsen Media Research. (1987b). *Television audience 1987.* Northbrook, IL: Author.

Noble, D. (1985). The underside of computer literacy. In M. Gurevitch & M. R. Levy (Eds.), *Mass communication yearbook* (Vol. 5, pp. 585–612).

Noble, K. B. (1986, May 11). Commuting by computer remains largely in the future. *New York Times*, p. E22.

Norman, D. A. (1983, October). The computer always rings twice. *Psychology Today*, pp. 46–50.

Nussbaum, B. (1983, June 12). "Reskilling" workers. *New York Times*, p. E19.

O'Brien, T., & Dugdale, V. (1978). Questionnaire administration by computer. *Journal of the Market Research Society, 20*, 228–37.

O'Connor, J. J. (1981, September 6). State of the art: Television. *New York Times*, sec. 2, p. D19.

On-line computer telephone directory. (n. d.). Kansas City, KS: OLCTD.

Ornstein, R. E. (1972). *The psychology of consciousness.* San Francisco, CA: W. H. Freeman.

Osgood, C. E. (1960). The cross-cultural generality of visual-verbal synesthetic tendencies. *Behavioral Science, 5*, 146–69.

Pace, E. (1982, October 14). Videotex: Luring advertisers. *New York Times*, pp. D1, D4.

Pacific Telephone. (1981, March). *Openline.*

Packard, V. (1972). *A nation of strangers.* New York: David McKay.

Packard, V. (1980). *Lonely in America.* New York: Simon & Schuster.

Paisley, W. (1983). Computerizing information: Lessons of a videotex trial. *Journal of Communication, 33*, 153–61.

Panko, R. (1977, July). Outlook for computer mail sunny, but dark clouds on the horizon. *Communication News*, p. 32.

Patterson, D. A. (1983, March). Microprogramming. *Scientific American*, pp. 50–57.

Pauly, D., & Foltz, K. (1983, June 20). Baby Bell's teething pains. *Newsweek*, p. 55.

Peled, A. (1987, October). The next computer revolution. *Scientific American*, pp. 57–64.

Perlez, J. (1983, June 8). Computers pose a peril for poor, Lautenberg says. *New York Times*, pp. B1, B22.

Personal computers grow. (1987, September 13). *New York Times*, p. F1.

Perspectives in Computing, 6(2) (1986). Donald T. Sanders, Ed.

Peterson, F., & Turkel, J. K. (1985, July 30). Start making sense of jargon. [New York] *Daily News*, p. XQ6.

Phillips, A. (1982). *Attitude correlates in selected media technologies: Pilot study*. Unpublished manuscript.

Phillips, A. F. (1983). Computer conferences: Success or failure? In R. N. Bostrom & B. H. Westley (Eds.), *Communication yearbook 7* (pp. 837–56). Beverly Hills, CA: Sage Publications.

Phillips, G. M. (1983, May). *The rhetoric of computers*. Paper presented at meeting of the Eastern Communication Association, Ocean City, MD.

Phillips, G. M. (1983, September). Gerald Phillips: Maintaining a master and slave relationship. *Today*, pp. 17–18.

Phillips, G. M. (1986, May). *Artificial intelligence as a tool for analysis of oral and written communication*. Paper presented at meeting of the Eastern Communication Association, Atlantic City, NJ.

Phillips, G. M. (1987). *Composition on the computer: Expert systems and artificial intelligence*. Unpublished paper.

Pinsky, L. (1951). Do machines think about machines thinking? *Mind: A Quarterly Review of Psychology and Philosophy*, 60, 397–98.

Polich, J. M. (1982). Hemispheric memory for random forms revisited. *Brain and Cognition*, 1, 360–70.

Pollack, A. (1982, May 30). Light, cold, molecules: The fantastic stuff of new computers. *New York Times*, p. E16.

Pollack, A. (1982, June 17). The home computer arrives. *New York Times*, p. D1.

Pollack, A. (1982, July 29). Preserving memories. *New York Times*, p. D2.

Pollack, A. (1982, September 13). Commercial uses for artificial intelligence. *New York Times*, pp. D1, D2.

Pollack, A. (1982, October 3). Latest technology may spawn the electronic sweatshop. *New York Times*, p. E18.

Pollack, A. (1982, October 28). Effort causes U.S. concern. *New York Times*, pp. D1, D9.

Pollack, A. (1983, January 16). When the grand master is a "ghost." *New York Times*, sec. 3, p. F23.

Pollack, A. (1983, February 18). Teletext is ready for debut. *New York Times*, pp. D1, D3.

Pollack, A. (1983, February 27). The birth of silicon statesmanship. *New York Times*, pp. F1, F30.

Pollack, A. (1983, March 27). Big IBM has done it again. *New York Times*, pp. F1, F28.

Pollack, A. (1983, May 11). Finding home-computer uses. *New York Times*, pp. D1, D7.

Pollack, A. (1983, June 6). Home computers steal show. *New York Times*, pp. D1, D5.

Pollack, A. (1983, June 16). Japanese seek a computer standard. *New York*

Times, pp. D1, D6.

Pollack, A. (1983, July 21). The diversity among RAMS. *New York Times*, p. D2.

Pollack, A. (1983, September 6). Computers mastering speech recognition. *New York Times*, pp. C1, C7.

Pollack, A. (1983, September 22). Moving data from *a* to *b*. *New York Times*, p. D2.

Pollack, A. (1983, October 6). Touch screen: Views mixed. *New York Times*, p. D2.

Pollack, A. (1983, October 16). Slugging it out on the software front. *New York Times*, pp. F1, F8.

Pollack, A. (1983, November 5). The publicity effect of IBM "sting." *New York Times*, p. 37.

Pollack, A. (1983, December 1). Integrating the software. *New York Times*, p. D2. Also see S. Cook (1984).

Pollack, A. (1984, January 5). Audiotex: Data by telephone. *New York Times*, p. D2.

Pollack, A. (1984, April 5). Selling phone information. *New York Times*, p. D2.

Pollack, A. (1984, July 15). Humbled Hitachi comes up fighting. *New York Times*, sec. 3, pp. 1, 12, 13.

Pollack, A. (1984, October 31). Knight-Ridder cuts videotex staff. *New York Times*, p. D7.

Pollack, A. (1985, January 20). The daunting power of IBM. *New York Times*, sec. 3, pp. F1, F8.

Pollack, A. (1985, February 5). AT&T videotex plan reported. *New York Times*, pp. D1, D9.

Pollack, A. (1986, August 21). Analog values in computing. *New York Times*, p. D2.

Pollack, A. (1986, September 27). Video games, once zapped, in comeback. *New York Times*, pp. 1, 39.

Pollack, A. (1986, September 28). Softening up software publishers. *New York Times*, p. F12. Software manufacturers are beginning to reduce copy-protect restrictions on computer programs.

Pollack, A. (1986, September 30). U.S. sees dangers in chip lag. *New York Times*, pp. D1, D5.

Pollack, A. (1987, September 15). More human than ever, computer is learning to learn. *New York Times*, pp. C1, C12.

Pollack, A. (1988, March 4). Setbacks for artificial intelligence. *New York Times*, pp. D1, D5.

Porat, M. U. (1974). *Defining an information sector in the U.S. economy* (Information Reports and Bibliographics, Vol. 5, No. 5). Stanford, CA: Institute for Communication Research, Stanford University.

Porat, M. U. (1977). *The information economy: Definition and measurement.* Washington, DC: Department of Commerce, Office of Telecommunications.

Porter, S. (1983, October 7). Learning computers—by the book. [New York] *Daily News*, p. 46.

Pournelle, J. (1984, August). Rolling your own. *Popular Computing*, pp. 81–83, 86.

Prial, F. J. (1984, January 9). Paris's electronic phone book. *New York Times*, p. D7.

Printing out: Many computer mags folding. (1984, September 30). [New York] *Daily News*, pp. 49–50.

Profile of computer buyers. (1983, May 11). *New York Times*, p. D7.

Prokesch, S. (1987, March 22). Stopping the high-tech giveaway. *New York Times*, sec. 3, pp. F1, F8.

Putting everything together. (1983, September 4). *New York Times*, p. F11.

Quality Education Data. (1988a). *Microcomputer and VCR Usage in Schools, 1982 to 1988* (2nd ed.). Denver, CO: Author.

Quality Education Data. (1988b). *Microcomputer Usage in Schools: A QED Update*. Denver, CO: Author.

Quinn, J. B., Baruch, J. J., & Paquette, P. C. (1987, December). Technology in services. *Scientific American*, pp. 50–58.

Recording Industry Association of America. (1987). *Inside the recording industry: A statistical overview—1987 update*. Washington, DC: Author.

Reinhold, R. (1984, January 13). Life in high-stress silicon valley takes a toll. *New York Times*, pp. A1, A12.

Reinhold, R. (1984, March 29). Reasoning ability of experts is codified for computer use. *New York Times*, pp. A1, A16.

Reinking, D. (1987a). Computers, reading, and a new technology of print. In D. Reinking (Ed.), *Reading and computers: Issues for theory and practice*, (pp. 3–23). New York: Teachers College Press.

Reinking, D. (1987b). Preface. In D. Reinking (Ed.), *Reading and computers: Issues for theory and practice* (pp. ix–xi). New York: Teachers College Press.

Rennels, G. D., & Shortliffe, E. H. (1987, October). Advanced computing for medicine. *Scientific American*, pp. 154–61.

Renner, L. (1984, February 8). "Timesharing": A computer widow's lament. [New York] *Daily News*, p. 39.

Resnikoff, H. L. (1982, October 2). *Information science and technology: Implications for higher education curricula*. Unpublished manuscript.

Restak, R. (1984). *The brain* (rev. ed.). Garden City, NY: Doubleday.

Rheingold, H. (1983, December). Our machine Friday. *Psychology Today*, p. 33.

Rice, R. E. (1982). Communication networking in computer-conferencing systems: A longitudinal study of group roles and system structure. In M. Burgoon (Ed.), *Communication yearbook 6* (pp. 925–44). Beverly Hills, CA: Sage Publications.

Rice, R. E. (1984). Mediated group communication. In R. E. Rice (Ed.), *The new media: Communication, research, and technology* (pp. 129–54). Beverly Hills, CA: Sage Publications.

Rice, R. E. (1987). Computer-mediated communication and organizational innovation. *Journal of Communication*, 37, 65–94.

Rice, R. E., & Bair, J. H. (1984). New organizational media and productivity. In R. E. Rice (Ed.), *The new media: Communication, research, and technology* (pp. 185–215). Beverly Hills, CA: Sage Publications.

Rice, R. E., & Boan, K. M. (1985). Periodicals on computer-mediated communications technologies and their use. *Journal of Communication Re-*

search, 13, 70–77.

Rice, R. E., & Case, D. (1983). Electronic message systems in the university: A description of use and utility. *Journal of Communication, 33*, 131–52.

Riding, A. (1985, September 16). Brazil's protected computers. *New York Times*, p. D8.

Risberg, J., & Ingvar, D. H. (1973). Patterns of activation in the grey matter of the dominant hemisphere during memorizing and reasoning: A study of regional cerebral blood-flow changes during psychological testing in a group of neurologically normal patients. *Brain, 96*, 737–57.

Rivlin, R., & Gravelle, K. (1984). *Deciphering the senses: The expanding world of human perception.* New York: Simon & Schuster.

Rochester, J. B., & Gantz, J. (1983). *The naked computer: A layperson's almanac of computer lore, wizardry, personalities, memorabilia, world records, mind blowers, and tomfoolery.* New York: William Morrow.

Roe, K. (1987). Adolescents' video use: A structural-cultural approach. *American Behavioral Scientist, 30*, 522–32.

Rogers, E. M., Daley, H., & Wu, T. (1982). *The diffusion of home computers: An exploratory study.* Stanford, CA: Stanford University Institute for Communication Research.

Roper Organization. (1983, April). *Trends in attitudes toward television and other media: A 24-year review.* New York: Television Information Office of the Roper Organization.

Roper Organization. (1985, May). *Public attitudes toward television and other media in a time of change.* New York: Television Information Office of the Roper Organization.

Rosch, W. L. (1988, June 28). 20-MHz 386s hustle with muscle. *PC Magazine*, pp. 93–142.

Rosemond, J. (1982, May 2). The war over video games. [New York] *Daily News*, p. You11.

Rosenfield, I. (1988). *The invention of memory: A new view of the brain.* New York: Basic Books.

Rubin, A. M., & Bantz, C. R. (1987). Utility of videocassette recorders. *American Behavioral Scientist, 30*, 471–85.

Rumelhart, D., & McClelland, J. (1986). *Parallel distributed processing.* Cambridge, MA: MIT Press.

Samuelson, R. J. (1985, September 9). Our computerized society. *Newsweek*, p. 73.

Sandberg-Diment, E. (1982, August 10). Learning the machine's language. *New York Times*, p. C2.

Sandberg-Diment, E. (1982, August 17). The children seem to know no fear. *New York Times*, p. C2.

Sandberg-Diment, E. (1982, August 31). How to choose printer's typeface. *New York Times*, p. C3.

Sandberg-Diment, E. (1982, November 16). Primers—in old-fashioned print. *New York Times*, p. C6.

Sandberg-Diment, E. (1983, January 18). Processing words. *New York Times*, p. C7.

Sandberg-Diment, E. (1983, April 26). Machine as SAT instructor. *New York*

Times, p. C3.

Sandberg-Diment, E. (1983, May 31). Words and numbers combined in a program. *New York Times*, p. C2.

Sandberg-Diment, E. (1983, July 5). Software on a disk acts as a guide to the I.B.M. *New York Times*, p. C4.

Sandberg-Diment, E. (1983, September 13). Hacking the English language to bits and bytes. *New York Times*, p. C4.

Sandberg-Diment, E. (1983, October 11). Splitting the Apple, four ways. *New York Times*, p. C4. Also see S. Cook (1984).

Sandberg-Diment, E. (1983, November 1). One area of programming that is helpful to all. *New York Times*, p. C7.

Sandberg-Diment, E. (1983, December 6). "Windows" and "gateways" loom in near future. *New York Times*, p. C6.

Sandberg-Diment, E. (1984, January 10). Integrated software makes its mark. *New York Times*, p. C5.

Sandberg-Diment, E. (1984, January 17). Does everyone need to learn programming? *New York Times*, p. C3.

Sandberg-Diment, E. (1984, February 3). Bailing out of the mainframe industry. *New York Times*, pp. F1, F36.

Sandberg-Diment, E. (1984, June 26). But is it writing? *New York Times*, p. C5.

Sandberg-Diment, E. (1984, December 25). Value of windowing is questioned. *New York Times*, p. 35. Also see S. Cook (1984).

Sandberg-Diment, E. (1985, February 17). A data base that thinks by "seeing." *New York Times*, p. F15.

Sandberg-Diment, E. (1985, June 9). When technology outpaces needs. *New York Times*, p. F13.

Sandberg-Diment, E. (1985, July 30). The value of learning languages. *New York Times*, p. C4.

Sandberg-Diment, E. (1985, August 6). Solving the puzzle of programming languages. *New York Times*, p. C5.

Sandberg-Diment, E. (1985, October 20). Making graphics glitter. *New York Times*, p. F14.

Sandberg-Diment E. (1985, November 5). Micro-CAD painting outdoes connecting the dots. *New York Times*, p. C5.

Sandberg-Diment, E. (1985, November 11). Computer-aided design dooms lesser tools. *New York Times*, p. C4.

Sandberg-Diment, E. (1986, January 21). Waving to the future from the electronic cottage. *New York Times*, p. C3.

Sandberg-Diment, E. (1986, February 25). Windows are open at last. *New York Times*, p. C6.

Sandberg-Diment, E. (1986, March 2). A built-in electronic buddy system. *New York Times*, p. F14.

Sandberg-Diment, E. (1986, August 17). Turning the PC into a landlord. *New York Times*, p. F13.

Sanders, D. H. (1985). *Computers today*. New York: McGraw-Hill.

Sanger, D. E. (1983, March 13). Waging a trade war over data. *New York Times*, sec. 3, pp. F1, F26.

Sanger, D. E. (1984, June 23). Antitrust inquiry on IBM. *New York Times*, p. 37.

Sanger, D. E. (1984, July 5). An electronic OED edition. *New York Times*, p. D2.

Sanger, D. E. (1985, March 24). Supercomputers: Super-shortage of experts. *New York Times*, pp. 29, 70, 71.

Sanger, D. E. (1985, April 18). Now, "smart" credit cards. *New York Times*, p. D2.

Sanger, D. E. (1985, July 21). Computer makers are waiting to hit bottom. *New York Times*, p. E7.

Sanger, D. E. (1985, August 5). Philip Estridge dies in jet crash; guided IBM personal computer. *New York Times*, p. D8.

Sanger, D. E. (1985, September 9). Breaking a computer barrier. *New York Times*, pp. D1, D27.

Sanger, D. E. (1985, December 15). Smart machines get smarter. *New York Times*, pp. 3F, 8F.

Sanger, D. E. (1986, January 5). The electronic college is still a dim prospect. *New York Times*, Winter Education Survey, sec. 12, pp. 50–51.

Sanger, D. E. (1987, February 18). Advanced chip for IBM unit. *New York Times*, pp. D1, D18.

Sanger, D. E. (1987, February 24). The widening computer gap. *New York Times*, pp. D1, D9.

Sanger, D. E. (1987, March 30). Chip dispute: Reading between the lines. *New York Times*, p. D11.

Sanger, D. E. (1987, October 11). Computer fails as job-killer: Reports that expert systems would put people out of work have been grossly exaggerated. *New York Times*, sec. 12, pp. L15, L16.

Sanger, D. E. (1987, December 9). Computer makers see strong '88 sales rise. *New York Times*, p. D1.

Santoro, G. M. (1986, November). *The computer connection: Computer-mediated communication and the Penn State heart*. Paper presented at meeting of the Speech Communication Association, Chicago, IL.

Schank, R. C. (1972). Conceptual dependency: A theory of natural language understanding. *Cognitive Psychology*, 3, 552–631.

Schank, R. C., & Childers, P. G. (1984). *The cognitive computer: On language, learning, and artificial intelligence*. Reading, MA: Addison-Wesley.

Schank, R. C., & Riesbeck, C. (1981). *Inside computer understanding*. New York: Lawrence Erlbaum.

Schiro, A. (1982, August 16). For secretaries, now it's word processors. *New York Times*, p. B12.

Schlender, B. R. (1988, January 25). Microsoft predicts industrywide sales of personal computers will surge 26%. *Wall Street Journal*, p. 5.

Schmich, M. T. (1985, August 4). Peril in the office. [New York] *Daily News*, pp. 5, 9.

Schmidt, P. (1985, April 14). The computer as tutor. *New York Times*, Spring Education Survey, pp. 50, 56.

Schneider, K. (1987, June 29). Services hurt by technology: Productivity is declining. *New York Times*, pp. D1, D6.

Schoenbach, K., & Hackforth, J. (1987). Video in West German households:

Attitudinal and behavioral differences. *American Behavioral Scientist, 30,* 533–43.

Schultz, A. (1945). On multiple realities. *Philosophy and Phenomenological Research, 5,* 533–75.

Secondhand games for video buffs. (1983, July 7). *New York Times,* p. C3.

Sekuler, R. (1985, February). From quill to computer. *Psychology Today,* pp. 36–42.

Selnow, G. W. (1984). Playing videogames: The electronic friend. *Journal of Communication, 34,* 148–56.

Selnow, G. W., & Reynolds, H. (1984). Some opportunity costs of television viewing. *Journal of Broadcasting, 28,* 315–22.

Semler, E. (1988, June 5). What technology can do for the disabled. *New York Times,* p. E32.

Seneker, H., & Pearl, J. A. (1983, June 20). Software to go. *Forbes,* pp. 93–102.

Serrin, W. (1982, July 4). Worry grows over upheaval as technology reshapes jobs. *New York Times,* sec. 1, pp. 1, 29.

Serrin, W. (1984, March 28). Electronic office conjuring wonders, loneliness, and tedium. *New York Times,* p. A16.

Severo, R. (1984, December 10). Computer makers find rich market in schools. *New York Times,* pp. B1, B9.

Shannon, D. (1982, May 9). Copycatting in the software patch. *New York Times,* p. F17.

Shannon, L. R. (1987, December 8). The promise, the reality, and the hope. *New York Times,* p. C9.

Shapiro, H. D. (1984, March 25). The demise of the canceled check. *New York Times,* sec. 3, p. F11.

Sharkey, N. E. (Ed.). (1986). *Advances in cognitive science 1.* New York: Halsted Press/John Wiley & Sons.

Sherman, M. (1985, March 24). The home robot is still in toddler stage. *New York Times,* p. 32.

Sherwin, R. (1987, October 6). PC choice strictly personal. [New York] *Daily News,* pp. XQ1, XQ15.

Shifren, D. (1985, April 18). Computer chess leaves behind its checkered career. *New York Post,* p. 47.

Short, J., Williams, E., & Christie, B. (1976). *The social psychology of telecommunications.* New York: John Wiley.

Shortliffe, E. H. (1983). Medical consultation systems: Designing for doctors. In M. E. Sime & M. J. Coombs (Eds.), *Designing for human-computer communication* (pp. 209–38). New York: Academic Press.

Siklossy, L. (1976). *Let's talk LISP.* Englewood Cliffs, NJ: Prentice-Hall.

Silk, L. (1982, November 3). The search for reality. *New York Times,* p. D2.

Sime, M. E., & Coombs, M. J. (Eds.). (1983). *Designing for human-computer communication.* New York: Academic Press.

Simons, G. (1981, February). Are computers alive? *Creative Computing,* pp. 62–67.

Simons, G. (1983). *Are computers alive?: Evolution and new life forms.* Boston, MA: Birkhauser.

Simons, H. W. (1978). In praise of muddleheaded anecdotalism. *Western Journal of Speech Communication, 42,* 21–28.

Sims, C. (1985, December 10). Computer design risks are seen for engineers. *New York Times,* p. C7.

Sims, C. (1986, September 30). Federal Express to end electronic mail service. *New York Times,* pp. D1, D17.

Sinclair, J. D. (1983, December). The hardware of the brain. *Psychology Today,* pp. 8–12.

Siwolop, S. (1983, March). Touching all the data bases. *Discover,* pp. 68–71.

Slack, J. D. (1984). *Communication technologies and society: Conceptions of causality and the politics of technological intervention.* Norwood, NJ: Ablex.

Slade, M., & Biddle, W. (1982, October 31). Is big brother prone to error? *New York Times,* p. E7.

Sloan, D. (Ed.). (1984). The computer in education in critical perspective [Special issue]. *Teachers College Record, 85*(4).

Sloane, L. (1983, December 3). Pros and cons of bank cards. *New York Times,* p. 30.

Sloane, L. (1985, August 10). Fees for using teller machine. *New York Times,* p. 32.

Small business and the PC: Getting the job done. (1984, June 3). *New York Times,* p. 22C.

Smith, H. (1984, March). *Computer-human communication: Effects of interactive computers in the home.* Paper presented at meeting of the Eastern Communication Association, Philadelphia, PA.

Software sales. (1988, February 8). *Wall Street Journal,* p. 27.

Solomon, R. J. (1988). Vanishing intellectual boundaries: Virtual networking and the loss of sovereignty and control. *The Annals of the American Academy of Political and Social Science, 495,* 40–48.

Sontag, S. (1986, September 28). What's new in electronic games. *New York Times,* p. F19.

Source, The. (1983). McLean, VA: Source Telecomputing Corporation/Reader's Digest Association.

Sproull, L. S., Kiesler, S., & Zubrow, D. (1984, January 26). Encountering an alien culture. Unpublished paper.

Staff. (1984, June 15). *The Wall Street Journal,* p. 33.

Stahr, L. B. (1984, January). The electronic university. *PC World,* pp. 246–49.

Statewide debit-card system introduced. (1984, September 4). *New York Times,* p. D4.

Steinfield, C. W. (1986). Computer-mediated communication in an organizational setting: Explaining task-related and socioemotional uses. In M. L. McLaughlin (Ed.), *Communication yearbook 9* (pp. 777–803). Beverly Hills, CA: Sage Publications.

Sterling, T. D. (1988). Analysis and reanalysis of shared scientific data. *The Annals of the American Academy of Political and Social Science, 495,* 49–60.

Stevenson, R. W. (1985, October 20). The networks and advertisers try to recapture our attention. *New York Times,* p. E8.

Stoan, S. K. (1982). Computer searching: A primer for the uninformed scholar. *Academe, 68,* 10–15.

Stone, A. (1982, November). A home-computer primer. *Natural History,* pp. 84–93.

Stores reassess video games. (1983, January 24). *New York Times,* pp. D1, D6.

Study says U.S. is failing to avert job drain. (1982, September 8). *New York Times,* p. A2.

Sullivan, J. F. (1986, May 5). Schools urge girls to use computers. *New York Times,* p. B2.

Sullivan, P., & Flower, L. (1986). How do users read computer manuals? Some protocol contributions to writers' knowledge. In B. T. Petersen (Ed.), *Convergences: Transactions in reading and writing* (pp. 163–78). Urbana, IL: National Council of Teachers of English.

Sullivan, W. (1981, August 23). Data service maps the way in labyrinths of information. *New York Times,* p. E9.

Surrey, D. (1982, November). "It's like, good training for life." *Natural History,* 70–83.

Tank, D. W., & Hopfield, J. J. (1987, December). Collective computation in neuronlike circuits. *Scientific American,* pp. 104–14.

Tannenbaum, J. A. (1988, January 11). Consumer electronics may lack blockbuster, but not new gadgets. *Wall Street Journal,* p. 29.

Tannenbaum, J. A. (1988, March 8). Video games revive—and makers hope this time the fad will last. *Wall Street Journal,* p. 37.

Tannenbaum, J. A. (1988, June 8). At consumer electronics show, gimmicks abound—but is there a new blockbuster? *Wall Street Journal,* p. 27.

Taylor, D. (1986). *Personalizing the impersonal and other tales of communication in the computer age.* Unpublished paper.

Technology. (1984, November 9). *Wall Street Journal,* p. 33.

Technology links nation's libraries. (1983, September 11). *New York Times,* sec. 1, p. 35.

Texas Instruments. (1983, Summer). Education: Beyond the classroom and into the home. *Home computer newsletter.* Lubbock, TX: Author.

Text of U.N. document on satellite direct TV broadcasting. (1982, December 11). *New York Times,* p. 6.

Toong, H. D., & Gupta, A. (1982, December). Personal computers. *Scientific American,* pp. 87–107.

Trevino, L. K., Lengel, R. H., & Daft, R. L. (1987). The influence of communication technology on organizational structure: A conceptual model for future research. *Communication Research, 14,* 553–74.

Tucker, M. S. (1985). Computers in the schools: What revolution? *Journal of Communication, 35,* 12–23.

Turing, A. M. (1937a). On computable numbers, with an application to the *entscheidungsproblem. Proceedings of the London Mathematical Society, 42,* 230–65.

Turing, A. M. (1937b). On computable numbers, with an application to the *entscheidungsproblem*: A correction. *Proceedings of the London Mathematical Society, 42,* 544–46.

Turing, A. M. (1950). Computing machinery and intelligence. *Mind: A Quar-*

terly Review of Psychology and Philosophy, 59, 433–60. [Reprint with a different title: Turing, A. M. (1956). Can a machine think? In J. R. Newman (Ed.), *Machines, music, and puzzles* (pp. 2099–2123). New York: Simon & Schuster.]

Turkle, S. (1984). *The second self: Computers and the human spirit.* New York: Simon & Schuster.

Turner, W. (1982, April 29). Publishers foresee clash with AT&T on electronic news. *New York Times,* p. A26.

Tydeman, J., Lipinski, H., Adler, R., Nyhan, M., & Zwimpfer, L. (1982). *Teletext and videotex in the United States: Market potential, technology, public-policy issues.* New York: Data Communications/McGraw-Hill.

Tyler, M. (1979). Electronic publishing: A sketch of the European experience. In *Teletext and viewdata in the U.S.: A workshop on emerging issues, background papers* (pp. 1–23). Menlo Park, CA: Institute for the Future.

Ullman, H. (1984, January 13). False notions about computers. *New York Times,* p. A16.

Ulrich, W. (1985). The telecommunications explosion. In T. Forester (Ed.), *The information technology revolution* (pp. 106–66). Cambridge, MA: MIT Press.

Updegrave, W. (1985, June 23). Home banking: Edging in the door. *New York Times,* p. F9.

von Neumann, J. (1958). *The computer and the brain.* New Haven, CT: Yale University Press.

Waldrop, M. M. (1987). *Man-made minds: The promise of artificial intelligence.* Chicago, IL: Frank R. Walker.

Wall, W. L. (1988, May 31). Few firms plan well for mishaps that disable computer facilities. *Wall Street Journal,* p. 27.

Walton, R. E. (1983, September). *New work technology and its work-force implications: Unions and management approaches* (HBS 84–13). Boston, MA: Harvard University Graduate School of Business Administration, Division of Research.

Waltz, D. L. (1982, October). Artificial intelligence. *Scientific American,* pp. 118–33.

Watt, D. (1983, July). Games designed for learning. *Popular Computing,* pp. 65–67.

Watt, D. (1984, May). *Popular Computing,* pp. 113–34.

Watzlawick, P., Beavin, J. H., & Jackson, D. D. (1967). *Pragmatics of human communication: A study of interactional patterns, pathologies, and paradoxes.* New York: W. W. Norton.

Weal, E. (1983, July). Does the manual measure up? *Popular Computing,* pp. 166, 169.

Weaver, D. H. (1983). *Videotex journalism: Teletext, viewdata, and the news.* Hillsdale, NJ: Lawrence Erlbaum.

Webster's new collegiate dictionary. (1981). Springfield, MA: Merriam-Webster.

Weil, H. (1982, October). Hooked on computers. *Express,* pp. 58, 60–62, 64, 67.

Weinberger, D. (1986). Computer literacy is not literacy. In R. Atwan, B. Orton, & W. Vesterman (Eds.), *American mass media: Industries and issues* (pp. 431–32). New York: Random House.

Weingarten, F. W., & Garcia, D. L. (1988). Public policy concerning the exchange and distribution of scientific information. *The Annals of the American Academy of Political and Social Science, 495,* 29–39.

Weizenbaum, J. (1984). *Technostress: The human cost of the computer revolution.* Reading, MA: Addison-Wesley.

Wessel, D. (1988, April 19). Service industries find computers don't always raise productivity. *Wall Street Journal,* p. 37.

West, S. (1984, July/August). The new realism. *Science 84,* pp. 30–39.

Whaland, N. (1981, February). When is a program intelligent? *Creative Computing,* pp. 44–49.

Wicklein, J. (1979). *Electronic nightmare: The home communications set and your freedom.* Boston, MA: Beacon Press.

Wiener, N. (1950). *The human use of human beings: Cybernetics and society.* Garden City, NY: Doubleday.

Wigand, R. T., Shipley, C., & Shipley, D. (1984). Transborder data flow, informatics, and national policies. *Journal of Communication, 34,* 153–75.

Wilford, J. N. (1987, March 10). Advanced supercomputer begins operation. *New York Times,* p. C3.

Williams, F. (1982). *The communications revolution.* Beverly Hills, CA: Sage Publications.

Williams, F. (1987). *Technology and communication behavior.* Belmont, CA: Wadsworth.

Williams, F., Phillips, A. F., & Lum, P. (1984, November). *Gratifications associated with communication technologies.* Paper presented at meeting of the Speech Communication Association, Chicago, IL.

Williams, F., & Rice, R. E. (1983). Communication research and the new media technologies. In R. Bostrom & B. H. Westley (Eds.), *Communication yearbook 7* (pp. 200–224).

Williams, L. (1988, May 2). Studies find more reading for information and less for fun. *New York Times,* p. D10.

Winslow, R. (1985, July 26). Integrated software has yet to satisfy great expectations. *Wall Street Journal,* p. 23. Also see S. Cook (1984).

Winston, P., & Horn, B. K. (1981). *LISP.* Reading, MA: Addison-Wesley.

Winston, P. H. (1977). *Artificial intelligence.* Reading, MA: Addison-Wesley.

Witten, I. H. (1982). *Principles of computer speech.* New York: Academic Press.

Wollman, J. (1982, December 23). Video cassettes soothe the psyche. *New York Times,* p. C3.

Wollman, J. (1984, February 9). Teaching at home with help of computers. *New York Times,* pp. C1, C8.

Wood, F., & McHenry, L. (1980). Regional cerebral blood-flow response in a patient with remitted global amnesia. *Brain and Language, 9,* 123–28.

Wood, F., Taylor, B., Penny, R., & Stump, D. (1980). Regional cerebral blood-flow response to recognition memory versus semantic classification tasks. *Brain and Language, 9,* 113–22.

Wood, L. (1984, October). DECtalk: Computer speech that's almost human. *Popular Computing,* pp. 121, 123.

Word Processing. (1984, November 28). *New York Times*, A guide to the personal computer, Vol. 2, pp. 24, 48–51.

Wrege, R. (1983, July). Across space and time. *Popular Computing*, pp. 82–86.

Zinsser, W. (1983). *Writing with a word processor*. New York: Harper & Row.

Zuboff, S. (1982). New worlds of computer-mediated work. *Harvard Business Review*, 60, 142–52.

Zuboff, S. (1988). *In the age of the smart machine: The future of work and power*. New York: Basic Books.

Zweig, P. L. (1985, June 3). Time, AT&T, two banks seen unveiling venture on electronic services to home. *Wall Street Journal*, p. 6.

Index

Computer friendships. *See* Friendships
Computer-human interactions as communication, 65–67
Computer-human communication, 8, 67, 95–210
Computer literacy, 71, 169–70, 213
Computer-mediated communication, 30–31
Computer obsession, 3, 143, 177, 213, 215, 216–18
Computerphobia, 3, 213, 215, 218–20
Computer politics, 229–33
Computers: dedicated, 1, 113, 131; interest in buying, 1; reactions to, 2–3, 3–6; popularization of, 19–20; as companions, 207–208; as technologies, 24; and scientific inquiry, 24; historical development, 25–30; as a labor-saving device, 30, 33; speed of, 30, 33, 145, 199–200; total information generated globally, 30; as a unique medium of communication, 30–31; motives for buying, 31–34; costs, 32; as a highly selective medium for communication, 117–18; as social and asocial, 118; emotional expression, 118
Computer Space, 129
Concept learning computer programs, 187–89
Conflict, 122–23, 177
Control, 37
Coordination, eye-hand, 144
Cornell University's Computer Graphics Laboratory, 159
Creativity, 144
Cross-modality perception, 52
Culture: computerization as a cultural system, 123–24
Cybernetics, 64–68

Data searches. *See* Searches by computer
Debit-cards, 112
Deciphering, 222–25
Deliberative communication, 62
Delta Drawing, 158
Democracy, 121
Department of Defense, 230
DIALOG, 139–40
Digital communication, 72–77
Digital computer, 74
DirectVision, 139
Discrimination by information manipulation and restriction, 230–31
Displacement and social disengagement:

by media, 36–37; by computer, 119–20, 143, 148; stimulating the use of other media, 124–25, 143, 236
Distribution: household computer penetration 1, 2, 31; motives for buying computers, 31–34
Dow Jones Company, 106

Economic: transformations, 20–23; issues, 225–29; dislocations, 228. *See also* Unemployment
Education: institutions, 33; individualized computer programs, 152–56, 166–70; microcomputer trends in schools, 157; computer uses by 7th and 11th graders, 158; social consequences of computer use, 166–70
Efficiency, 201
Electronic banking, 110–12, 213
Electronic bulletin boards, 100–103
Electronic cottage, 148, 221–22
Electronic encyclopedias, 103–105
Electronic mail, 98–103
Electronic newspapers, 103–105
Electronic Numerical Integrator and Calculator (ENIAC), 26
Electronic shopping, 107–109
Electronic sweatshop, 228
Electronic Yellow Pages, 105–106
Eliza, 161–62
Entertainment, 113–14, 142
Epideictic communication, 62
Equality, 150–51
Erasable programmable read-only memory (EPROM), 50
Estridge, Philip D., 2
Ethical issues, 37, 236
Evans, Christopher, 198–203
Experimentation in writing, 146
Expressive and emotional communication, 127–28, 207
Expressive technologies, 128
Extravision, 139

Facts, 35, 43–44, 116, 235
Family interaction, 142–43, 147, 148
Fantasy theme analysis, 214–33
Feedback: synchronistic, 60; asynchronistic, 60–61
Films, 17–18
Forensic communication, 62
Friendships: computer, 36, 102–103, 119, 121, 220–21, 235–36

About the Series

STUDIES IN RHETORIC AND COMMUNICATION
General Editors:
E. Culpepper Clark, Raymie E. McKerrow, and David Zarefsky

The University of Alabama Press has established this series to publish major new works in the general area of rhetoric and communication, including books treating the symbolic manifestations of political discourse, argument as social knowledge, the impact of machine technology on patterns of communication behavior, and other topics related to the nature or impact of symbolic communication. We actively solicit studies involving historical, critical, or theoretical analyses of human discourse.

About the Authors

James W. Chesebro is on the faculty of the Department of Communication Arts and Sciences, Queens College of the City University of New York. He received his doctorate in Speech Communication from the University of Minnesota. Donald G. Bonsall is a computer specialist at Queens College.